GRIDIRON GAUNTLET

GRIDIRON GAUNTLET

THE STORY OF THE MEN WHO INTEGRATED

PRO FOOTBALL IN THEIR OWN WORDS

ANDY
PIASCIK

Taylor Trade Publishing

Lanham New York Boulder Toronto Plymouth, UK

Published by Taylor Trade Publishing
An imprint of The Rowman & Littlefield Publishing Group, Inc.
4501 Forbes Boulevard, Suite 200, Lanham, Maryland 20706
www.rlpgtrade.com

Estover Road, Plymouth PL6 7PY, United Kingdom

Distributed by NATIONAL BOOK NETWORK

Library of Congress Cataloging-in-Publication Data
Piascik, Andy, 1957–
    Gridiron gauntlet : the story of the men who integrated pro football in their own words
/ Andy Piascik.
        p. cm.
    Includes index.
    ISBN 978-1-58979-442-9 (cloth : alk. paper) — ISBN 978-1-58979-443-6 (electronic)
    1. National Football League—History. 2. African American football players—
Biography. 3. Football—Social aspects—United States—History. I. Title.
    GV955.5.N35P53 2009
    796.332'64—dc22
                                        2009009660

∞™ The paper used in this publication meets the minimum requirements of American
National Standard for Information Sciences—Permanence of Paper for Printed Library
Materials, ANSI/NISO Z39.48-1992.
Manufactured in the United States of America.

To Eileen Steele Piascik
(1924–2008)
She taught me a lot

CONTENTS

ACKNOWLEDGMENTS

Two books, *Outside the Lines: African Americans and the Integration of the National Football League*, by Charles K. Ross, and *Tackling Jim Crow: Racial Segregation in Professional Football*, by Alan H. Levy, were valuable to the research I did for this book. Ditto for the following articles from *The Coffin Corner*, newsletter of the Professional Football Researchers Association: "Not Only the Ball Was Brown: Black Players in Minor League Football, 1933–1946," by Bob Gill and Tod Maher, and "Outside the Pale: The Exclusion of Blacks from the National Football League, 1934–1946," by Thomas G. Smith (originally published in *Journal of Sports History*).

Sean Lahman, Ken Crippen, and T. J. Troup offered encouragement throughout. I consider them friends as well as colleagues. I'm grateful to family members of some of the subjects in the book, especially Irma Powell, Vera Mann, Marilyn Mann Matthews, Marjorie Mann Geisberg, and Rochelle Ford.

Although they declined to be interviewed, the late Bill Willis and Ollie Matson offered important encouragement, as did Ollie's wife, Mary Matson. Thanks also to Bob Boyd, Veryl Switzer, and Wally Triplett for their time and insights.

Finally and most importantly, I'd like to thank the twelve men who made this book necessary: Eddie Bell, Harold Bradley, John Brown, Emerson Cole, Henry Ford, Sherman Howard, Eddie Macon, the late Bob Mann, Joe Perry, Charlie Powell, George Taliaferro, and Bobby Watkins. In addition to the time they gave, all of them were patient and supportive as this project unfolded. They were pioneers, and I hope this book does them right. I owe a special debt of gratitude to George Taliaferro for his unwavering belief in this book and for putting me in touch with several of the other men whose stories appear here.

INTRODUCTION

The year 1933 was a significant one for the National Football League. For the first time, the 14-year old league operated with a two division format. Previously, all of the league's teams were lumped together, and whichever finished atop the standings was declared the champion. With the league split in two for the first time, the division winners would play in the inaugural NFL Championship Game on December 17 in the home park of the Western Division winner.

In addition to the realignment, the NFL fielded fewer teams in 1933 than it ever had in its history. From a peak of 22 teams in 1926, the league had gradually decreased in size until, by 1933, there were ten. The league hierarchy had decided that it was best businesswise to weed out the teams in smaller cities and become a big city enterprise. Teams in such cities as Akron and Canton, the backbone of the NFL in its precarious formative years, were rapidly becoming things of the past.

The geography of the NFL was different 76 years ago in another way, as were the identities of some of its teams. The Redskins played in Boston and would not move to Washington until 1937, while the Cardinals played in Chicago, a city they would call home until 1960. The Pittsburgh franchise, playing its inaugural season in 1933, was still several years away from being called the Steelers. The team instead went by Pirates, a name lifted from its baseball brethren.

It was a common practice then for NFL teams to take the nickname of the baseball team with which they shared a city. In 1933, there was a franchise in Brooklyn called the Dodgers and one in Cincinnati called the Reds (no relation to today's Bengals), and there had once been the New York Yankees, the Washington Senators, and three different incarnations of the Cleveland Indians. Then there were the Giants, who for many years were called the New York Football Giants to distinguish them from their baseball counterparts.

The Portsmouth Spartans were one of the last of the small city teams that remained from the NFL's shift to a big city league. The Spartans moved from Ohio to Detroit in 1934 and changed their name to the Lions. That left the Green Bay Packers as the last of the small city teams.

Amidst all the flux, the most significant change is one we can pinpoint to December 3, for that day marked the last time until 1946 that blacks played major league pro football. Few knew at the time that such a change was coming, certainly no one outside the NFL's inner sanctum. No agreements would be signed—at least none that we know of—and no announcements concerning the change were made to the public. As surely as both of those things had occurred, however, black players would be absent from NFL rosters in 1934 and for the 11 seasons that followed.

All of the NFL's ten teams were in action on that long ago Sunday afternoon as the 1933 season neared its completion. There wasn't much drama left to the regular season as the Chicago Bears and New York Football Giants had already clinched spots in the Championship Game. Absent were the comically expansive playoff scenarios of today, which meant that 80 percent of the league's players were playing out the string on the season's penultimate weekend.

For that reason it is likely that many players around the league—members of the Bears and Giants excepted (but perhaps even including them)—were looking forward to the imminent end of the season. Then as now, pro football was a physically demanding job, and it's safe to assume that virtually everyone who played that day had incurred an assortment of injuries and ailments during the season. Rosters were smaller, and everyone played both offense and defense, not to mention special teams (a term still 30 plus years in the future), a fact that increased the likelihood that a player would get hurt at some point during the season.

With many teams losing money and profits small for those that did manage to make it into the black, owners preferred to employ as few players as were needed to get through a season. Players did not ask to be taken out of a game for anything but the most serious injury. To do so was to risk loss of a job. Those too damaged to play healed as best they could with little hope of compensation for a workplace injury.

Some players were also undoubtedly thinking of their end-of-season travel plans, as six teams were finishing the season on December 3. For many, that meant catching a train or bus or both to some faraway place either that evening or the following day. In 1933, most players rented rooms in the cities where they played and returned to their hometowns when the season ended. There they would rejoin families and resume their work or look for whatever offseason jobs could be had in a country wracked by an unemployment rate that was approaching 40 percent.

Among the players in action that day were Joe Lillard of the Cardinals and Ray Kemp of the Pirates, the 12th and 13th blacks, respectively, to play in the NFL. Both had experienced a great deal of hostility and discrimination in their brief careers, and both undoubtedly suspected that a day might come when their employment would be abruptly terminated. Probably neither, however, suspected that it would happen when it did.

In New York on December 3, Kemp played with the Pirates in their 27–3 loss to the Giants. The 25-year old tackle had been signed in the summer, played in Pittsburgh's first four games, and then was released. He re-signed with the Pirates on December 1 and played in the game against the Giants two days later. After the NFL's color line descended, Kemp played some semipro football and then embarked on a long career as a college coach.

A halfback, the 28-year old Lillard had quite an impressive sports resume and was arguably one of the best athletes in the United States. He had been a star halfback at the University of Oregon as well as for the Cardinals, he had played baseball for the Negro League Chicago Americans, and he had played basketball for the Savoy Big Five, a team that was soon renamed the Harlem Globetrotters. Unlike the latter day Globetrotters, the Savoy Big Five did not play exhibition games designed primarily to entertain fans. They played to win and win they did, so much so that they were regarded by many as the best basketball team in the world.

Signed by the Cardinals for the 1932 season, Lillard contributed immensely to the few games the team won in his two seasons with field goals, touchdown passes, and long kick returns. Evidence of his versatility and of how he performed many jobs at a high level is what he did in what turned out to be his last pro game. That day,

Lillard moved from halfback to quarterback when teammate Roy Lamb went down early with an injury. The results weren't spectacular, but the Cardinals managed a tie against a superior Redskins team, one of only two games the Cardinals did not lose that year. Like Kemp, Lillard played semipro football after 1933.

Lillard had on a number of occasions stood up to unfair treatment and racial slurs, acts that led to his being suspended by the Cardinals for part of the 1932 season. The league office, owners, and coaches resented any acts of resistance by the hired help, all the more so in Lillard's case since he obviously did not appreciate the opportunity they had bestowed on him. Whether Lillard's unwillingness to quietly submit hastened the NFL's move to imposing the color line is uncertain, but there were signs that a shift was coming prior to the end of the 1933 season. Chief among them was the steady drop in the number of black players since 1923. Given that trend and absent any organized protest or resistance, it's likely the color line would have come to pass regardless of anything that Lillard did or did not do.

So even though Lillard was one of the best players on a team in obvious, desperate need of playing talent (the worst team in the NFL in 1933, in fact), he was released. Taken together, the utter ineptitude of the Cardinals and the fact that Lillard did not play for them or anyone else after 1933 even though he was better than probably 75 percent of the players in the NFL, are perhaps evidence enough to establish that the league had consciously moved to a "whites only" policy. Besides the case of Lillard, another compelling bit of evidence is that none of the many other outstanding black players played in the NFL in the next 12 years: Kemp, for one, but also Ozzie Simmons, Wilmeth Sidat-Singh, Mel Reid, Bobby Vandever, Brud Holland, and yes, Jackie Robinson, not to mention Kenny Washington, Marion Motley, Bill Willis, and Woody Strode, all of whom were available prior to being signed in 1946.

Among the NFL's decision-makers during those 12 years were some of the most storied individuals in the history of the game:

George Halas, Bears owner/coach, NFL founder, member Pro Football Hall of Fame;

Tim Mara, Giants owner, member Pro Football Hall of Fame;

Art Rooney, Pirates/Steelers owner, member Pro Football Hall of Fame;

Charles Bidwill, Cardinals owner, member Pro Football Hall of Fame;

Bert Bell, Eagles owner, later NFL commissioner, member Pro Football Hall of Fame;

George Preston Marshall, Redskins owner, member Pro Football Hall of Fame;

Dan Reeves, Rams owner, member Pro Football Hall of Fame;

Dan Topping, Dodgers owner, later owner of the baseball Yankees;

Curly Lambeau, Packers general manager and coach, member Pro Football Hall of Fame;

Steve Owen, Giants coach, member Pro Football Hall of Fame;

Joe Carr, NFL president, member Pro Football Hall of Fame;

Wellington Mara, Giants secretary, later owner, member Pro Football Hall of Fame

There was no Bill Veeck among them, no Paul Brown or Branch Rickey. Their commitment to apartheid was seemingly stronger than their commitment to winning championships. The Bears under Halas did not employ a single black player in their first 32 seasons. The Giants began play in 1925 and did not sign any blacks until 1948. The Steelers were all-white from the day Ray Kemp was released until 1952.

Over the years, team owners and league officers from the 1934–1945 period vehemently denied that a color line had been imposed, so much so that they sometimes resembled the Player Queen in *Hamlet* (thou doth protest too much, Mr. Mara). With the exception of George Preston Marshall, who consistently and proudly proclaimed his determination to employ only white players, a claim he made good on until 1962, they instead put forward the lie that there had been no blacks capable of playing in the NFL. As loathsome as Marshall's views and policies were, he at least did not pretend there were no blacks good enough to make his team. Unlike the others, he was honest enough to admit that he simply didn't want them around.

The NFL's early years are in striking contrast to the whitelist years of 1934–1945. Although the total number of blacks on NFL rosters had never been high, there had been at least one in all of the NFL's first 14 seasons beginning with Fritz Pollard and Rube Marshall in the inaugural year of 1920. Pollard and Marshall were two of a group of blacks who played for semipro teams in the years before the formation of the NFL. Among those from that group who did not continue on once the NFL was formed were Charles Follis, Doc Baker, Henry McDonald, and Gideon Smith.

The total number of blacks in the early NFL reached a high of six in 1923. The number declined thereafter until 1932, when Lillard was the only one; then Pittsburgh's signing of Kemp made two for part of 1933. Some had noteworthy careers of above average length, especially Duke Slater, who played ten years and was one of the NFL's best players throughout. Fritz Pollard, who was elected to the Hall of Fame in 2005, played six years, as did Inky Williams, while Sol Butler played four. Paul Robeson was outstanding in his two seasons before he embarked on a long and distinguished career as a singer, actor, and activist.

The NFL's employment of black players from 1920–1933 also contrasts with professional baseball, which blacks were a part of in its early years until 1889. From then until 1947, no blacks played in the major leagues. So although pro football's record is reprehensible on many levels, it was at least ahead of baseball. That was true in the 1920s, and it was also true in the 1946–1947 period, which marked the beginning of the final integration of pro sports. By the time Jackie Robinson took the field for his first game in Brooklyn, Marion Motley, Bill Willis, Kenny Washington, and Woody Strode had completed their first seasons.

The thirteen men who played in the NFL prior to 1934 make up what we might call the First Generation of black players in pro football. None of the thirteen is still living, but their accomplishments live on in the stories of some of the men in this book, including Harold Bradley (whose father was one of them) and Sherman Howard (who knew a number of them while growing up in Chicago). The thirteen men are:

Fritz Pollard (1894–1986) Akron, Milwaukee, Hammond, Providence, 1920–1923, 1925–1926

Rube Marshall (1880–1958) Rock Island, Duluth, 1920, 1925

Paul Robeson (1898–1976) Akron, Milwaukee, 1921–1922

Inky Williams (1894–1980) Canton, Hammond, Dayton, Cleveland, 1921–1926

John Shelburne (1894–1978) Hammond, 1922

Duke Slater (1898–1966) Rock Island, Milwaukee, Cardinals, 1922–1931

Jim Turner (1899–1932) Milwaukee 1923

Sol Butler (1897–1988) Rock Island, Hammond, Akron, Canton, 1923–1926

Dick Hudson (1898–?) Minneapolis, Hammond, 1923, 1925–1926

Harold Bradley Sr. (1905–?) Cardinals, 1928

Dave Myers (1906–1972) Staten Island, Brooklyn, 1930–1931

Joe Lillard (1905–1978) Cardinals, 1932–1933

Ray Kemp (1907–2002) Pittsburgh, 1933

This book consists of the stories of twelve of the Second Generation of black players in major league pro football. All began their pro careers in the decade beginning in 1946. Each chapter is narrated by the players themselves. They speak of their football experiences, yes, but also their upbringings, influences, experiences in college and the military, post football careers, and much more.

The stories would be incomplete if they focused entirely on football. The men profiled here were all born from 1920–1933. Racial attitudes, customs, interactions—virtually everything pertaining to race—were far different in the United States then. Segregation was the law of much of the land and the reality in much more. Four hundred and forty blacks were lynched in the decade of the 1920s. Each man speaks about a wide array of subjects. Their football careers cannot be adequately understood without an understanding of the other parts of their lives.

The content of each chapter is entirely dependent on the individual. Some speak at great length about football while others devote more time to discussing their other careers. Some regard their college years or other periods of their lives as seminal moments; in those instances the chapters reflect that. Many speak about people who made a lasting impact on them—family members, teachers, community leaders, friends, classmates. Also influential were the accomplishments of prominent blacks they grew up reading or hearing about, athletes and others, Paul Robeson, Joe Louis, Marcus Garvey, and Jesse Owens among them.

The men profiled here were contemporaries of Jackie Robinson, Larry Doby, Roy Campanella, and Monte Irvin, yet their stories are little known by comparison. They faced many of the same hardships as their baseball counterparts while playing a game that was much more physically dangerous. A number of the men in this book spent their post-football careers working with young people, undoubtedly recalling the elders who had inspired them. Some express dismay that as a whole today's youth do not know of their experiences and, worse, that they don't care to. If this volume does anything, let it shed some light on what is, after all, the not very distant past.

One often neglected piece of history-telling is the work of everyday people. Undue emphasis is often placed on big deeds done by great individuals. Such individuals, the story goes, were somehow more determined, smarter, braver, more principled, and more innovative than everyone else. Without them not much would have happened. The push from below, often concerted, is left out of the narrative. Unfortunately, this is often the case with the telling of the story of the fall of football's color line in 1946.

A major effort to integrate pro sports involving thousands of people began in the mid-1930s. Greater emphasis was placed on baseball, then far and away the most popular spectator sport, but football was also very much on the agenda. Most of the people involved worked far from the spotlight, although their numbers included former NFL star Paul Robeson, who was later hammered and badgered by the state as a subversive for just that kind of activism. Their work resulted in picket lines, meetings, petition drives, protests, and other activities around the country demanding an end to the color line.

On a macro level, the World War II years that immediately preceded pro football integration were years of great domestic tumult. Nowhere was that more true than in the area somewhat inadequately referred to as civil rights. Many factors contributed to the tumult, but perhaps none was greater than the philosophies at the heart of the war itself: democracy, with its ineluctable component, equality, is better than dictatorship. Virtually everyone in the United States who propagandized about the importance of going to war did so by invoking the necessity of defeating ethnic intolerance and racial superiority.

Millions who signed on to the fight insisted that a concomitant struggle be waged against racism in the United States with something approaching the vigor of the fight against Nazis. This was the popular Double V or Double Victory campaign: victory over fascism abroad and victory over white supremacy at home. It was on the heels of this campaign that the Cleveland Browns and Los Angeles Rams employed two black players, both in 1946. Paul Brown did not act in a vacuum. He did what he did in an atmosphere created by thousands of people—perhaps millions—who were pushing against the walls of backwardness. That many of them may not have been specifically engaged in a struggle for the integration of pro football is beside the point.

This is not to say that pressure from below was the only ingredient. More visible actors performed on this stage as well. Paul Brown was one of them, as is clear from some of the testimony in this book. Rams owner Dan Reeves deserves some credit as well, although more because the Rams signed blacks in larger numbers than any NFL team than for the 1946 signings of Kenny Washington and Woody Strode. Credit for the latter belongs almost entirely to the people of Los Angeles, who told Reeves in no uncertain terms that the city's football stadium would not be made available to the Rams if they remained an all-white team.

But none of the risks that Paul Brown took compared to the punches to the balls that Kenny Washington endured. None of the angry glares or harsh words directed Dan Reeves's way hurt as much as the gouges on Marion Motley's body from the spiked shoes of opposing players. Washington, Motley, and many others, including the men profiled in this book, are the ones who kicked in the door of opportunity. In so doing, they endured more than a human being should have to. In the end, all Brown and Reeves endured, really, were a lot of victorious football games made possible in large part by the great black players on their teams.

I once heard about a very talented black player of the 1940s—unquestionably good enough to make the team, according to the man who related this—who left training camp without ever playing a single game. Apparently the insults, harassment, and isolation were too much to bear. Undoubtedly there were others at that time who did likewise. For lack of a better way of putting it, they didn't make it. The situation was too oppressive. In some ways this is their story, too, if only between the lines.

Similarly, some of those profiled here said or implied that they would have done more in their football careers absent the obstacles they had to overcome. That fact is perhaps so obvious that it's easy to overlook. It can be a haunting question, the kind that never entirely goes away: What more might I have accomplished? Those deprived of the opportunity bore the brunt of the blow, yet all of us who missed the great deeds never done lost out as well.

But this is not a sad tale. One of the themes that unites the men whose stories appear here is that of satisfaction at a job well done—in football, yes, but in the whole of their lives as well. In the grand scheme of things, the integration of pro football may be a small piece of our history, but it is nonetheless a part of the collective struggle to move forward. Understanding who and where we've been enables us to better know who and where we are. It can also guide us in the quest for higher ground and equip us to resist efforts to push us back.

JOHN BROWN

John Edward Brown
Born April 9, 1922, in Belen, Mississippi

Theodore Roosevelt High School in Gary, Indiana
North Carolina Central University

Center/linebacker
Undrafted, signed by Los Angeles Dons in 1947

Many of the best African American pro football players have come from traditionally black colleges. The list of players from these schools reads like a Who's Who of pro football: Walter Payton, Jerry Rice, Deacon Jones, Roosevelt Brown, Tank Younger, Willie Davis, Kenny Houston, Leroy Kelly, Roger Brown, Bob Hayes, Willie Brown, Lem Barney, Larry Little, Willie Lanier, Rayfield Wright, Claude Humphrey, Charlie Joiner, Art Shell, Mel Blount, Buck Buchanan, Harold Carmichael, Emmitt Thomas, L. C. Greenwood, Albert Lewis, John Stallworth, Rich Jackson, Ernie Ladd, Richard Dent, Aeneas Williams—a team of players from traditionally black schools would do pretty well against any group of players from the game's history.

There was not always that kind of relationship between the black colleges and the pro game. None of the thirteen African Americans who played in the NFL from 1920–1933, for example, attended a black school. Marion Motley attended South Carolina State College for one year but transferred to Nevada before ever playing varsity football. Tank Younger of Grambling is usually recognized as the first, but that's only if the NFL's rival from 1946–1949, the All-America Football Conference (AAFC), is ignored.

Year	Team	League	Games	Interceptions	Yards	Avg.	TDs
1947	Dons	AAFC	14	1	4	4.0	0
1948	Dons	AAFC	14	1	1	1.0	0
1949	Dons	AAFC 1	2	3	46	15.3	2
1950	Played in Canada with Winnipeg						
1951	Played in Canada with Winnipeg						
1952	Played in Canada with Winnipeg						

In fact, John Brown of North Carolina Central and Elmore Harris of Morgan State were the first players from traditionally black schools to play major league pro football. Both signed with teams in the AAFC in 1947, Harris with the Brooklyn Dodgers and Brown with the Los Angeles Dons. Brown played three years and then, after an unpleasant stint with the San Francisco 49ers in training camp in 1950, went on to play three outstanding seasons in Canada for the Winnipeg Blue Bombers.

In a way, the Dons of the AAFC were at the forefront of pro football integration. During the four years of their existence, the Dons featured eight black players, far and away the most during that time period. Among them were Hall of Famer Len Ford and George Taliaferro. John remains friends with Taliaferro to this day.

After his playing career ended, John became an educator and assistant coach at Southern University in Louisiana. He left the coaching staff after being bypassed for the job as head coach but remained on the Southern faculty for years thereafter. He is currently retired and living in Louisiana.

I was born in Belen, Mississippi, in 1922. I'm an only child. We moved to Cairo, Illinois, when I was two and to Gary, Indiana, when I was four. My grandfather and my father were cotton pickers in Mississippi, and my grandfather used to come North every year after the crops were in to try and find a place to live. I'm told he was really headed to South Bend but he was hired by the railroad in East Chicago, Indiana as a boxcar builder and never made it to South Bend. When he took that job, him, my mother, my father, my aunt, my grandmother, and me all moved to Gary.

Once we got to Gary, my father got a job in the tin mill. My mother worked at a laundry and she ironed sixty shirts a day. She made $10 a week, which wasn't much but she saved out of that. I had an uncle who played football and basketball and I basically tried to mimic him. He was seven years older than me. I was an avid sports fan and I was around the coaches at school all the time. I played football and basketball and I also played tennis. I'll tell you who died recently who was from Gary—Hank Stram the football coach. He was a good guy. Tom Harmon was a Gary fellow. And George Taliaferro, we went to the same high school. He was a few years behind me. We had a lot of pretty famous people athletically and otherwise whom we recognize and remember. We all know about each other.

Gary is very segregated now but back when I lived there it wasn't. I lived in a neighborhood that was predominantly black, but we had a lot of European immigrants from most of the Slovak countries. We had about five or six white families on our block, and you'd have five or six black families on the blocks that were predominantly white. We all played together. And we had one Japanese family on our block who had a daughter named Violet who was very pretty and all of us fell in love with her. The immigrants, you know, they did it the right way. I mean they did it a lot more educated than the blacks did it. They'd buy a home and send for their family and live together for three or four years and then buy another home and send for more family.

Gary was divided north and south by the main street, which is called Broadway. All the streets on the east side of Broadway were named after presidents. Like there would be Washington, Adams, and Madison, and that was one way to learn the presidents. And the streets on the other side were named after states and they were in the order that they came in the union. I lived on Connecticut and there was Massachusetts, Pennsylvania, Delaware, Maryland, and Virginia. If you took a long walk you could learn a little bit, although you didn't appreciate it until you were older.

My grandfather was a staunch supporter of Marcus Garvey. When I was young I thought my grandfather was as solid as the earth and I followed him everywhere he went. He would take me to the Garvey meetings because when you're a kid, your people sort of indoctrinate you into whatever it is that they believe because they want you to believe, too. So we had a definite idea about our culture as blacks and how we arrived in the United States and that sort of thing. You would never have thought of my grandfather as an educated person but he'd quote the Bible like any minister or anyone who'd been trained to do so.

Every Sunday the older people in my neighborhood would meet on my front porch, and since my bedroom was right there, I'd raise the window and listen to them talk. They'd be arguing about politics and Garvey and President Roosevelt and I'd listen to them, so I grew up knowing about things. I was mostly interested in the Garvey meetings for recreation because they had things for youngsters to do. We used to go on field trips to Chicago and that was a big deal, but I really wasn't interested in the philosophy as much.

The other times we got to go to Chicago was from the baseball league I played in in the summer. We played baseball for the school but we didn't play during the school year, we played in the summer. We had preps, juniors, and seniors. The preps were ten to twelve, the juniors were thirteen and fourteen, and the seniors were up to sixteen. We played eight other schools, home and home, and I used to pitch. As our reward for playing, we would go to Chicago on the Fourth of July and on Labor Day, once to see the Cubs and once to see the White Sox. I remember Lon Warneke and Charlie Grimm and Kiki Cuyler with the Cubs, but I was a St. Louis Cardinals fan when I was a youngster because they usually won. I can remember the names of many of their players even now as I'm sitting here talking—Enos Slaughter, Joe Medwick, Dizzy Dean, Daffy Dean.

You know, I had an opportunity to meet Joe Medwick when I was in the army and that was sort of thrilling. He had led the league in hitting and runs batted in, and he came over as part of a USO [(United Service Organizations)] troupe. We had played a football game, and him and Leo Durocher and two or three other guys were there. At the banquet that night, I was sitting next to Joe Medwick and I thought I was in hog heaven. I was looking at him and I'll never forget how big his wrists were. So I asked him, I said, "Joe, who do you think was the toughest pitcher you ever faced?" He said, "Well, John, I guess [Carl] Hubbell gave me the hardest time. But you know, when I'm hitting, I don't give a damn who's pitching." I've never forgotten that.

We had eight high schools in Gary and they were all segregated except for Froebel. As a matter of fact, three of my coaches in high school were graduates of Froebel. I have never understood why just one school was desegregated, but that's the way it was. The school I went to, Roosevelt, was an all-black school and we had another black school, Pulaski. Roosevelt was unique because it was K through 12 and I went there for thirteen years. Gary had a great education system. The school system was copied and promoted all over the world. People came from all over the world to study the system.

See, Gary is a steel mill town, and they tried to get the students out of school at the same time the parents were getting off work.

They had shifts at the mills, 8–4, 4–12, and 12–8, so we went to school eight hours, 8:15–4:15. And they tried to weave the school system into the type of work the students were likely to do after they graduated from high school if they didn't go to college. It was well done, really. I always appreciated my high school education because you took a lot of things that, when you became older, you really appreciated.

For example, we had a course called Auditorium, and if you ask George Taliaferro, he'll tell you what Auditorium was. In Auditorium, there were five or six classes that met in the auditorium and for the first half hour we sang songs. Then we listened to music and we were to identify the music and the composer and maybe the year. These were Brahms and Bach and Beethoven and Rachmaninoff and that type of music. I've forgotten some of them but there was a time I really knew them. And when you hear it on the radio or on the TV as background to movies, you still recognize it. The second half, you watched a play that each division in the school put on—the chemistry class or the biology class or the history class—they had to give a program and the students had to act in them. They would act for the students in the audience and then the students in the audience would critique the play after it was over and say what was good about it, what was bad about it, evaluate the acting, what they got out of it, etc., and it really was beneficial later in life.

Then for six weeks you took speech classes so most people who went to school in those days, you can understand them very well. They would ask you to get up and speak extemporaneously for about two minutes, and I remember the teacher called on one guy because he was asleep and not paying attention. This guy had an apple and he got up and he says, "This is an apple. It's red on the outside and white on the inside and when I bite it it's juicy on the inside," and he talked about the apple for about five minutes. He made up a little extemporaneous talk, and it broke up the class. It was really funny, and the teacher appreciated it. We had to do those sorts of things, so it was just a class where you got a lot of good information. You learned how to be fast on your feet and get up and speak to people.

We also elected a president and a secretary for the Auditorium class by vote of the student body, and they had to take charge and they had to learn parliamentary procedure. They would change the president and secretary about every four weeks or something like that so different people got to learn how to do it. I look back at it and I think it was really a great class. You had to go to the Auditorium class every day and you had to go every year you were in school so by the time you got to the 12th grade, you had taken it for twelve years. I think many students from Gary will tell you it was a great class and it was one of the classes that made up the eight-hour day. It was called a work/study/play system and it was a good system.

Like I said, in the summer I used to play baseball, we played handball—we had sixteen handball courts at Roosevelt—and we had an indoor swimming pool. You just learned to do a lot of different things athletically. Tennis. Basketball. I was in the band, too. I used to try to play the clarinet and saxophone but I could never learn to read music. I could memorize play but I couldn't play by reading music.

All through high school, we only played one integrated school, a school in Chicago. Otherwise we went all over the place to play other black schools. They had a national basketball tournament for blacks and they had it in Gary for two years. There were sixteen schools and schools came from all over the place, from down South, from everywhere. One year we went when it was in Dayton, Ohio. Two years when I was in high school we went to a tournament in Fayetteville, North Carolina and we won. Then we went to a tournament in Tuskegee, Alabama so we traveled a lot. It was educational, really, because we went all over a good part of the Midwest, the North, and the South. We went to Blue Field and Charleston, West Virginia, to Memphis and Tulsa, to Cairo and Carbondale, Illinois. We played a team called the Kansas Vocational School in Topeka, Kansas. We played two schools in St. Louis. Those were good trips. That was the best part of being an athlete—the travel. That was why you wanted to make the team. The guys from Froebel, they would say they wished they could go on those journeys.

We went in a sort of convoy of cars with coaches and teachers and they'd be glad to get away, too. Sometimes we'd have to stop and stay over on the way because it was too far to travel in one day. And then we would stay over night when we got there, depending on where we were. Like the basketball team, when we went to St. Louis, we played on Friday night and then we played on Saturday and then one of those schools would come up to Gary and we would do the same thing. Or we would play in Ft. Wayne on Friday and Dayton on Saturday or vice versa. So you got a chance to meet a lot of athletes, and after I got into college I would run into them.

My coach's name in high school was John D. Smith and he tried to see to it that all the kids that graduated from Roosevelt went to college. When we'd go on these trips we'd always visit a college and try to meet a coach or an athletic director. That was one of the coach's goals, really—to stop and see schools and start us thinking about going to college. And the coaches knew where there were restaurants owned by blacks. If they didn't, we would eat at a place in a bus terminal or train terminal. Sometimes they wouldn't let you use the restroom and that sort of thing, but at that time we weren't really thinking about segregation. You were with your buddies having fun. You were thinking about, "I'm in Louisville and I've never been to Louisville."

I had quite a few offers to go to black colleges. I also went up to South Dakota State for a visit with another fellow on my team, a boy named James Hardy. They were going to take us and everything but we went in the wintertime and damn near froze to death. You know, Gary is cold in the winter, but it wasn't as cold as South Dakota. The other thing was there weren't many black people up there so we just made a choice not to go there, that's all.

I decided to go to North Carolina Central University. It was called North Carolina College for Negroes when I first got there in 1940, and then my last year after I came back from the army they changed the name to North Carolina College at Durham, and then later on they named it North Carolina Central University. I played football and basketball. It was kind of a scholarship deal, but it was a work scholarship. You had to have a job. I graduated from Roosevelt on June the 10th 1940, and we took off for North Carolina on June 14th. There were five of us, two from St. Louis and three from Gary, and we had to work all summer. We did the work they hire people to do now. We cut the grass, we worked in the dining hall, we worked in the dormitories—cleaned toilets and waxed the floors—that kind of thing. They only had one person who worked for the college, the supervisor that distributed the work that had to be done.

I loved that school. To this minute, I love it. That's the truth. I didn't ever want to graduate, didn't ever want to leave. I didn't know what the hell I was going to do but I loved that school. I was there in North Carolina last year for a CIAA [(Central Intercollegiate Athletic Association)] tournament. I loved that school. And I loved college. That's the other thing, I loved college.

Let me tell you, there was an adjustment. The first day after we got to school, coach took the five of us to our dormitory and we got our rooms. The next day, he came and picked us up and took us to downtown to show us how to get there. It was a Sunday, and he took us to look in the windows of the stores and that sort of thing. A group of white kids passed by in a car and they yelled out at us, "Niggers," and we said, "Uh-oh." Nothing happened, you know, they were in a car and they kept going, but that was my introduction. But we didn't come in contact with a lot of whites in Durham. That was downtown, you know, that wasn't in the black community.

In the black community, they had black businesses, just a great community of educated blacks. They had Farmers and Mechanics Bank, which was the only bank that didn't go broke during the Depression. They had an insurance company owned by C. C. Spaulding. It's kind of famous and it now has a 16-story building in downtown Durham. John Merrick was another one. It was not a wealthy community but when students would graduate, the boards of the banks and the insurance companies would hire them. It was a progressive area. That's why I liked North Carolina. And I still like it. I had a lot of black inclinations from my Marcus Garvey history and it all fits in. I don't know how it fits but it fits.

I played football and basketball my whole time in college. In fact, basketball season was still on when I got drafted into the service in March 1943, and I went kicking and screaming. I was in until December 1945, and I didn't ever want to go to war. I wasn't a patriot and I didn't want to sacrifice my life. I mean, I love the country. It wasn't because I didn't love it, I just didn't want to fight for it. I just wanted to be free, just live my life, and I just wasn't into the military. It's just what happens to you, I don't know, when you run into some of the faults. They talk about the greatness of our country but I think about its faults because I've seen some of them. I think about the greatness of it also, but we've done things that I don't think we ought to be too proud of.

One of the faults that I'm talking about that I didn't pay too much attention to at the time but that I found out about after the war when I lived in Los Angeles was the internment of the Japanese. They interned most of the Japanese and didn't touch a German or Italian. The Germans were giving us more hell than the Japanese, but they moved all of the Japanese people and interned them. I lived over on the West Side of town when I lived in Los Angeles and the West Side was where the Japanese lived. They had really nice homes and they were neat and the lawns were pretty and everything. So I've seen some of the faults.

Right now, I'm really perturbed that they don't have a draft, especially in the situation we're in as black people. Much as I didn't want to go, I learned a lot and I matured in the military, and I think it would be beneficial to young black guys. For one thing, we lost a couple of generations of young black men. You know, almost all of the black people we have in college are women. I live in Louisiana, and the prisons are just full of young black men. So many black kids come up and they only have mothers. They don't know who their fathers are—they deserted them and don't care for them and that sort of thing. The military may be one way out of poverty. Maybe I'm wrong. People who say they're so patriotic, they won't allow their children to go into the military. That just blows me wide open. If they don't want their kids in there, why should I want mine in there?

I was in the quartermasters. They're the guys who drive trucks and deliver food, rations, clothing, and that's what we did. When I first had my training I was in the cavalry—not the mechanized cavalry but the horse cavalry, and I didn't know one end of a horse from the other end. But I ended up in the quartermasters. Actually, I was supposed to go to Officers Candidate School, and if I had become a captain, I might have stayed in and made a career of it. But I ran into some racial stuff.

What happened was, I was a platoon sergeant, and I was pretty good at it and my captain tried to set it up for me to go to OCS. We were in Texas about fifteen miles from Mexico and it was all black enlisted men but white officers. I was one of the few college guys in the outfit because that was rare at that time, but I never got to go to OCS. I don't know for certain that it was my color. More than likely it was, but maybe it worked out because if I had gone to OCS I might have ended up with the infantry. If I had been a captain with the quartermasters, that would have been okay, but there was no guarantee of that. I could have ended up with the infantry and I saw what happened to the infantry when I got to Italy. You'd see those guys lined up dead all the time.

When I went overseas I was in a convoy of over 150 ships, and in the daytime all you could see was battleships and aircraft carriers way off on the horizon. It took us nineteen days and we were in an overcrowded liberty ship stacked four high, sleeping in hammocks. We were four deep and a guy, he'd be maybe two or three feet above you with another guy two or three feet below you. Another ship ran into us and knocked a big hole in us, and the convoy left us because we endangered the whole convoy because of German submarines.

The captain of this one ship called us on the radio and our captain gave him the name and the number of the ship. And he says, "What is your problem and how long will it take to repair?" They told him our steering mechanism had been damaged and it would take about six hours to repair. Because the rest of the convoy left, we were a sitting duck out there. And this other captain says, "Go ahead, we've got you covered." And that guy circled us the whole time. That's the closest I ever came to combat.

Two days later we went into Gibraltar and right up the Mediterranean and you could see the people in Spain on the shore looking at us. Part of the outfit went on to Oran and then the rest of us went up there later. In the meantime, we went all over North Africa. I never got in Black Africa but I was in four countries: Libya, Algeria, Tunisia, and Morocco. I was in Casablanca so I joke that I was at Rick's Place. That's not true, but I really liked Casablanca. And I really liked Algeria. I could have lived in Algeria.

When I was in Florence, Italy we played a football game called the Spaghetti Bowl on New Year's Day in 1944. They had about 40,000 soldiers there, and it was the GIs versus the officers. Most or all of the officers had been in college and they had played a lot more football than we had, but we beat them pretty handily. Then they built a basketball court in Florence and they named it Madison Square Garden and General Mark Clark sent down an order that every division had to have a team. We had a tournament and the

92nd Division won the tournament and my team got second place. I met two or three generals as a result of playing ball. They picked me out to question me and that sort of thing. I met General Roosevelt, the president's son, and some other generals and my colonel, he liked that, and later on he helped me get out of the army sooner than I would have. You press a little flesh here and there and you get a lot of perks—it's a perk world.

I went back to college when I was discharged and caught right on after being gone two and a half years. I finished in 1947. Kenny Washington and [Marion] Motley and [Bill] Willis signed in '46. I felt good because until then, I never dreamed I'd play pro ball. Not at all. And then suddenly, you know, we had a chance. I went with the Dons in '47. My rookie year was the same year as Jackie Robinson's rookie year. The pro guys, we all knew each other, whether it was baseball, football, or basketball, and we talked to each other. Like Larry Doby, who played baseball for Cleveland that same year, I knew him because he played basketball for Virginia Union and we played against each other. We were good buddies. I didn't know Jackie real well but I knew him. After knowing him, you say, "I wonder how he took some of the stuff he took?" I took some of it but Jackie had a temper. I mean, a real temper—he'd bite a snake.

The Dons sent me a contract for $4,500 in the spring of 1947. We had a big gathering in the student union and I have a picture of me signing my contract. It wasn't a no-cut contract and when I got to camp the first time in Ventura, you had to make the ball club or you didn't get any of that money. Our coach Dudley DeGroot had been the coach of the Redskins and he was a great guy. He had a Ph.D. and he had been on the 1912 Olympic team. He was a fine guy, and he helped me an awful lot.

I'll tell you one thing he did. He found me a place to live with a lady named Mrs. Adams and I rented there. It wasn't just me, there was a black guy named Bert Piggott from the University of Illinois, and we both roomed there. We didn't have a car and every day he'd pick us up and drive us to practice in Pasadena across the street from the Rose Bowl, which was a pretty good ways, and every day he'd bring us back from practice. And when we had to go on road trips, same thing, he'd come and pick us up to take us to the airport.

Bert and I were roommates on the road. He was from a small town in Illinois. I forget the name of it. As a matter of fact, I talked to his wife about a month ago. He's deceased. He used to be the football coach at North Carolina A&T for quite a while—right up until he died, really. He only played a year and the next year he was cut. And we had another black player that year, Ezzert "Sugar Foot" Anderson.

Actually, we started out with about fifteen blacks in training camp that year. We had a couple of guys that should have been on the team but I just assumed that they had a quota. The Browns had three—that seemed to be the limit. No team had over three until they became a little different in their thinking. But we had a kid from a junior college in California in camp, and I've forgotten his name, but he was one hell of a football player. And then they had a kid named Ben Whaley. He was a guard from Virginia State University and they cut him after only a few games. I played center and I knew what he could do and to me, he was the best guard on the team. He was one of the guys they cut who shouldn't have been cut. He became an assistant coach at North Carolina Central. I don't know if he's still alive but the last I knew, he was living in Durham.

We had another black guy in camp, a quarterback from New Jersey, Oscar Givens, and he could throw with both arms. He went to Morgan State, and I played basketball against him in college. De-Groot wanted to keep him but somebody higher up made some decisions and they got rid of him. DeGroot was a fair-minded person. He really was just a fine person, and I know he wanted to keep him. What they did after camp broke up, they sent Givens to Hawaii to play and he played over there for a year but he never came back to the pros. Oscar Givens was one hell of a football player.

Mel Hein was our line coach and he was also a nice person, just an absolutely nice person. He played center and he was an all-pro and taught me everything he could. Angelo Bertelli, he was another one, just a very nice person. He was our number one quarterback, and he always complimented me in front of the guys. He just liked me and I guess he had some influence, I don't know. But I was a really good blocker, okay, my forte was pass blocking—protecting the passer. I don't know, maybe the fact that he always complimented me in front of the guys helped me. "Way to go, Brownie," that sort of stuff. He just liked the way I delivered the ball to him.

We had one coach and one player who were prejudiced. They showed it in the little things they did. When they're prejudiced against you, other people may not see it but you know it. They don't ever say "I hate you" or "I don't like you" or anything, but you can feel it. It's like a horse and he knows there is a damn snake around, he just knows it. I learned that in the cavalry. You can't say how you know it because he hasn't done anything to you, he hasn't said anything out of the way, it's just the way he says things and the way he looks at you.

I liked Los Angeles but it was kind of phony. That's what I disliked about it. The people we came in contact with were doing bit parts in movies and that sort of stuff, and they were sort of artificial, that's the way I saw it. And the other thing, I'll tell you, we had an earthquake tremor and after that earthquake tremor I knew I wasn't ever going to live out there. Myself and Nat King Cole and a fellow by the name of Claude Shinar—him and his brother had a band called the Shinar Twins—we were in a pool hall and all at once that damn tremor started. So the tremor lasts I guess about five seconds or so, and all at once all those balls on the table started moving and we took off out of that pool hall. We got outside and Claude Shinar said, "Nat, why were you running?" And Nat Cole said, "Well, you know, my dad is a preacher, and I wasn't going to die in no pool room." That was a big laugh and then we went off and got our hair cut next door at the barbershop. I live down here in hurricane country and at least with a hurricane you've got time to do something about it—they know it's coming. With those earthquakes, they just come up on you and you don't know anything. So I never wanted to live out there. My wife wanted to but not me.

A lot of the athletes and entertainers used to go on the East Side to get our hair cut. We used to meet up in the barbershop and that's where I met Nat King Cole. He went to Wendell Phillips High School in Chicago. I'm from Gary, and we used to play them in high school so we'd talk. We didn't become great friends but we knew each other very well. I used to go to his house when he had a party—he used to have a lot of parties—and he used to have a lot of pretty girls there. His wife couldn't stand all of that. Lenny Ford and myself, we'd be over there with all these party people and they'd burn holes in the furniture and that kind of thing. She couldn't stand it and I don't blame her, really. But he had a lot of parties. He had a swimming pool and we'd be out there because of the babes—we weren't out there because we were going in his pool.

I met Bill Cosby when he was a young kid. And I met the guy from the Rams and UCLA who became a movie star, Woody Strode. He played ball up in Canada when I was up there. He was really a philosophical person and I used to tell him to take that philosophy and get away from me. Woody was a brooder. He married a Hawaiian girl who was beautiful but she was sorry. She liked to drink and she liked to check out on him and that sort of thing. And Kenny [Washington] I knew. He was a life lover. He loved life and he enjoyed it, he really did. He became a detective in Los Angeles. Yeah, we all knew each other. A fellow by the name of Cliff Wilson took a girl away from Jackie Robinson and married her. We used to tease Jackie about it but you never teased him if you were by yourself. Like I told you, he had a temper, so you always made sure three or four other guys were there. Yeah, we used to tease him all the time about his girlfriend running off with Cliff Wilson and getting married.

Lenny Ford came up to the Dons my second year, and I'll tell you, Lenny was one of the best football players I've ever been around. He was about 6'5", weighed about 255, 260, and he was a terror. We played both ways then and he played defense and on offense he caught passes. He played basketball, too, see, so he had pretty good skills. He could catch and he could outrun all of the other ends. He was happy-go-lucky and he thought he owned the universe. "I ought to be able to do anything I want," you know, that kind of attitude. He was a great football player, no question about it, but he drank a little more than I thought he should. I didn't see much of him after he went to Cleveland. I came down from Hamilton once when I was playing in Canada to see him when the Browns were in Detroit to play.

I remember we played a game against the Chicago Rockets in Chicago and I intercepted a pass and half of Gary must have been there. I ran it back about 35 yards. I didn't score, but I intercepted this pass and the stands went crazy. I was happy that it happened. That was really a pleasing moment in my life because all of my friends and all of the people I grew up around were there to see it. That was one big moment for me, it really was.

There were a few incidents I can recall. We had a tackle named Buddy Tinsley and I have a picture of he and his wife because we eventually became best friends. That's how I ended up going to Canada to play, because of him. But when we were on the Dons together, we were playing an exhibition game against Brooklyn in the Coliseum and we were beating Brooklyn pretty good. Well, Buddy came out of the game and he was over on the sidelines and athletes get hyper during a game—during a game, before a game, halftime, doesn't matter. They're all hyper and everything just like they're about to blow up. I wasn't over there because I was still in the game but I could hear Buddy talking to Ben Whaley and he said, "You know what, you niggers sure can play football."

Well, I'll tell you, the place got quiet. We had four black guys on the team—me, Ben Whaley, Lenny, and George Taliaferro. We said, "We're going to get this guy." We got over there and we were close to him, and now he's crying because the other guys told him what he said. He says, "You know, I meant it as a compliment"—which he did—"I meant it as a compliment and I'm from west Texas, and in west Texas that's what we call niggers." We got so tickled that we just fell out. We said, "Aw, go ahead," you know, and that's the way it went and that was the end of it. And later on we became best friends. He graduated from Baylor and lives in Damon, Texas. Buddy Tinsley.

Another time, we were playing Chicago and they had a Notre Dame player that played center. We went up there and something happened during the game, I forget what, but he said to me, "Nigger," and Lenny Ford decided we were going to get the guy. But he was as tough as we were. And that getting people, you know, it's not always that easy because you aren't going to deviate from what you have to do in order to try to get somebody. But that's the only time I've ever been called a bad word to my face like that.

I had another incident with Don Kimbrough, who was a teammate of ours from Texas A&M. We played an intra-squad game in Bakersfield and Bakersfield is out in the desert and they said the temperature was 113. We're playing the game and guys were falling out and I was running around like I was in a swimming pool because the heat didn't bother me. And Don's playing on the other side and because he was so tired, a situation arose in the game where I had a chance to really rack him, but he was important to our team so I just tackled him. I said, "You owe me one." And he says, "Okay."

So the next day he came over to me, and he was Texas A&M all the way. He had that stature and that army military background and everything and actually, I learned some things from him. I learned when you get on an elevator and there are women on the elevator, you take your hat off and speak and that sort of thing. It's funny, you learn a lot of things along the way that you aren't aware of, that you don't know. Anyway, the next day he brought me a box of cigars and he says, "John, here's a cigar that few white folks and no niggers smoke." I said, "Well they certainly must not be for me, Don, because I'm not a nigger." He says, "But you're my friend, take them, won't you Johnny?" So I said, "Yeah, I'll take them if I'm your friend." So I took the cigars and I wish I hadn't because I burned my clothes with them and everything. But that was another situation.

They allowed us to play poker on the Dons with a quarter limit, so we were playing one night and Lenny Ford was in the game and he's getting beat every hand. We used to play with the joker—it wasn't wild but you could use it as an ace or you could use it in straights and flushes. So we were playing and Bob Nelson, he was a center—real prejudiced, although he didn't do anything out of the way other than this particular night—and a guy beat him in a hand by using the joker and he said, "Ah, ya'll niggered me." That's what they called the joker, but we didn't know that. Well, everybody got real quiet, you know. Nelson looked at Lenny and me, and Lenny was losing about $35 in quarters if you know what I'm saying, and he says, "Shit, lets get the game on. So he niggered you. Deal the goddamn cards." And that was the end of that. But, you know, you had little things that happened and it happened, that's all, and with no intent at the time, really, they just happened.

Overall, I have to say they accepted us. We were just football players and on the field, we were okay. I never saw anybody from the Dons do anything or say anything when we played against Buddy Young or Marion Motley. We just didn't fit in most of the social situations or anything of that nature—on my team anyway. I don't know how they did on other teams. You know, after practice we'd go our way and they'd go their way.

The first time I met Bill Willis and Motley would have been on the playing field. The Browns also had another guy, Horace Gillom. He used to punt. And then after the merger, they got Lenny Ford. Motley and Willis and Gillom all played for Paul Brown in high school and at Great Lakes and Ohio State. When it came to signing black players, they weren't going to sway him. He just wanted to win and he was going to do whatever it took. Like I said, even the Browns had a limit of three or four blacks at a time but they had more than the other teams. And Otto Graham was their quarterback and he was some athlete. The Browns had a basketball team and I played against them when I was getting my master's degree from Northwestern. We had a pick-up team and they came to Evanston and played us. They had Gillom and Graham—he was an All-American basketball player for Northwestern—and they beat the pants off us. They beat us to death. I don't know if Motley played on the basketball team because he had real flat feet. His feet used to hurt all the time and he'd be walking like he was walking on hot coal. We used to tease him about it but when he was playing football, you didn't know he had flat feet.

George [Taliaferro] came up in '49. Before he signed with the Dons, I took him over to Chicago because he wanted to be a Bear. I had been a pro for two years so I had a lot of nerve. I figured I knew the ropes so I took him over to meet [George] Halas and I told Halas that George had been offered a contract by the Dons and could he get a contract with the Bears. And Halas said, "Nooooooo." He said, "Blacks aren't tough enough for the National Football League," something in that vein. George was disappointed and I guess Halas really believed that until he got J. C. Caroline. When he got J. C., he fell in love. And then he got [Willie] Galimore from Florida A&M and they had another kid [Bo] Farrington from Prairie View. You know how it is. You're trying to win and if there is a better athlete somewhere else, you get them. So eventually he came around.

When the All-America Conference broke up in 1950, we went to different teams in the NFL and I went to the 49ers. They had Joe Perry and Bob Mike, but they weren't anything like the Dons in terms of their racial feelings. They did not respect black players. I was the best center they had and the two guards they had—[Visco] Grgich and [Bruno] Banducci—they loved me. They weren't really big guards like they have now, they were small, and like I said, I was a good blocker and they liked for me to be playing with them. You know, when I had played against them the previous three years, I used to block them all the time because they were small and they weren't any quicker than I was. I could block them pretty easily. But the 49ers' coaching staff didn't have the same type of respect for black players that the people on the Dons' coaching staff did and they cut me.

Bob Mike I knew because he went to Florida A&M, and we had played against each other in college. Bob was a smart boy. I knew him well. I don't remember exactly but he got into some problem with the 49ers because they didn't like the fact that he was fooling with a white woman. You know, I didn't like the 49ers organization. I didn't care for them. They were nothing like the Dons. The Dons were a first class outfit. [Ben] Lindheimer was the owner and when he got sick the whole league collapsed. If that hadn't happened, the league would have continued because we were outdrawing the NFL.

When the 49ers cut me I could have gone to Green Bay. They wanted to sign me, but my teammate from the Dons Buddy Tinsley had signed in Canada and when I talked to him he told me I ought to come up there because I would get paid more. And sure enough, the Winnipeg Blue Bombers offered me more than the Packers did and it was a no-cut contract, which you couldn't get in the NFL, and I said okay. Except when it got cold, I loved Winnipeg. I still get phone calls from up there. I lived there for seven years and I never was going to leave. Just loved it. But my wife finally wore me down. I had two daughters at the time and she wanted to know who they were going to marry. She didn't want them to marry white kids and she finally wore me down.

Although I loved living in Winnipeg, and I loved playing there, I still have one regret. See, if I had stayed in the States for another year I'd have a pension from the NFL, that's the biggest thing. Plus, I didn't play long enough in Canada because they also have a pension system that came in after I retired. I got hurt and I decided not to play after that. But if I had known they were going to have a pension I would have played another year because I could have. I made the all-pro team up there two years in a row and there's no question I could've played another year.

After I left Winnipeg, I came to Southern University in 1957 and I've been in Louisiana ever since. I was the defensive coordinator and I taught physical education. I retired from coaching first and then I retired from teaching in the '80s. Now let me tell you what I used to do. When I was living in Winnipeg, I used to get job offers all the time from black colleges to come and be an assistant coach because I knew a lot of the guys from when I was in school. To me, it was a chance to travel, a free visit to places like Tennessee, you understand, even though I had no intention of taking any of the jobs. Finally my wife said, "Are you going to take one of these jobs?" And I said, "Shoot no, I'm not thinking about going." And she says, "Why not?" We'd bought a house in Winnipeg, and I was partners in business and we were doing pretty well, but she was always concerned about what was going to happen to our daughters. I didn't object to them marrying a white boy but my wife did so we moved. That's why we moved. And I ended up staying at Southern University for about 30 years and I've been in Louisiana since 1957.

I made the plans for the house I live in now. That goes back to my Gary education. I got two degrees in high school, both a diploma and a vocational diploma. I know quite a bit about drafting. It's not a work of art but it's a nice home. I made my own plans and then had it critiqued by an expert. I stay in touch with some people I've known but not necessarily people I played with. One player I stay in touch with is George Taliaferro. He's a great guy and I know him well. And like I said, I go back to North Carolina Central pretty regularly. I love that school.

BOB MANN

Robert Mann
Born April 8, 1924, in New Bern, North Carolina

J. T. Barber High School in New Bern, North Carolina
Hampton University
University of Michigan

Wide receiver
Undrafted, signed by Detroit Lions in 1948

As much as any African American player of the post-World War II era, the career of Bob Mann was marked by excellence unrecognized and potential greatness stifled by prejudice. In his first year with the Detroit Lions, Bob was the team leader in receptions (ninth in the NFL) and second to Tom Fears among rookies in receiving yards. The following year Bob led the NFL in receiving yards and was second in receptions with 66, a total that was the fourth highest in pro football history at the time behind only Fears, Don Hutson, and Mac Speedie. Yet Bob got no mention on any of the major all-pro teams that year.

In addition, despite his great 1949 season, the Lions traded Bob the following summer. With salaries dropping because of the NFL-AAFC merger, Bob objected when Lions' president Edwin Anderson insisted that he take a pay cut. Detroit's trade of Bob had a racial dimension as well. When his offseason employer, the Goebel Brewing Company (Anderson was Goebel's top boss), was accused of discriminatory hiring practices, Bob found himself in the middle of the disagreement. Although Bob was apparently not involved in the ensuing boycott of Goebel, he was traded to the New York Yanks.

Year	Team	League	Games	Receiving				Rushing		
				Receptions	Yards	Avg.	TDs	Attempts	Yards	Avg.
1948	Lions	NFL	12	33	560	17.0	3	6	46	7.7
1949	Lions	NFL	12	66	1,014	15.4	4	—	—	—
1950	Packers	NFL	3	6	89	14.8	1	—	—	—
1951	Packers	NFL	11	50	696	13.9	8	2	9	4.5
1952	Packers	NFL	12	30	517	17.2	6	—	—	—
1953	Packers	NFL	10	23	327	14.2	2	—	—	—
1954	Packers	NFL	2	—	—	—	—	—	—	—

1 kickoff return for 16 yards

Incredibly, he was cut during training camp a few weeks later. At 26 and just a year after being one of the two best receivers in the NFL, Bob was unemployed. He filed suit against the NFL, claiming that he had been blackballed as a troublemaker by a gentlemen's agreement among team owners. Commissioner Bert Bell, who knew all about such gentlemen's agreements from his days as an owner when the NFL refused to employ black players, disputed Bob's contention. Undoubtedly in part because of the suit, Bob scored a partial victory when the Green Bay Packers signed him late that season.

Bob bounced back to have another excellent year in 1951. He finished fourth in receptions, fourth in yards, and third in touchdown catches but was again completely bypassed by all the major all-pro selectors. He also was not chosen for the Pro Bowl. Bob posted another good season in 1952 and teamed with Billy Howton and Tobin Rote as the Packers led the NFL in passing. He had another solid year in 1953 but suffered a career-ending knee injury in 1954. Released while hurt and unable to play, Bob again sued and won his season's salary from the Packers.

Bob holds the distinction of being the first African American to play for two NFL franchises: the Lions in 1948, along with Mel Groomes, and the Packers in 1950. In addition, he was one of the first black players to play for the University of Michigan. The Wolverines had the greatest season in school history in 1947, when Bob was a senior, as they finished with a 10–0 record, outscored opponents by an average of 34 points per game, and posted the most one-sided victory in the history of the Rose Bowl.

Also an outstanding baseball player (he signed with the Kansas City Monarchs but his hopes for a career were ended by a shoulder injury), Bob attended law school after his football days and was an attorney in Detroit into his eighties. A man with a great sense of humor, Bob evinced no bitterness at having run into pro football's wall of prejudice. He died on October 21, 2006, at age 82.

New Bern is a small city with between 10,000 and 13,000 people, probably about 40 or 45 percent African American. My father was a physician and he was a highly regarded member of the black community. It was a small town and we were all poor because nobody had any money really during the Depression. He was just a country doctor in a small town, and I don't think he made a lot of money, but I think he was a good doctor.

My mother worked in the local school system. I don't think she always worked but I remember her going to work in some of the county schools. She used to play baseball with us sometimes and she was a pretty good athlete. My father said he played baseball at some time but I know he did not play football. I also have a brother who was a pretty fair athlete.

My father read a lot and knew a lot about current events and things like that. He knew a lot about baseball and baseball history, too, both about the Negro Leagues and the majors. There was no television, of course, but he could tell you the whole Yankee team and what inning somebody hit a home run or what inning some-body did something else. Guys he hung around with at the barber shop were like that, too. They really read and knew about those players. I can't remember that we had a black paper there, but they used to read the *Chicago Defender*, which was where they got news about the Negro Leagues.

It was a highly segregated town. We didn't have any public trans-portation so it wasn't a matter of riding in the back of the bus be-cause there were no buses. Being in the city was not as bad as, say, Mississippi, but it was not good. You couldn't eat here and you couldn't go there, but it wasn't as bad as places further South.

You might get in a neighborhood and get chased out but it was such a segregated place, it didn't happen much. One side was black, one side was white, and we didn't have much intermingling. Because it was so segregated, I never did play with any whites until I got to Michigan. Even when it came to sandlot ball, it was all blacks or all whites. They were in one part of the city and we were in the other and the schools were all-black or all-white and I didn't know the players on the team at the white schools. We had a separate but unequal school.

Football was the only sport I played in high school because that was about the only sport we had. We didn't have a track team and we didn't have a gym for basketball or even a paved court outdoors, just a dirt one. I never bounced a basketball on a hardwood court until I went away to Hampton. We didn't have a baseball team ei-ther, but there were plenty of fields to play on so we played sandlot ball. Our football team played against other black schools in Wilmington, Goldberg, and other places around North Carolina.

I played baseball better than I did football, really, and I think I might have been better suited for it. When we played sandlot games, I was always chosen with the older guys and that was unusual. They didn't usually let a younger kid play with the big guys but I did. I always played infield and I could throw and catch and run and I could hit the curve ball so I think I probably would have been better at that.

There was a guy in my hometown, a pitcher, and he could have made it to the major leagues if they had been open to blacks. I don't know about personality and those things, but based on the physical part, he could have made it, I'm positive. He was the best in the city, but he didn't have anywhere to go. Anytime the best hitters can't hit you, you're doing something right.

The first black athlete I knew of was Kenny Washington. You probably know of him and Jackie Robinson at UCLA. And Brud Holland from Cornell. I didn't really know many colleges but I knew Cornell because of Brud Holland and UCLA because of Kenny Washington and Jackie Robinson. Kenny Washington was a tremendous athlete. He really didn't get to play until an age where he wasn't performing at his best.

I remember him signing with the Rams. He was playing for a semipro team—the Hollywood Bears or the Hollywood something. He had been playing for years before that—he'd taken a beating running the ball all the time. I mean, he was still a heck of a player but I think he had better years before then. I got to know him when I went out to play in the Rose Bowl and then later on. He was a nice guy, a nice person. He was larger than I thought. He had a nice wife, just a nice family person.

I met Jackie Robinson after I was through playing football. I met him and Campanella and another guy—can't think of his name but he was a relief pitcher—so I met a lot of those guys. Jackie was a tremendous athlete and the way he took all that stuff they were doing to him, I mean, he was amazing. He was a very fiery guy, and he just took it at first, but I know that's not what he preferred to do.

I did real well in high school athletically and then I went to Hampton. I don't think they were doing a lot of recruiting but my sister and brother went there and my mother had a sister that went there so I chose Hampton for that reason. My brother played football at Hampton. He was ending up when I was a freshman. He broke his leg—a compound fracture—when he was a senior. I remember his ankle had broken at the shin and he held his leg up and the rest of it just bent over. That was a terrible injury. He handled it pretty well, though.

My sister ended up teaching at Texas Southern in the athletic department. She taught dance and physical education. My brother ended up working as an engineer in Washington for the Agency for International Development. He traveled a lot. He went to Chile and he was in Ghana and other places. Eventually I didn't have any relatives in New Bern, and I didn't go back for years.

Hampton played against other black schools. We played Morgan State, who always had a good team. We played against Virginia State, we played against Virginia Union and some other schools I can't think of right at the moment. There were a bunch of good athletes that weren't getting taken by the white schools. There was a guy named Big Train Moody. I'm not sure if he went to Morgan or some place in Atlanta, but he was a fullback and he was outstanding.

It was really interesting, the kind of athletes they were getting. They said the coach from Morgan used to go up to Jersey and places like that further North to recruit guys. I don't know if that's true because there wasn't much recruiting going on then but that's what they said. And Morgan always had good teams. There was just a lot of talented black athletes around who weren't welcome at the white schools.

I remember one guy when I was at Hampton. I played both ways, offense and defense, and I could always run fast. So I was playing defense and a runner went through and I thought it was just a matter of time before I caught him. He weighed like 230, 235 pounds, and I weighed probably about 165, and the longer we ran the further he got away from me. I just mention that because that's the kind of athletes we were getting during that period of time.

I heard Bear Bryant once on the radio in my car. Of course he was smart. He knew he couldn't keep winning if he's selecting from one group and some other teams are selecting from two groups. I mean, he had the worst of that—just mathematically he had the worst of that. There was a guy from the western part of North Carolina who played against Bear Bryant, a lineman, and he was outstanding. I can't think of his name but he went to some place like Minnesota, and common sense told Bear Bryant, he knew he couldn't keep winning like that.

There were a lot of guys like that from the South, outstanding football players. In my day, most of them went to schools like Hampton or else didn't go to school. Later on guys from the South went to school up North. Somebody asked me once since I was from North Carolina, why didn't I go to Duke. I told them I couldn't even breathe, they made me stop breathing when I went past Duke. There were a bunch of good athletes that got passed up by the white schools.

I loved Hampton. It was wonderful. It's just a beautiful place—nice life, girls, you know, it was just a beautiful situation. Just wonderful really, a great experience. But my father wanted me to transfer because he wanted me to go to a school that had a medical school. He said I'd have a better chance to get in. I didn't really want to be a doctor but I didn't know what I wanted to be. He asked me where I wanted to go and I said Cornell or UCLA because they were the schools I knew about because of Brud Holland and Kenny Washington and Jackie Robinson. He said one of them is too expensive and one of them is too far so that ended that. He chose Michigan, and he was paying the bills. It was totally his decision. I really wasn't particular about leaving but I didn't really object much because I knew it was for the better because he said it was for the better.

I had some good years at Hampton. I remember one real good game, I think I had a three touchdown day. I remember playing Virginia State and making the winning touchdown in the last few minutes. I was a tailback/quarterback and Jimmy Griffin, the coach at Hampton, he was a small guy but a tremendous athlete. He moved me to end and broke my heart. But it was the best thing that ever happened to me in terms of football. It's less pounding at end. I don't know if I would have made it professionally as a runner. May have, may not have. I had played tailback all my life. It's more thrilling than end because you get the ball and run it. You play receiver, you may not touch the ball, you know, they didn't throw that much.

I only needed ten hours to graduate when I left Hampton to go to Michigan and I lost 30 hours transferring. I don't know what credits they took from me, but whatever it was, I didn't care. The war was going on and it kept me in school awhile longer so I really didn't mind. War is dumb, you know that? War is really dumb.

When I went to Michigan I thought I was going to the North Pole. My last year at Hampton I went up North to New Hampshire to work in the summer. It was beautiful up there. I went up in June and in North Carolina in June it's warm, the water is warm. Well I jumped in this lake—boy, I like to have froze. It was like ice. In fact, it probably had just gotten through being ice.

I played some that first year in Michigan but I got hurt. I don't remember what game it was but I had a torn medial collateral ligament. In fact, the doctor told me I'd never play again, and I ended up playing ten more years. I'm fortunate in that he knew he didn't know about knees so he just didn't bother, which was cool. I had a doctor tell me once that I needed to keep exercising my thigh muscles, both top and bottom, in order to strengthen my knee and he was right. I still do some calisthenics and exercises.

I went into the service in '44, went into the Navy. I didn't go overseas, thank goodness. I was just trying to get out of there. I was stationed at Staten Island. Wonderful duty. I was out every night. Took the ferry over to lower Manhattan I guess it is—it was a quarter or something to come across. They had all the jazz joints on 52nd Street at that time so I'd stay in there half the night. I never was a drinker but I've always gone in bars, so I'd always tip the bartender when I sat down and get a Coke. He wouldn't bother me and I could see a show, see Billie Holiday and everybody.

There were three jazz joints on 52nd Street. I can't remember the names but it was nice—two on one side and one on the other side. It was just wonderful. You could walk right across the street and hear some more jazz. It was a ball, really a ball. If you liked jazz you'd go down there—I think Joe Williams sang there a couple of times. I can't remember the other people, but it was just wonderful. I'd say literally I'd go every night except one night a week I'd stay in and sleep because I wasn't getting much sleep. But the rest of the time I'd go down there and it was just wonderful. You couldn't see it any cheaper. I'd give the guy a few dollars and he wouldn't bother me—I'd just stay at the bar and hear all the sounds.

At Michigan, it was totally different from Hampton. The number of blacks on campus was very small—shoot, they probably didn't have a hundred really. And they weren't particular about me playing, that was the first difference. I went out for the team, and I asked for a uniform and they finally gave me one, but they wouldn't let me play for awhile. My chances of playing were proportionate to the toughness of the game. If the game was tough I had a better chance of playing. The coach, Fritz Crisler, was not dumb, he was smart—he was a genius, really. He knew if he wanted to win, his chances were better if he let me play, so whatever his prejudices were, if any, he put them aside.

I never had a problem with the players at Michigan. I mean, they all knew I should have been starting, and the guys that were playing at my position at end would tell me, "We don't know why you're not starting." I said, "Go ahead, don't even worry about it." Ann Arbor was very prejudiced, the restaurants and things, but the students weren't. You didn't really have to deal with them, so they were okay.

By the time I got there, they had had a few black athletes in that area. Buddy Young was playing one year before I did—he played at the University of Illinois. He was a tremendous runner. And Bill Willis had been at Ohio State. I think Paul Brown did a lot to break that up, both in college and the pros. He was just a beacon. He had such a big impact. I remember the Browns played a game against Philly, and I remember reading an article that said they didn't have a chance, they didn't even have a ball yet, they're so upstart, all this stuff. And Lenny Ford, who also played at Michigan—a tremendous athlete, good football disposition—he told me, "We're gonna kill them." And they did. I don't know the score, but they beat Philadelphia something terrible. But nobody wanted to give them credit. And they had Marion Motley and Bill Willis and Lenny Ford and Horace Gillom.

Did you know that Paul Brown was the first one to drop the kicker back? Horace Gillom took three steps when he punted, and if you ever saw Horace Gillom, he'd kick it long and high. So Paul Brown figured that out. He's smart, he just moved Horace back fifteen yards instead of ten. Paul Brown was unusual. He had his rules, but it's not just about rules. He changed to fit a guy's talent in. And he was the first one to give guys an extra day off. He knew they could get it done in one less day. The other teams didn't know it but finally they started doing it, too.

We had some good teams at Michigan. We had an excellent coach and some outstanding athletes. The 1947 team was undefeated, and we won the Rose Bowl, 49–0. Like I said, we had some talented football players. You know, you don't need a whole lot of talent, maybe just six or seven real good athletes, especially at the skill positions, and you've got a chance to win any game. Crisler did such a good job. I think Michigan went to a bowl this year and they didn't want to go and they weren't ready to play. That's the coach's fault. Crisler kept us ready to play. I mean, when we went to the Rose Bowl, they pressure you, party you so much, and you've got to remember what you came there for. And Crisler did an excellent job. He was an unusual coach.

And we had some good athletes. Lenny Ford was outstanding and he made all-pro, too, with the Browns. He was a big guy, just under 6'6", and he had good athletic ability, was mean, just had a good football disposition. He was the kind of player you have to make arrangements for, like Barry Sanders. If you played the Lions and didn't make arrangements to stop Barry Sanders, you're not going to win the game, it's that simple. If you didn't make some kind of arrangement for Lenny, he'd disrupt your whole team. He was just that vicious and aggressive—he was a good athlete.

And he had the right attitude for football. You have to have a different attitude for football and he had the right attitude to be a defensive football player. He had a meanness that a whole bunch of football players have. Football players are just different, especially on defense. I was reading somewhere, they said Tiger [Woods] could have played football. Maybe he could, but he'd have to have a certain attitude. I remember a player at Green Bay, they were asking for volunteers to break up the wedge. Now I wouldn't volunteer to do it. I've got more sense than that, but if I did it I wouldn't just run straight into it, I'd roll into it. This guy ran straight into it face up—you know, I've got more respect than that for my body, but a lot of guys didn't.

Lenny and I gravitated toward each other. We had three brothers on the team at Michigan and that was it—me, Lenny, and [Gene] Derricotte, and we were all good athletes capable of making outstanding plays. You gravitate toward the guys that have something in common and Lenny and I were close. Derricotte and I were room-mates but we weren't close. I mean he was alright, but he didn't run with Lenny and me. We were running around and Derricotte had a different attitude, but he was an outstanding athlete and except for his passing he would have played more. But [Bob] Chappius threw the ball better than he did, and Crisler wanted to pass. He put Chappius at tailback and moved Derricotte [to defense].

Lenny and I remained friendly after college. He would call me from Cleveland and I would call him from Green Bay. As I recall, I think he went to law school. He was married to a judge, Judge Geraldine Bledsoe Ford, who died maybe a year ago. Lenny died in his forties. I think he died of a heart attack. He was a great guy.

I graduated before June in the middle of the semester. I knew the Lions were interested. They didn't draft me but I got invited to camp. They could have signed Lenny, too, but they didn't. He went with the Los Angeles Dons [of the rival All-America Football Conference] because they gave him more money. I became a starter right from the beginning and did quite well. I think I was able to evaluate talent and that's not always easy because you have a tendency to make yourself better than you are. But I always tried to be honest about it and just looking at the receivers, I had a feeling I should make the team. I said, "I can do this and I can do that," and it's not really a hard job. If you're honest about what your talent looks like, if you're honest about what your job is and you try to do that better than anybody else, I don't care what you're doing, you ought to do pretty well.

I met a guy in a restaurant recently and I told him all you had to do was get open and catch the ball. I believe in simplifying things and, shoot, that's all I had to do. Playing in the NFL, it's not hard, but it's specialized. I worked at that hard: getting open and catching the ball. You just need to work at it. I used to stay after practice and run patterns by myself. They didn't throw many passes in those days—they throw more passes now in one game than we threw all year. If you got three or four thrown to you, you were lucky. Now, boy, every other play is a pass. I would love to play now. Frank Tripucka was the quarterback, and he wasn't bad, they just weren't throwing that many passes. Frank's son [Kelly] played here for the Pistons and I think he was announcing basketball games. I always intended to contact him but never did, just to see how his father was doing.

Mel Groomes was on the Lions and then Wally Triplett came in my second year. He was a good athlete. Wally was tough. I mean, he would go in there and try to make that extra yard and they were taking shots at him. There comes a time when you got to know—and I see this happen now—two guys are tackling you and you're not going to make but maybe another yard, you need to get down. That's common sense. That's where a lot of fumbles occur, when the guy's still struggling, he's not going to make any more yardage, he's got to make sure he protects the ball. You hear these guys say, I heard a tackle tell the defensive end, "If you get there before I do, hold him up. I'll be there." See, you got to miss that part. It's just common sense, you got to get down. But Wally wouldn't do that.

I was just thinking of this guy at Green Bay, I don't remember who he was, but he tackled Wally and Wally didn't like the tackle. Wally's what, 180 or 185, and this guy weighed about 230 and was a good physical guy. So the guy said, "Okay, you want to do that now or you want to do that after the game?" I'm standing right next to him, and Wally and I cracked up laughing, you know, it's just absurd talking about doing something to him. But Wally was tough, and he could run that ball. He was a good athlete. But sometimes you need to get on the ground.

I liked Detroit. It was an unusual city. Detroit was still very segregated at that time. You only had one part of the city you could live in. They called that part Black Bottom, right where the stadium is now. It was bad in one way and great in another. The places that were available were just wonderful.

They had a hotel name of the Gotham Hotel and it was run by a guy who was in the number business and he took care of it. He made sure the menu was good and he asked me to bring him a menu from some place when we went on a trip so the chef could cook what was on the menu. It was just wonderful. Anybody who was a star had to come to the Gotham because you couldn't stay at the white hotels so you saw all the stars, all the female stars, you know, and you got to know them and it was just a wonderful situation. Segregation was bad but it had some good points.

I lived near the hotel and every entertainer that came here had to stay at the Gotham, so you got to know all of them. They used to tell me so and so is in town and, boy, she's fine, so I used to go and see her firsthand because she had to eat in the dining room. So like I said, there were just some things about it that weren't too bad.

You'd see all of them come through the hotel, all the entertainers. Duke Ellington, Lena Horne, they all stayed at the Gotham Hotel. I'm trying to think of one, but I can't think of the name, she came in there and they'd say boy, is she fine—Barbara McNair. She stayed there. Everybody stayed there, and the man who owned the hotel— well two men owned it, I think—they took excellent care of it.

In 1949, I was first in [receiving] yards and second in receptions. But like I said, now one receiver will get a chance at 12 passes and that was unheard of when I was playing. It was totally different. They didn't have the pass patterns or anything. I would love to play now. Here's something of a trivia question: I was traded for Bobby Layne. Bobby Layne was a character, he was something else.

The way I left here was interesting and it was just a lot of mess, really. I'm not talking about ability, it was just a lot of mess. I was working for Goebel [Brewery], and the president for Goebel was Edwin Anderson, who was also president of the Lions. And they didn't have any black drivers at the beer company and we got into I'll just say a discussion, not really an argument, and then it crept over into my contract. I said I'd just quit working for the brewery and they said they wanted to cut my salary, and that didn't seem right to me because I just had that year I spoke of. So I just said the heck with it and they traded me to the New York Yanks for Bobby Layne.

Buddy Young, Sherman Howard, and George Taliaferro were all with the Yanks, but we did not get to be close friends because I wasn't there long enough. But we got to know each other. Buddy was an unusual guy, he really was, just a carefree guy. The white guys on the team loved him and they protected him. If you wanted to get into a fight, you just hit Buddy Young dirty and somebody would fight, it was that simple. He got along with the guys wonderfully and his association was just interesting.

Buddy had two or three white guys on the team who loved him. They went someplace, they had a game in the South, and they wanted to eat and they weren't going to serve him and they used the n-word. The guys he was with, two big tackles, some of those guys loved violence and they probably would have torn the place up. So they served them.

Somebody kind of roughed Buddy up once and the Yanks had a tackle, I think his name was Johnson, from someplace in Texas. He said, "Listen, man, if you want do that we're going to have a big problem because we're not going to have you do this. If you want to be in a fight just do that one more time." You know, they looked out for Buddy and it was wonderful. He had a good relationship with them.

New York cut me and I went home and Green Bay called me at the end of the season. I got there on Saturday and played on a Sunday. I think I was the first black player for the Packers. There were two black males in the whole city, three including me. One worked for the railroad but he didn't have to do anything. He chauffeured the head of the railroad who didn't go out. And the other one was a porter. So there were two other black guys in the city—and no black females at all.

I had a talk with the coach, and I don't know if I should say this but I'm going to say it anyway. There were no black females in Green Bay so I said, "Coach, I need to be able to get in and out of town, go somewhere like Chicago." I didn't want to mess around with the white girls and he didn't want me to so it worked out great. When we played in New York he paid for me to stay overnight for an extra night so it worked out. He was understanding, and I had some sense. I used to go to the archway in Chicago—it's a wonderful spot—and it was like, "Here's a professional football player coming into town," so it was nice.

Man, I used to burn up going down that road to Chicago. I was fortunate. There was a guy here who was an engineer for Chrysler and he used to tune my car for me. He tuned that sucker and you talk about running, boy. There weren't that many cops on the highway in those days, either. That car was like a suicide vehicle, which I didn't know then. It was like driving a boat. It's not like a European car. It was just like driving a yacht going down the highway.

I got along fine in Green Bay and most of the guys on the Packers I got along with beautifully. The guy closest to me was Dick "the Bruiser" [Afflis] but I got to know all the guys. One of them I had intended to call the other day but I haven't called him yet, Stretch Elliott. It was interesting, some of those guys came out of segregated situations and in less than 24 hours they were integrated. I told some of them that. I told them, "You were segregated, and now you come up here playing with somebody who's black. Shoot, you can't integrate much faster than that." I didn't have a problem with anybody.

It's interesting because a guy called me two days ago, Ray DiPierro. He played at Green Bay and he and I were roommates. He's white and he didn't have a roommate and there were no other blacks on the team for me to room with. But anyway, we just roomed together—what the heck, there was no reason why we shouldn't.

We had a problem going South. We went to New Orleans and played the Eagles and we had to stay in a private home. The lady was the best cook in the world. Boy, she could really cook. That lady cooked all those New Orleans dishes. One of them, I can't remember the name of it, it was baked fish and rice and it was just delicious. And the gumbo and the deviled crabs and fried oysters—just delicious. If you had to miss something, that's the way to miss it, I guess. We made the best of a bad situation. We should have been staying with the team but it just ended up not being as negative as it could have been.

I think I only had one player say something racial and I don't remember who that was. I mean, I had guys call me names but not racial and I've always been able to handle that part of it. [Chuck] Bednarik hit me in my mouth and some of the guys tried to make that out to be racial but it wasn't. I know how to put things racial and nonracial. I don't have any problems doing that even now and it wasn't racial. I told the guys, "He hits everybody. Every Sunday he hits somebody. He's crazy." It was just my day to get hit and he hit me in my mouth and knocked loose two teeth that I had replaced. It was just who he was. He just hit people every day. He was an ornery sucker, that's what it was.

I roomed with Dick "the Bruiser." He was insane, just cuckoo. He was my roommate for some time. He was totally insane. Oh, he loved violence. Loved violence. He should've been paying to play rather than them paying him. He was a character, believe me, he was something else. You would've loved him. He was crazy as a loon. He was as coo-coo as they make them. He would start fights on the field, off the field. Loved violence. But he was a good athlete, too, a really good athlete. He could do a handstand and do push-ups. I mean, it's hard to think a guy could do that, it's hard enough to do a push-up. And he was quick and he was tough and he had the right disposition.

As I said earlier, I had met Kenny Washington at the Rose Bowl so I got to know him before any of the other black players. He would take us around to the clubs and things when we were out there. He would come pick us up and there was a doctor who liked the athletic scene and he loaned us his car so we got around and Kenny was wonderful. Later on I met Bill Willis and Motley. I met them the first time when they came up and played us in Green Bay. They came up to the room because they wanted to talk. They were great guys.

I remember reading a piece about Motley. Excellent player. I can't remember what game it was, but his helmet came off and the writer said just to even things up he should be forced to play without a protective headpiece. The Browns made a career out of running that draw play to Motley. And I remember Bill Willis playing nose tackle at his weight, which was just 215 pounds. He had all his weight in his chest and he'd get down and really explode into the center. And he was so mobile. They'd have to play him somewhere now with that kind of athletic ability, they'd just have to find some place for him to play. Probably defensive end. Bill Willis was an outstanding athlete. And he was a good guy, too. They had Willis, Motley, and Lenny on the same team. They had a good personality plus an excellent coach.

The difference between a coach like Crisler or Paul Brown and some of the other guys is amazing. There's a bible study I had conducted where I was talking about different gifts that we have. One thing I pointed out is how Crisler figured out that when we were going to kick a field goal or an extra point and I weigh 178, I can't block as well as some guy who weighs 250. I'm surprised nobody thought of that. I mean, just think about that. Here I am trying to keep out some guys weighing 250. You'd do better if you had another guy doing it. I think part of the problem was getting them in—they didn't have free substitution. But Paul Brown and Crisler figured that out quick.

Now to show you about coaches, we had an assistant coach at Green Bay, Hugh Devore, that came in from Notre Dame. So we have a practice drill where one guy tries to get by two guys. Now it looks like common sense would tell Hugh Devore that that's not my job description. I have to get down and try to get past two guys on the team that weigh at least 550 pounds total? The two guys saw me get down, and they said, "We're going to kill you, man." I said, "You're not going to kill me because I'm backing up the other way," just kidding with them. When the head coach saw this he said, "Get him out of there." But why wouldn't Hugh Devore know that?

What situation am I going to be in where that would come up? Common sense would tell you no situation. And why would he not know that? And the last thing I would do would be to charge at them. No way. That's suicide. I mean, I wouldn't try to duck my job but I'd try to figure out some way to get around them. Then another coach had the guys blocking somebody, doing some insane drill, and they asked me, "Why don't you tell him?" I said, "That's not my job." But he should have known better. Talk about coaches, boy, there are certain things you got to have. Like the Lions now, I don't think they have a clue, really.

I was playing first string when I got hurt [in 1954], and then they cut me. I got hurt in an exhibition game, and strangely enough, Bednarik was the one that hurt me. I'm not going to say he did it intentionally because a pass was thrown and he ended up falling against the back of my knees. It was just an exhibition game in Hershey, Pennsylvania so I don't think he did it intentionally. Not that I would put it past him. I just don't think he did it intentionally.

I had the anterior cruciate damaged. I don't know if they were torn but I couldn't play. You know, knees then were a mystery to most people. I could run straight and I knew I could run far but I couldn't cut either way. Nobody spoke about doing anything to it. Now they just go in and sew it up and you sit out, what, six, eight weeks and come back playing. But then they didn't know what the heck to do. I knew I couldn't play. I went from first string to getting cut so I sued Green Bay for my salary and I won, of course.

When I was playing for the Packers I used to come back to Detroit after the season. In those days we'd end up playing two games in California so I'd just stay out there for a month and then go back to Green Bay and then I'd come here. After I left Goebel, I got into real estate and I worked in it for a long time and did well, then I went to law school.

I went to law school when I got to be about 40 because I went to visit a guy that was a friend of mine, a judge. I was watching the proceedings and I thought I could do that and do it as well as he could. I met and talked with him in the judge's chambers and he told me about law school and he sounded like he knew what he was talking about. It looked like something I could do, and then it became something I wanted to do so I decided to go to law school.

I went right in Detroit to the Detroit College of Law, which has moved now to Lansing. People are always telling you what you can't do. It's amazing. Everything I've ever done, every team I ever went to, somebody was always telling me, "You can't do this, you can't do that." I made a career out of doing things people said I couldn't do. When I started playing football at Hampton they said I couldn't, and when I went up to Michigan they said, "This is the Big Ten," and when I went to the pros they told me, "You can't really do this, this is the pros." I just said, "Listen, I can do that better than he's doing it." I try to be very positive. You just see what you can do and try to do the best you can and work at it. They were just negative people. It seems like there are a bunch of negative people around. Somebody's always knocking you.

I've done mostly criminal law. I was in a civil case not too long ago, but I try to stay out of those things. I was just doing that for a friend—I didn't even know the terminology. If I get a client I can help out, I'll try to mentor them. I tell them, "Listen, if you need somebody to talk to, call me." Not the hardened guys but the kids. I try to get the kids to stay in school because once they drop out of school, they're dead. They drop out, they're in the street and they get with somebody else who dropped out and before you know it they have a real problem.

If I can help them, I don't mind doing something. I talk to my clients all the time, try to steer them right. I gave a speech years ago at a school and I was in contact years later with a lady that was in the class and she said how much I motivated her. I've done it throughout the years and I like to do it whenever I can because we've got too many kids we're losing.

If I see a new lawyer—I saw a guy the other day I hadn't seen in court before so I gave him a card and said, "I don't know if you need this card but if you need a brief or need to talk about a case, call me." I do that for any new lawyer I see. I say, "Maybe you don't need help but you always need somebody to talk to about a case. There are always briefs you might need." I just try to help everybody, my clients and any new lawyer that I see, and I'm sure most of them appreciate it, too.

I met my wife after I quit playing football. She's in Florida right now because she's got terrible arthritis. I have two daughters. I don't know their ages because they're always changing their ages so I don't know what their ages are. I say they're twins—they're not but one of them is getting younger and one is getting older so now I place them at the same age. One is 40 and one is between 40 and some other age. One of them is an entertainer in a couple of groups—she was in *Hello, Dolly!* and traveled to Europe in another play. She enjoyed that. And she's doing commercials now. She's got pictures in a couple of magazines and she's on a billboard in LA.

I'm not heavy into the alumni, either at Michigan or Hampton. I sometimes go to reunion functions for the Lions. I was inducted into the Hall of Fame in Green Bay in '87 or '88, I can't remember, and I talk to some of the guys. But I haven't been back to Green Bay since whenever I was inducted. I really don't like the autograph situation, you know, how somebody just comes up. I just never liked it much so I haven't been back but I intend to go back.

I'd like to retire in the next year at the most. I kind of would like to live here [Detroit] in the summer. Summers here are great. In Florida summers are not nice so if you miss the extreme weather both places, I think you fare a little better—I would anyway. I don't do well in the cold weather. The older I get the less I like it.

I was talking to somebody recently and he didn't know who Wilt Chamberlain was. Now I don't know, young as you might be, you ought to know who Wilt Chamberlain was. But a lot of people don't know the history. I was honorary captain for the first game at Ford Field, so I was down on the field. I spoke to one of the guys on the Lions, Shaun Rogers, a nose tackle, and he asked me about myself so I told him. He said, "Man, I'm glad to meet you. We don't know much about you guys." I said, "I know you don't." And that was good because he was interested. But too many people don't know the history.

JOE PERRY

Fletcher Joe Perry
Born January 22, 1927, in Stevens, Arkansas

David Starr Jordan High School in Los Angeles, California
Compton Junior College

Fullback
Undrafted, signed by San Francisco 49ers in 1948

Whenever sports pundits talk about the greatest running backs of all time, it is rare that they mention Joe Perry. That is true even when the field is as large as ten, as in the Ten Best Running Backs or Ten Greatest Running Backs. Usually such lists go something like this: Jim Brown, Walter Payton, Barry Sanders, Emmitt Smith, Eric Dickerson, O. J. Simpson, Earl Campbell, Gale Sayers, Thurman Thomas, and Tony Dorsett.

Because Joe is almost never on such lists, younger fans are likely to respond to a call for his inclusion by asking, Who the heck is Joe Perry? Well, consider a few facts and then consider that the better question is, Why the heck isn't Joe on these lists? He won two rushing titles in the NFL and one in the All-America Football Conference (AAFC). That total of three is equal to the number won by Payton, Sayers, Thomas, and Dorsett combined, and only half of the ten players listed above—Brown, Dickerson, Simpson, Smith, and Sanders—won more.

In addition, Joe was the career leader in rushing yards for five years, six if his yards from the AAFC are included. Sayers, Simpson, Sanders, Campbell, Dorsett, Dickerson, and Thomas never held the all-time top spot, and only Brown, Payton, and Smith of the ten players above held it for a longer time.

| | | | | | Rushing | | | | Receiving | | | | Total |
Year	Team	League	Games	Attempts	Yds.	Avg.	TDs	Receptions	Yds.	Avg.	TDs	TDs
1948	49ers	AAFC	14	77	562	7.3*	10*	8	79	9.9	1	12
1949	49ers	AAFC	11	115	783*	6.8	8*	11	146	13.3	3	11
1950	49ers	NFL	12	124	647	5.2	5	13	69	5.3	1	6
1951	49ers	NFL	11	136	677	5.0	3	18	167	9.3	1	4
1952	49ers	NFL	12	158	725	4.6	8	15	81	5.4	0	8
1953	49ers	NFL	12	192*	1,018*	5.3	10*	19	191	10.1	3	13*
1954	49ers	NFL	12	173*	1,049*	6.1	8	26	203	7.8	0	8
1955	49ers	NFL	11	156	701	4.5	2	19	55	2.9	1	3
1956	49ers	NFL	11	115	520	4.5	3	18	104	5.8	0	3
1957	49ers	NFL	8	97	454	4.7	3	15	130	8.7	0	3
1958	49ers	NFL	12	125	758	6.1	4	23	218	9.5	1	5
1959	49ers	NFL	11	139	602	4.3	3	12	53	4.4	0	3
1960	49ers	NFL	10	36	95	2.6	1	3	-3	-1.0	0	1
1961	Colts	NFL	13	168	675	4.0	3	34	322	9.5	1	4
1962	Colts	NFL	12	94	359	3.8	0	22	194	8.8	0	0
1963	49ers	NFL	9	24	98	4.1	0	4	12	3.0	0	0

*Led league

Completed 3 of 11 passes for 79 yards and 1 TD

Returned 33 kickoffs for 758 yards and 1 TD

Made 1 of 6 field goal attempts and 6 of 7 conversion attempts

Intercepted 1 pass for 24 yards

Played in AAFC Playoff and Championship Games in 1949

Played in NFL Conference Playoff Game in 1957

Named to Pro Bowl in 1952, 1953, and 1954

Named Most Valuable Player of NFL by United Press in 1954

Elected to Pro Football Hall of Fame in 1969

Still not convinced that Joe belongs somewhere in the Top 10 best rushers of all time? Then consider that his NFL average of 4.82 yards per carry is one of the best ever, better than seven of the ten players listed above, all except Brown, Sayers, and Sanders. If his two AAFC years are counted, Joe jumps past both Sayers and Sanders to 5.04. He averaged five yards or more per carry five times in his career, including two seasons of more than six.

Two 1,000-yard seasons in a row does not sound that impressive in this day and age, when as many as 23 running backs break that barrier in a given year, but when Joe reached that level in 1953, the NFL season was only twelve games. It was only the sixth time anyone had ever reached the 1,000-yard mark in the 34-year history of pro football. When he did it again in 1954, Joe became just the second player to do it twice and the first to ever do it in consecutive seasons.

Joe was especially dominant in 1954, when he averaged 31 yards more per game than the second-place rusher. Calculated over today's 16-game schedule, that works out to a difference of 500 yards for the year. If his statistics from his two best seasons are prorated to 16 games, this is what they look like:

1953:	1,357 yards	5.3 avg.	13 TDs
1954:	1,398 yards	6.1 avg.	11 TDs

Joe was incredibly durable as he played 16 seasons, a total equaled by Marcus Allen but never surpassed by a running back. At the time he retired, his 181 games played were the third highest ever behind only Lou Groza and Y. A. Tittle. From 1958–1974, Joe held the record for most games played by a running back.

The combination of durability and skill allowed Joe to pile up enough rushing yards to put him in the all-time Top 10 for almost 40 years. Even setting his AAFC stats aside, Joe was in the Top 10 for an incredible 36 years (1953–1989). That makes his stay in the Top 10 longer than anyone's, save Jim Brown. Given the ever-growing numbers put up by running backs, it's unlikely anyone will match that 35 year stretch anytime soon. Joe also once held the all-time record for yards from scrimmage, as he totaled 11,744 rushing and receiving yards for his career.

It's important to note that Joe did all this while playing in the same backfield as Hall of Fame running backs Hugh McElhenny and John Henry Johnson for nine and two seasons, respectively. In addition, for ten years he played with Y. A. Tittle, a quarterback whose preferred method of moving the ball was via the pass. That meant fewer carries than would have been expected for a back of Joe's caliber.

The time is way past for modern fans and pundits to get wise and recognize Joe as one of the greatest runners of all time. Along with his many individual accomplishments, he played for one of the most exciting teams in one of the most exciting eras of pro football history. Perhaps most important, Joe accomplished all he did at a time when he was one of only a few blacks playing in the pros. His presence was met by hostility—some went out of their way to injure him, yet Joe rose to the very top. In addition to his overwhelming credentials, keep that in mind the next time you see a program or a list of the Best Running Backs that does not include him.

My mom was very athletic and my dad was to an extent. He didn't really care about sports, though. He kept busy working to put food on the table. They were from Arkansas and that's where I was born. We moved to Los Angeles when I was very young. The area where I grew up is called Compton now, but back then we just said we lived in Los Angeles. My father was a miner in Arkansas but after we moved to California, he worked on a farm and in factories.

I have Indian blood from both my mother's side and my father's side. He was part Cherokee and Blackfoot and she was part Choctaw. My father wasn't that tall but he was big across and strong. I would say I was taller than my dad by the time I was eleven years old. You could tell he was part Indian because he had a temper. He didn't take anything from anybody and that's the way I am, too. My mom wasn't docile but she was quiet. She'd think about things and be a peacemaker. She'd say, "Now, wait a minute. Just cool down."

We played all kinds of sports when I was growing up: football, track, basketball, softball. We didn't really play too much baseball, we played softball. I tried basketball but I didn't last too long because they said I was too rough. We used to play on the neighborhood dumps because the black kids were not allowed to play on the fields. My sister Louella was a good athlete and she used to play with us. She was two years older than me, and she was fast. I don't know how old I was when I finally caught up to her, but when I was younger I couldn't keep up with her.

The area where I lived was mostly black but it had some whites and a sprinkling of Mexicans. I would say people mostly got along. The only trouble I remember was a riot involving some sailors during World War II. I was in high school at the time. There was a streetcar called Big Red that used to run right through Compton and these Caucasian sailors got into it with some of the neighborhood black guys when they got off the streetcar, and the black guys beat the you know what out of them.

Well, the next day a whole streetcar full of sailors came back and went after every black guy they could find. It went back and forth like that for about two weeks. I can't remember all the details too well, but what I do remember is that the police hardly seemed to be around. And I'm not talking about a fistfight between a few guys, this was a situation where you had these two groups of people battling in the streets.

The first year I played high school football, a player on the other team was killed during a game. It was an all-white school, South Gate, but it wasn't a racial thing. The kid got the ball on a kickoff and a bunch of players on our team gang tackled him and he broke his neck and died. When my mother heard about it, I thought my football days were over because she didn't want me to play football in the first place. She was okay with everything else but not football. She got upset one time when I hurt myself because I hadn't even told her I was on the team, so I was just waiting to hear what she was going to say about a boy getting killed. But she let me keep playing. She figured if I wanted to do something that bad, then it was okay with her. She was quite a lady.

The school I went to, Jordan, the majority was black. Then you had South Gate and Huntington Park and a lot of other schools that were either majority white or all white. I had a lot of Caucasian friends who went to Jordan, but not many of them played on the football team. The school had an exceptionally good baseball team, and a lot of the whites played baseball. We were also dominant in track, but in football, we were just mediocre.

I could've played on the baseball team but I preferred track and the two of them were at the same time. I had a good arm and I played every position and I could hit. After I had been playing for the 49ers a few years, I started off in spring training in the Pacific Coast League. I figured I could play baseball until football season started and then switch over. I did pretty well but then they told me they wanted to ship me out to a lower league, so that was it for baseball.

I was a running back from the time I started playing football in high school but, really, I did everything. I punted, kicked, passed, and ran. Same thing in track. I did all the sprints, plus the high jump, the broad jump, and the shot put. The 100 and 220 and the relays were my best. They tried me at the 440 but after awhile I said, "No thank you." Even though I'm over six feet tall I don't have long legs, and the 440 used to kill me. I used to cramp whenever I tried it. I kept up with the sprints in college, too. I ran against some of the fastest guys in the country and either beat them or stayed right there with all of them. Being that I was black and from such a small school, it used to create a disturbance in the headlines once in awhile because they didn't know how to deal with this guy from Compton Junior College beating these big-name runners.

Kenny Washington was one of my idols when he was at UCLA. In fact, I wanted to go to UCLA because of him and Woody Strode and Jackie Robinson. They were all great football players and we used to follow them very closely. Then when I was finishing up high school UCLA gave me the cold shoulder. I went out there to talk to them and they snubbed me. So instead I went to Compton Junior College and never looked back. USC wasn't an option, as I recall. I don't think USC was welcoming blacks at that time. Then after I tore it up at Compton, somebody from UCLA came around soliciting and I told the guy, "I wouldn't go there if you were the last school on earth." Oh, I remembered. Some things have gotten vague in my memory over the years, but that's one I remember to this day.

I started at Compton in the fall of 1944 and I only played one year and then I went in the Navy. The war was still on, and I was 18 and I figured it was just a matter of time before they drafted me, so I enlisted. It almost killed my mother. She did not want me to go in. When I got down to the induction center, the WAVE who was signing people up asked me, "Wouldn't you like to go to Great Lakes? You can go to school there and learn how to be a cook or a steward." I said, "Lady, if I wanted to learn how to be a goddamn cook, I would just stay at home with my mother. She knows how to cook better than anybody I know."

Well, she gave me a big sigh, and I said, "No, don't give me no sigh. You think every black person you see has to be a cook or a steward?" Oh, I created quite a ruckus. I don't take crap off anybody. She didn't know what to say so she called the top dog over and this guy came up to me and took me back into his office. I said, "Listen, I'll tell you the same thing I told her. I came because I wanted to volunteer. I don't have to volunteer for anything. If you don't want to accept me, then we'll just end this right now. Nobody's going to make a damn slave out of me."

I was very abrupt because I always believed you should say exactly what you think, and if somebody says something to me I don't like, I let them know about it right away. I figured it was going to be more of the same with him so I started to get up and he said, "No, don't leave. I understand what you're saying. I've got just the place for you." They sent me to the San Diego Naval Training Center and that's how my navy career started.

I forget now how many were in the platoon when I first got there but I was the only black in the whole platoon so I said to myself, "Oh boy. I wonder how this is going to turn out." Because I was the only one in there who had any college, I became the platoon leader. Nobody from up top made me the platoon leader, I was chosen by the rest of the guys even though I was the only black.

I had a great time. Some of the best friendships of my life were formed out of that platoon. I think you had guys from every state in the union there. I wasn't a tough ass, I just made it clear that I didn't take any crap from anybody. Once they recognized that, we got along fine. I'll never forget one guy, a gigantic guy, his nickname was Steamboat. He was one of the worst of the bigots from the South but after awhile, he and I became the closest of friends. It's a great feeling when you get with a group of guys from all different backgrounds from all over the whole country and all of a sudden you just all melt together. That's the only way I can say it, it was a great feeling.

It was in the Navy that I made the connection that led me to the 49ers. A guy by the name of John Woudenberg saw me play when I was based at the Alameda Naval Air Station and he told me later that his reaction was, "I think this guy would make a hell of a running back for the 49ers." He had been playing tackle for the 49ers and he told [49ers head coach] Buck Shaw and [owner] Tony Morabito about me.

After that, both Shaw and Morabito started coming over to Alameda to watch me play. Apparently they liked what they saw because after a few weeks they offered me a contract. My plan at that time was to go back to college once I finished in the navy but I was young and dumb and I needed a job so I said, "Why not?" and that's how my pro football career started. I don't know what would have happened if Woudenberg hadn't come along. I heard recently that John died not too long ago. He was living not too far from me here in Arizona.

The Rams had been scouting me, too. This is when there were two leagues, the NFL and the All-America Football Conference. The Rams actually offered me more money but I went with the 49ers and I've never regretted it right down to today. There was just something about Tony Morabito that made me think that signing with the 49ers was the right move. From that moment on, from the first meeting I had with him, a very close friendship began that lasted the rest of his life.

I would say friendship doesn't do it justice. It was really a father-son relationship, that's how close we were. He was just a straight shooter whose word was as good as gold. Once he told you something, that was it. I never once negotiated a contract with Tony because I knew that whatever he would decide to pay me would be more than fair. He would just call me up and tell me he was putting my contract in the mail without telling me how much it was and I would sign it without even looking at the dollar amount, that's how much I trusted him. I'm just about eighty years old now and to this day the two most influential people in my life were my mother and Tony Morabito.

One example of what I mean came in 1953 when I rushed for 1,018 yards to lead the league. Only a few guys had ever rushed for 1,000 yards at that time and after the season Tony gave me a bonus of $5,090—$5 for every yard. Obviously, he didn't have to do that. We didn't finish in first place so there was no extra money coming in for him from any playoff game. He just appreciated the effort I gave and wanted to express it. You've also got to keep in mind that there were a lot of players in the NFL in 1953 who didn't even earn

$5,090 for a whole year's salary. But I'm not even talking about the money. I'm talking about the gratitude he showed me by doing that, the feeling.

The 49ers had not had a black player before so when I got to training camp in 1948, I was the first one. I was the only one for the first few weeks of camp until Bob Mike came along later that summer, and then a few years later Charlie Powell joined the team. Bob Mike was a tackle who played at UCLA and, of course, with us being the only blacks they automatically put us together as roommates. It's funny when I think about how people thought back then, although when I think about it, a lot of people still think that way today. Just because you're black doesn't mean that you have to have a black roommate or that you'll get along better than with any of the whites on the team. You're human, you speak the same language, so there's no reason why you can't eat together or drink together or share the same room together.

Bob was a pretty big guy and he could run and they made a defensive tackle out of him, although personally I think he would've been better off at offensive tackle. I guess they wanted to see if they could make him into a defensive player. He was pretty good. Nothing spectacular. He lasted two years and that was it. We weren't close and we did not fit as roommates. He kind of had a UCLA attitude that I ran into with a few people. You know, "I went to UCLA and you went to Compton Junior College," that kind of an attitude where he was looking down at me. He found out quick that I don't take that kind of shit from anybody.

After Bob Mike, I roomed with Verl Lillywhite, and I believe he and I were the first black and white roommates in pro football. The year 1948 was his first year with the 49ers, too. He and I played against each other when I was at Compton and he was at Modesto Junior College. Then the following year I began to room with Lowell Wagner and he and I became the best of friends. I think we stayed roommates throughout the whole time he played for San Francisco.

I never had any problem with Verl Lillywhite, it wasn't anything like that. He and I were great friends. It just worked out that Lowell and I liked each other. We met, we hit it off, and we became roommates. That was it. The funny thing about Lowell, I could never figure out his nationality. He had black hair, medium complexion, and I could never figure out, "Is this guy Irish or what?" It was just a kind of thing where we blended very well and skin color didn't matter one bit. Whether we were on the field or off, he always had my back and I always had his.

Lowell was a quiet guy but, boy, don't ever get him mad because he would get mean. I never realized that until one day somebody grabbed something out of his hand or something, I really don't remember what exactly happened, but he got a look in his eye like he was going to kill somebody. I knew he would listen to me, so I said, "No, no, no," and the sucker he was mad at didn't know how lucky he was. Never mess with quiet people. I never did anyway. But Lowell was a great guy and a good cornerback. He was good and he was tough.

A lot of the guys on the 49ers my first year or two were from the South and I never had any problems with any of them. We got along great. Really, it was like one big family and I was part of that family. If somebody on the other team ever got any idea he wanted to start something, he had to mess with our whole team. The way they welcomed me and made me part of the team definitely made it easier.

I settled in San Francisco as soon as I joined the 49ers and lived different places and, then, about halfway through my career, we bought a home in the Excelsior district. I was really hooked into music because I was a disc jockey for about ten years. I used to go see different singers and bands when they came to town at places in the Fillmore district. Ray Charles is the one who stands out in my mind. One time when he was playing, he invited me up on the stage area and I went up and sat by him while he was playing the piano.

In the beginning with the 49ers, I played on defense as well as offense. That's what everybody did. That only lasted a little while and then the two platoon system came in. I had a good year as a rookie and then they switched Norm Standlee to defense when they went to two platoons and I played strictly on offense. The team had a good year, too. We only lost two games but both of them were to the Browns and we finished second behind them. I always had confidence in myself and my ability. I knew I could play and once I got going I saw I could do the job.

I ran behind some good linemen. Bill Johnson our center and Bob St. Clair, who came along later, were two of them. The guys who stand out in my mind are Visco Grgich and Bruno Banducci. They were two of the best guards in the business. Neither one of them was all that big, but they moved those guys they were blocking out of there. Without the two of them I never would have been as successful running with the ball as I was. Visco was quite a character. He and I had a lot of fun together.

Frankie Albert was a very good quarterback. He was another guy who was not that big but he was smart and he was tricky. Frankie's the one who gave me the nickname The Jet. He called a running play to me up the middle and when he turned to give me the ball, I was already past him. Then the next time he called that play, he went to hand off and the same thing happened and he said, "Joe, you're like a jet coming through there." From then on, for as long as I played, I was known as The Jet.

Sometimes we ran into problems on the road. Baltimore was a place where they didn't want to let me stay at the same hotel as the rest of the team and I would end up staying with a black family in town. I couldn't eat in certain restaurants, either, or take taxis that were for whites only. If I had to go somewhere, I had to call a cab company that had taxis for blacks.

One time we ran into a problem in Pennsylvania. What we used to do was, when we would travel east to play two weeks in a row on the road, we wouldn't go back to San Francisco in between games, we would stay somewhere where there was a hotel and a field where we could practice, and then we went on to play our next game. Well, this time Tony Morabito had arranged ahead of time for us to stay at this place in Pennsylvania, only when we got there they would not let me stay there. I got very upset and Tony got very upset, and it turned out that he took the whole team out of that place and moved us to a country club where they would let me stay with everybody else. That's another thing that tells you about the kind of relationship Tony and I had, the kind of guy he was.

I met Bill Willis and Marion Motley the first time we played Cleveland my rookie year. I was in awe of them because they were the two guys that started the whole thing in 1946. They had Fritz Pollard and some other guys before that, but Willis and Motley were the first in a long time. It was just like if you're a youngster and you meet someone you respect a great deal. I had been reading about these guys, and now here I was meeting them and they greeted me very warmly. Then once the game starts, you're out there and you're trying to kill each other.

That's just the way football was back then. Off the field you were good friends, but on the field you wanted to kill them. That's the way I played against everybody and it was no different with Willis and Motley or any of the other black players I played against. It was the same thing when I met Buddy Young in New York. I had heard about him and I went over to him before the game and introduced myself and there was a great deal of respect and camaraderie, but the camaraderie only lasted until the game started.

That's the way I played and that's the way a lot of guys played. They would hit you as hard as they could. That's the thing about football. They can hit you as if they're trying to kill you regardless of whether that's their intent or not. The ones who would hit you and call you a dirty name, those guys were doing it because of something racial. But there were guys I knew pretty well who I would say hello to who would hit you just as hard. That's just the way the game was played.

You had two or three bigots on every team so you heard stuff just about every game. "You better not come through here, nigger, or I'll kill you." Shit like that. I didn't mind, I'd just talk it right back to them. "Bring your momma because I'm coming." I always had an answer for whatever they had to say because I was raised to not take anything from anybody. I could take anything they had to say but if they had ever put their hands on me like they wanted to fight, that would have been something else. None of them ever did because they knew if they ever did, I would've whipped their ass.

In addition to the bigots, you had guys who were just dirty football players. They didn't really care about race, they just tried to hurt everybody, but they would do it by dirty means. It was one thing to block or tackle a guy with as much force as you could, but certain guys would come in with their elbows or jump on the pile late and all sorts of stuff like that. You'd be down at the bottom of the pile and this guy is grabbing your crotch and this other guy is trying to twist your leg into a pretzel, just dirty stuff that was done with the sole intent of injuring you.

Meanwhile, the official is standing there watching all this and if you say something, they'd tell you it was all part of the game. They'd say, "Shut up, they're not hurting you. It's a man's game." So I'd say, "Okay, be sure you tell him to shut up when I put my foot up his ass." I put together some old film the 49ers had and there's one play in there where a guy is just pummeling me as he's tackling me. That kind of stuff went on all the time. After awhile you knew who the dirty players were, so you just looked out for them.

I don't want to get into a whole thing comparing the players of today and yesteryear, but my personal opinion is that as a whole, the players then were tougher. They were made out of blood and guts and that's the way they played. The equipment was very minimal and every once in awhile if there was enough tape, they'd tape your legs. But if there wasn't enough tape, then you didn't get taped. It was more on guts then than material or anything else.

The guy I admired the most as a football player was Marion Motley. Here was a guy who was almost 250 pounds and could run like a deer when he got going. He was so big and strong, it would take ten guys to bring him down. He also played linebacker and, let me tell you, I played for sixteen years and he was as good or even better than any linebacker I ever saw. Then he blocked for Otto Graham and nobody got past him. He and Bill Willis made a big difference for the Browns.

Skin color didn't matter to Paul Brown, he was going for the best players. That was the difference between him and a lot of other coaches. Tony Morabito and Buck Shaw were like that, but even they were a little behind Paul Brown. Cleveland had Bill Willis, Motley, Horace Gillom, and Lenny Ford when some teams still didn't have any blacks. Listen to the names of the players I just called, how good they were. If you were going to be biased or prejudiced, you wouldn't get the Motleys or whoever, you'd get some Caucasian player instead and if those Caucasian players weren't as good, then you were hurting your team through just plain stupidity. It seems simple now because things have changed but that's the way it was then. At least I hope things have changed.

Buddy Young was the only guy who played when I played who maybe was faster than me. And I say maybe. He was a sprinter in college, too. I think the fact that he was so short made him tough to tackle. He was so low to the ground guys didn't have much to hit or grab onto. And he was strong, believe me. He was built solid and he would break tackles and get away if they didn't hit him right. We were supposed to race once in a match race but it never happened. It would have been interesting. I can't say I would have beaten him but it would have been close.

The 49ers always came up a tad short. It was frustrating. The Browns had everything—good offense, good defense, good kicking game. When we came up short, it was always because we weren't good enough on defense. I know my first two years when we were still in the All-America Football Conference, we scored more points than the Browns but they beat us out because their defense was better. I think both years we scored around 35 points a game and yet we still finished in second place. We even got 56 in a game against the Browns one time and won something like 56–28, but they beat us later on and finished first. They were tough. They were tough against everybody. Even after we went into the NFL, they beat up on just about everybody.

I don't blame the players we had on defense because we had a lot of good ones, it just seemed like we were always drafting for offense. If you do that and you don't pay attention to your defense, then you're not going to win championships. I don't know if Buck Shaw and the others did it because they thought it would mean more exciting football, but we always had a few holes on defense and a good team like the Browns will eventually find them. We certainly were exciting because we moved the ball and scored a lot of points, but putting all the emphasis on offense cost us. That was true after we joined the NFL as well.

We were definitely powerful on offense. Frankie was good and Y. A. Tittle was an outstanding quarterback. Smart. Great arm. Tough. He'd stand in the pocket with the rush coming for as along as he had to. He's an example of a guy from the South who I got along great with. Hugh McElhenny was as good an open field runner as you'll ever see. We complemented each other because I was best running up the middle and Hugh was a great outside runner who would zig and zag all over the place. Sometimes he zigged and zagged so much that the same guy would miss him twice on the same run.

Then we had John Henry Johnson for a couple of years and that meant we had a backfield made up of four Hall of Famers. Nobody else has ever had that and I don't believe anybody else ever will. I guess I might have carried the ball more if I hadn't had two backfield mates who were so good, but we got the job done. Besides, having a guy like McElhenny could really open things up for me because they couldn't key on just one guy.

It was the same thing with our receivers. Gordy Soltau and Billy Wilson were one of the best combinations in the league and that made our offense better and that's what it's all about because that's how you win. I didn't worry that I might get the ball more in a different situation because I didn't care about that. We had a good situation right there with the 49ers.

The playoff we lost to the Lions in 1957 was the worst game of all. That whole 1957 season was up and down because we played a lot of close games. We won most of them but we lost a few, and if we had won one more we wouldn't have had to play the Lions because we ended up in a tie for first place. Plus it was the year Tony died. He died right at Kezar Stadium during a game when we were playing the Chicago Bears. He had already had one heart attack before that and then during the second quarter against the Bears he had another one and they took him out of the stands to the hospital.

Our defense was on the field so I was on the sidelines and I remember standing there looking up into the stands because there was all this commotion, and I knew right away what had happened. We all knew it was just a matter of time before Tony's heart gave out and the time came during that game. He was probably dead before they got him out of there because we found out later that it was a massive heart attack. They told us about it in the locker room at halftime and many of us were in there crying. I don't know what the score was but we were behind, and then we went out and won the game in the second half. That was one of the saddest days of my life.

I definitely thought we had the best team that year, but the Lions came back in the playoff game and beat us. We were ahead in the third quarter by three touchdowns or something [27–7] and they came back and got closer, then we made some mistakes and the next thing you know, they won the game 31–27. That was another time when you had guys crying in the locker room. Cleveland finished first again that year and that was one time when I know we would have beaten them. The Lions killed them [59–14] and we would have killed them, too.

When I mentioned my relationship with Tony Morabito, I don't want to forget Buck Shaw. He was a very good coach and a great person. I got along very well with him the whole time he was there and I thought the 49ers made a mistake when they got rid of him. Some people said that football had passed him by, but I don't think that was true at all. I guess they wanted to go in a different direction. What did I know? They sure as hell didn't ask me what I thought. I was just one of the peons. I guess Buck showed them things hadn't passed him by because he went to Philadelphia and led the Eagles to the NFL championship, and the 49ers were still waiting.

They brought in Red Strader and that didn't work out so they let him go after just one year and hired Frankie Albert. I got along well with Frankie, too. I got along with all the coaches I played for except for Red Hickey. I played with Frankie for five years and everything was fine and then everything was fine when he became the coach. We were okay as a team under Frankie, nothing great, although we did come close in '57. We had the same problem we had in the beginning of my career: just not enough defense. Maybe it was because Frankie was a quarterback and he was looking for offensive players, I don't know, but we kept drafting players for offense instead of defense just like with Buck Shaw.

Then they brought in Hickey in 1959 and I did not get along with him. It was just one nitpicking thing after another and I did not like him at all. I finally told [49ers general manager] Lou Spadia, "You better trade me or I'm going to kill your coach. Not just beat him up but kill him," and that's when they got rid of me. I did not want to leave the 49ers, but if it meant getting away from Red Hickey, then I had to go. They traded me to the Baltimore Colts in 1961.

I played two years for the Colts and then [Baltimore head coach Don] Shula cut me. Weeb Ewbank was the coach my first two years and he was fine, then Shula came in that year [1963] as the new, young coach and I didn't like him. Vic Morabito contacted me about coming back to the 49ers after I was released by Baltimore. Hickey was still the coach and Vic told me not to worry, he would make sure nothing happened like the first time around. Then the team started off slow and Hickey got fired, so that took care of that. Playing that last year increased my pension, plus I got to retire as a 49er, which was important to me.

After I played that last year, I worked for the 49ers for awhile as a coach and a scout. I did a lot of things over the years. You had to work on the side in those days because nobody got rich playing.

Everybody was in business or had a job. I owned my own business, I worked for a car dealership, I was in business selling supplies to bowling alleys, I worked in the wine business, I owned my own gas station, a lot of things. I was a jack of all trades, a master of none. I'm retired now and my wife Donna and I moved to Arizona a few years ago. I like the weather down here better.

Donna is a great lady. She was always right there in my corner no matter what I was going through. We were living in California but she has a daughter from a previous marriage living here, and she wanted to be closer to her daughter, so we moved. We enjoy our life. We bought a little place on a lake and we enjoy it thoroughly.

I used to see a lot of the players I played with before we moved. They had reunions and a 49ers' alumni group that organized dinners and things like that. The dinners and other events were always a good opportunity to see the guys and talk about the old days. I think there was even a group who used to meet in the parking lot before games at Candlestick and tailgate. There wasn't anybody I played with who I didn't get along with and some of them were the best friends I've ever had in my life. We really were like a big family.

Getting elected to the [Pro Football] Hall of Fame was the biggest thrill of my football career. That is the top honor that shows that you have the recognition as one of the best by people who followed the game very closely. It was very fulfilling and very emotional for me, too, because my mother had died not long before that, plus Tony was gone, and they were the most important people in my life.

One thing I don't like is that the 49ers don't count any of the records from my first two years. In fact, they don't count anything that anybody did from the first four years because it was done in the All-America Conference. They say it's because it was the All-America Conference, not the NFL, but how about all the records and statistics of the players from the American Football League? Those are counted in the team record books and the NFL's record books, yet they don't count anything from the All-America Conference. To tell you the truth, I don't think the NFL got over the job the Browns did when they came into the league, the same kind of job they did on us in the AAFC.

The team was the same, the owners were the same, we wore the same red and gold colors the 49ers wear to this day, we played in

Kezar Stadium just like we did in the NFL, and the league was just as good. I don't get it. It was just as tough for me to run for those yards in '48 and '49 as it was after that. The Hall of Fame counts all those yards and all the records from the AAFC, why can't the NFL?

What really bothers me is that the 49ers don't do it in their own media guides. All these new teams, I understand why they don't care about the AAFC, but teams like the 49ers, the Colts, and the Browns—you think Otto Graham and Motley weren't good enough to play in the NFL before 1950? Or me and Tittle and all the other guys? I can't even remember what the answer was they gave me when I asked them about it, it was so stupid. If somebody wants to come out with something that makes any sense, I'll be glad to listen. But nobody has because I don't think there's any answer they could give. It's like they're saying those four years of the history of the San Francisco 49ers don't exist. Hey, I was there. I know they exist.

When I heard that Motley died, I made a point of flying back to Ohio for his funeral, that's how much I thought of him. He and I remained friends all through the years. As a football player, I think he's one of the greatest. He was just a great fullback, one of the greatest blocking backs you have ever seen in your life. But don't forget, he was also a great runner. Because he was so big and strong and could block and play linebacker, people have a tendency to forget how great a runner he was. Marion could really run.

I don't think the kids today have the kind of feeling I was trying to express earlier about what it was like for me to meet Motley and Willis the first time. We had never had one of our people or one of our race or however else you want to say it on the football field before, and these were the first two guys to do that. I knew all about what they had done before I met them, and I felt a great deal of respect for them and I wanted to be sure they knew how important it was to me that they had done what they did and made it possible for me to be playing, too. In addition to the fact that he was a great player and my friend, that's the other reason I had to go to Marion's funeral. People don't know and they should. And some people who used to know have forgotten. I'm not one of them. That's why I went.

SHERMAN HOWARD

Sherman John Howard
Born November 28, 1924, in New Orleans, Louisiana

Wendell Phillips High School in Chicago, Illinois
Iowa University
University of Nevada

Running back
Undrafted, signed by New York Yankees in 1949

Growing up in a tough Chicago neighborhood during the Great Depression, having lost both of his parents by the age of 13, Sherman Howard could have grown up at war with the world. He could also have grown up, as far too many modern athletes apparently have, believing he was owed things. But he didn't.

Raised by an aunt and mentored by numerous adults, including some of the greatest athletes who ever lived, Sherman instead appreciated those around him and drove himself to excel. As a young man, he displayed that excellence in athletics and in pursuing an advanced education. Later, it showed itself in a long career as an educator.

At 84 he has not forgotten the legendary figures and tradition he grew up with. Buddy Young was a schoolmate and a close friend. Jack Johnson, Jesse Owens, Ralph Metcalfe, Paul Robeson, Duke Slater, Fritz Pollard, and Sol Butler were a part of his early years. He attended high school and college with Earl Banks, who later had a distinguished career as head football coach at Morgan State University. In college, he played with and befriended Emlen Tunnell, and later he came to know Jackie Robinson, Marion Motley, Bill Willis, and George Taliaferro. There was a lot of athletic wisdom

Year	Team	League	Games	Rushing Attempts	Yards	Avg.	TDs	Receiving Receptions	Yards	Avg.	TDs
1949	Yankees	AAFC	12	117	459	3.9	3	1	24	24.0	0
1950	Yanks	NFL	12	71	362	5.1	3	12	278	23.2	5
1951	Yanks	NFL	12	94	343	3.6	4	21	447	21.3	3
1952	Browns	NFL	5	34	95	2.8	0	11	219	19.9	3
1953	Browns	NFL	12	7	42	6.0	0	0	0	—	0

Year	Kickoff Returns Returns	Yards	Avg.	TDs	Interceptions Interceptions	Yards	Avg.	TDs
1949	4	95	23.8	0	1	26	26.0	0
1950	8	240	30.0	1	0	0	—	0
1951	0	0	—	0	0	0	—	0
1952	1	22	22.0	0	0	0	—	0
1953	1	6	6.0	0	1	3	3.0	0

Returned 1 punt for 12 yards

Played in AAFC Playoff Game in 1949

Played in NFL Championship Game in 1953

passed on, but there was also something that Sherman took to heart: Make a contribution. Give something back.

Sherman began his career in 1949 with the New York Yankees of the All-America Football Conference. The Yankees and the arch-rival Cleveland Browns had five black players who were among the best in football—Sherman and Young for New York and Motley, Willis, and Horace Gillom for the Browns. One result was huge crowds, crowds that included tens of thousands of African Americans, the first time large numbers of blacks were drawn to major league pro football.

Sherman had a splendid first season in the NFL after the two leagues merged. Along with Buddy Young and George Taliaferro, he was part of what may have been the fastest backfield up to that time. He scored nine touchdowns on only 83 touches to finish seventh in the league and was especially dangerous as a receiver, with five scores on just 12 catches and a 23.2 average.

Sherman remained a valuable player through the end of his career, by which time he was a member of the Browns. Robbed of some of his effectiveness by injuries, he retired after five seasons and embarked on his long career as a teacher, coach, and athletic director. Blessed with a wonderful memory and a fine eye for detail, Sherman is retired and lives just outside of Chicago.

I was born in New Orleans and then eventually moved to Chicago with my mother and my aunt when I was ten years old while my father remained in New Orleans. He was a stevedore and my mother was a housewife. She only lived here three or four years when she passed from cancer. In fact, in 1938 when I was thirteen my mother and father died two weeks apart, my mother from cancer and my father from a heart attack.

In those days they worked twelve, fourteen hours a day six days a week on the docks and that was hard on him. You started at six and got off at six. The eight hour days didn't come in on the docks until 1940, '41, and it was all physical labor, very demanding work in that New Orleans heat. That's all I really remember about New Orleans is how hot it was.

At the time as a youngster, I didn't understand the importance of losing both my parents. Later on you realize it but not so much then. It was quite a blow, don't get me wrong, but I guess it wasn't as bad because of my aunt and a lot of what you could call surrogate parents. I had a brother but he was a lot older than me and he wasn't around so I was like an only child. I had playground instructors, athletic directors, people like that looking after me, although my aunt was the main one who raised me.

We lived on the South Side of Chicago on 38th Street, right down the street from Wendell Phillips High School. I knew a lot of guys who worked at White Sox Park because it was a very short distance from my house. We had a big stove in the middle of the house with coal heat. In those days you warmed up by the stove and then jumped in bed so you could go to bed warm, and you got up early and started the fire in the stove so everyone would be warm. I always slept on a pull out couch all through my coming up. Then when I went in the service, I slept on a cot at camp because that's all they had. So I never slept in a real bed until I got married. But as they say, it doesn't matter how you start out, it matters how you end up.

Chicago was very segregated, no question about it. There were certain places blacks just did not go. Blacks weren't allowed in Marshall Field's and there were very few blacks in the transportation jobs or post office jobs. It was the Depression so many families were on welfare, or relief, as they called it then. Part of it was that jobs were just hard to come by, but part of it was that those jobs were just not open to blacks. If you could find a job and make $10 a week, that was pretty good money because rent was $10 a month, I remember that specifically, and that was for a pretty nice apartment.

You never went west from White Sox Park, you always went east. Going west was a very dangerous move. You did not venture around certain areas of the city on your own. We used to play softball in certain areas and they took us on a truck and told us, "Once you play the game, get back on the truck. Don't go anywhere else in that neighborhood." That's the way it was at that time. I remember one boy tried to go swimming in one of the swimming pools out of our area and they tried to drown him. So it was a little rough.

They had two high schools that were primarily black and the school I went to, Phillips, was one of them. When you played other schools, you were not as welcome as one of the white schools. You would not get the best reception, let's say, even with the officials. I remember one time one of our players ran for a touchdown but the referee said he stepped out of bounds. Our coach complained that he was not out of bounds and the referee made a footprint with his cleats and said, "He stepped out of bounds right there." We didn't like it but you knew if you complained you wouldn't get any results, so you accepted it.

Growing up, there was always something to do. We did everything. They had a lot of playgrounds at that time so you played football, baseball, basketball, volleyball, you pitched horseshoes, ice skating, everything. Then you had your indoor activities such as ping pong, marbles, and wrestling. I was a pretty good marble shooter and horseshoe pitcher.

We roller-skated, played checkers, Chinese checkers—I know a lot of kids now that never heard of checkers or Chinese checkers. They say, "What is that?" But at that time, you sought recreation outside the house because there wasn't recreation in the house except for radio, and we didn't have a radio for a long time. Then when we did get one, you had to get all close to it, and it was always what the adults wanted to hear anyway. You participated in anything to keep busy. You didn't stay home, you only went home to go to bed.

I think all of those activities helped later on. I used to swim at the Boys Club, just all different kind of athletics like basketball, where you jumped and ran around and moved around in different ways. It really helped your body develop athletically. Kids today play soccer and take karate and those were not very popular then. Seems like some kids play soccer all year round and we never played soccer. Or nowadays kids sit and watch television three, four hours a day. We kept busy. We were always involved in some kind of activity.

One of the guys I grew up with was Buddy Young. He was a little younger than me but we were very good friends. We went to the same high school, but I knew him even before high school because of the Old Timers Club. They organized activities for young people and they had citywide track meets and football and basketball. They had a junior division that involved the younger kids and Buddy was primarily a track man at that time. He went out for football at another high school and the coach didn't want him to play because he thought he was too small, but he came to Phillips and gained recognition as a football player and a track man.

I knew Buddy had great potential for athletics even at that time, although I thought primarily in track because the NFL was not open to blacks. Then during the war when he played in the service out there at Fleet City, they recognized his talents right away. When he came out of the service, he went to Illinois and made them Big Ten champions and starred in the Rose Bowl. His twin sister Claudine was a good athlete, too. We were all close. I've known the family for years.

There were always great athletes around our area. The original Harlem Globetrotters came from my high school. They were called the Savoy Big 5 then. Jesse Owens and Jack Johnson, the fighter, and Bernie Jefferson, who went to Northwestern, lived right near us. They were some of the guys who came around and inspired me. One guy I remember real well was Sol Butler, who was one of the first blacks to play in the NFL and was on the '28 Olympic team. He played against Jim Thorpe and all those guys and he was a terrific track man.

The thing I remember most about Jack Johnson was his flamboyancy. I didn't use that word then but thinking back about it now, that's the word I use. He was always jolly, always upbeat, and whenever he came around he always gave us inspirational speeches. You know, "Do the best you can, work hard, whatever you learn try to be the best at it," things like that. That was his attitude. Jesse Owens would tell us the same thing.

Sol Butler was just fabulous working with kids. He had the techniques and skills to show you how to be the best. You might not have the opportunity to use them but at least he taught you the best way. I found that the skills Jesse and Sol taught us in track, you could take anywhere. It was the same thing with the football skills we learned—how to come out of the hole, how to move your body, how to use your body, everything.

We also had something called the Varsity Club, which were guys that had lettered in college. Jesse Owens and Ralph Metcalfe and guys who had been in the Olympics were all members. Ralph lived right near me at 31st and Federal. He went to Marquette University and became an alderman and was president of our Varsity Club one year. Jesse never wanted to be president, but whenever we needed a speaker he would call them and they would come and speak. We had Woody Hayes one year and Whizzer White came one year.

The guy who just recently got inducted into the [Pro Football] Hall of Fame, Fritz Pollard, was another member. Even when I went on to New York as a player Fritz would come around and give me encouragement. He played in the '20s with Paul Robeson and Jim Thorpe and Duke Slater and Inky Williams. Fritz and Inky both went to Brown University and played football there. Fritz was also a coach. If I'm not mistaken, they all played on the same team for awhile. I had a picture of those guys—they had a hell of a group. They beat the Bears for the championship in '21 or '22, and then not too much later blacks were barred from the NFL.

Duke Slater was another guy I knew coming up. He was a judge. You could ask anybody from Notre Dame, [Knute] Rockne and all of them, and they would all tell you about a picture of Duke blocking one whole side of Notre Dame's line. He played at Iowa and then he was a big, big star for the Chicago Cardinals. Everyone who played against him talked about what a great player he was. He even made Grantland Rice's All-American team, and Rice was the guy who started the All-American team. When you mentioned Duke's name to [George] Halas or any of them on the Bears or Hunk Anderson or any of them on Notre Dame, they all remembered Duke. And he would come around and speak. Whenever you wanted someone to give an inspirational speech to young guys, you would always call Duke Slater.

I always tell everyone we were very, very fortunate to have people like that around us. Even in baseball, which I was never very interested in—this was way before Jackie Robinson and we never thought at that time that blacks would ever get into the major leagues—we knew guys like Bobby Anderson from the Negro Leagues. They were good in that area, they had performed, and they believed in giving back.

When I was with the New York Yankees Paul Robeson was always around because he was performing in the theater, and he would come to games on Sundays whenever he was in town. He'd come in the dressing room after the game or show up every now and then at a little place where we all went to socialize—a very down to earth guy, always telling you things to inspire you. You know, "Make a contribution in life."

I had seen Robeson as a kid because my principal knew him real well and he came to sing for us at my elementary school. Then when

I was in college, he came to Reno one time to speak and I called him and he said, "Come on down," so we had a nice little conversation. He was telling me inspirational things. You know, "Stay in school and get your degree," so I had known him before I got to New York. Then when I got to the Yankees he remembered me, so it was very nice.

One time I was sitting at a banquet in New Jersey with the president of Rutgers, who went to school with Robeson, and he just admired him so much. He told me about so many things that Robeson went through and he could not imagine how he could do it and still maintain the strength that he had. In addition to football, he spoke six or seven languages, excelled in music, and I think he was valedictorian of his class. That's just amazing under the circumstances that existed in 1919, 1920.

It was around the time I was in New York that Robeson started having trouble with the government. He was not the type of man to sacrifice his own personal integrity to set aside someone else. You've got to be strong-willed to deal with people like that and that's what I always admired about Robeson. He would never say anything that was derogatory or insulting to anyone.

In 1949, my first year with the Yankees, there were only about five or six blacks in pro football, and Jackie Robinson would come around and give you encouragement and tell you what to expect and to not let the frustration get to you. After he retired, he was a guest speaker at many affairs that I went to. The last time I saw him I didn't know he was going blind. We had a Legends of Athletics banquet and he was sitting there and I spoke to him. I mentioned my name and he said "Hi," but he didn't move and I asked one of the guys that was there, and he said Jackie was blind. That was just one of the most shocking and tragic experiences for me, and shortly after that he passed.

At Phillips I played football, basketball, and ran track. Duke Slater was a legend at Iowa and he was one of their primary recruiters. He talked to me and another fellow, Earl Banks, who was a coach at Morgan State for years, about going to Iowa, but first I had to go into the Army. I was in Europe two and a half years in the transportation corps helping transport tanks and guns up to the front. They had segregated outfits and in the transportation corps, you had white officers but all black personnel.

We came in right after D-Day. The Germans had destroyed all the ports so you couldn't get in and they had to park all the ships outside the city. Then they used what they called ducks to get all the equipment to the shore. These ducks could float on the water, and once they came out of the water, they became cars. The wheels would come out and you could transport them on the ground. We were able to get tanks, guns, food, and everything else into these places where they had destroyed the ports.

We were supposed to go into Cherbourg but we never got there. They had snipers there and we lost two or three guys, so we were told not to go near there. It was the first time I ever saw churches with those high, high steeples—I never saw churches like that in the United States. Well that's where those snipers would hide. You wouldn't even think of guys being able to hit you from that far but they would go up in those steeples and hit you from 500 yards.

Not long after I got back to the States, I went to Iowa. I played varsity football my freshman year, which you could do at that time because so many guys were in the service. There were only three blacks on the football team: me, Earl Banks, and Emlen Tunnell. All told on campus they had 20,000 students and I think there were 50 blacks. We couldn't stay in the dorms, you had to live with a black family, and there were other things like they wouldn't cut your hair, stuff like that. I ran into a few incidents in terms of prejudice and I felt I didn't have to take it so I decided to leave after one year.

One of the things that happened was, there was this girl Betty Jo who was president of the student council and she talked to me about what issues I felt were important to the blacks there. She and I and some of her friends became very friendly and some of the guys, they resented it. These are white girls and white guys I'm talking about. Betty Jo would tell somebody not to interrupt me while I was talking and that was a no-no, then the girls would tell you different things that other people would say about them in the dorms. When somebody wrote "Nigger Lover" on Betty Jo's mirror, that was when I said it's time to leave.

I guess I was supposed to grin and bear it but I realized I didn't have to because I was on the GI Bill and I could go anywhere I wanted. Now if I was on scholarship, I would have had to back off and lay low. That was one of the advantages you had at the time because of the GI Bill. It was a very independent bill that gave everyone opportunity. I could have gone to Yale, Harvard, anywhere. In fact, I got my master's at the University of Chicago with it so I got the education I wanted out of the GI Bill.

I wanted to go to UCLA but UCLA would not take some of my credits, so that's how I ended up at Nevada. I was on the GI Bill so I could pick my own school and not have to worry about tuition. I had heard about Nevada because of Marion Motley and Horace Gillom and when Nevada took all my credits, I went and played football, basketball, and ran track, but basketball was too much of a conflict with my studies.

At that time there were areas in Reno you couldn't go. For example, you couldn't go in the gambling houses. But the campus was beautiful and the people on campus were very liberal and supportive. We still have a relationship with people I went to Nevada with. It was a good experience for me. They put me in the Hall of Fame there a few years ago.

When we played Tulsa, they had never had a black player and their coach said he couldn't guarantee my safety. Well our players said that if I didn't play, they weren't going to play. Tulsa had some guys who went into pro ball who I later found out were very, very embarrassed about the situation. Jim Finks was one of them. He was the quarterback on that team. They had never had a black player in Wichita, either, and I had to stay with a black family. That happened many times.

That even happened in pro ball when we played in Baltimore. They brought Buddy and I down from New York the morning of the game and met us at the train station and then took us straight to the ballpark because we couldn't stay in the Belvedere Hotel. And in Houston, we couldn't stay with the team, we had to stay with a private family. Same thing in Dallas. Now when I got to Cleveland, Paul Brown would not allow that. If you couldn't stay with the team, he wasn't going to take his team there. One incident did occur before I got there and Paul said it would never happen again.

I left Nevada in 1949. I had another half year left but the Yankees [of the All-America Football Conference] wanted to sign me. Buddy was with New York and I thought that would be a pleasure for me to go there. The guys who was our mentors, Mr. Bobby Anderson and another guy—they didn't have agents then—but these two men advised me to go with the Yankees. The Giants were also interested and offered $5,000 plus bonuses, but the Yankees were paying much more money and it was a better deal for me.

My first year, we were scrimmaging every day and some of the guys hardly played but I was out there every day, sometimes for the whole scrimmage. One of the coaches told me, "We have to be sure you're first-string material. When your opportunity comes, take it." Now I was always a starter, but I understood because it was a new era, a breakthrough, and there was a lot of pressure on [Yankees' head coach] Red Strader. When I got in against the Buffalo Bills, I ran for about 45 yards on the first play and I never did have to sit down anymore.

We had some good players with the Yankees: Tom Landry, Otto Schnellbacher, Martin Ruby, Arnie Weinmeister, John Mastrangelo, Harmon Rowe, Barney Poole, Joe Signaigo, Bruce Alford, and George Ratterman. And we had the Springfield Rifle from Notre Dame, Angelo Bertelli. You talk about throwing the ball. He was the closest to Sammy Baugh I've ever seen. That ball left his hands just like his nickname, like it was shot out of a rifle. But he had hurt his knees. He'd come out there with braces on his knees, and it was no wonder he couldn't play. His arm held up but his knees wouldn't.

I play golf together with Bobby Kelly, and he was on that Notre Dame team and he says the same thing: "Boy, could Angelo throw that ball." Bertelli died the same time as Motley, you know. I don't know if they died on the same day, but I remember it was in the paper the same day. Then after Bertelli couldn't play because of his knees, Ratterman took over as our quarterback. He was another Notre Dame guy.

When Motley and Willis went up with the Browns, boy, that was really something. See, when Paul Brown first started at Massillon [High School] he had some great black athletes so he was familiar with black athletes. What he did with the Browns was nothing new for him. He had Horace Gillom and some others at Massillon and they say Horace's brother was an even better football player than he was.

Paul knew all about Marion Motley because Motley played for Canton [McKinley High School], and he coached Bill Willis at Ohio State. Bill was the bulwark of Paul's Ohio State team. I mean, without Bill there would have been a whole lot more touchdowns scored against Ohio State. Everybody said that he saved four or five games for Ohio State when Paul was coach, that's how good he was.

Those guys were all from Ohio so that made the transition to the Browns easier. They were all well known, at least in Ohio among football people. Those people who didn't know them, once they saw them play, you can bet they didn't have any objections. They had a punter like nobody had ever seen before, they had a powerful fullback, and they had an A-1 defensive lineman, and they were the bulwark of the Browns when they first started.

Once I asked Willis how he knew when the center was going to snap the ball because it seemed like he knew exactly when the center was going to snap it. He would get off that ball faster than anybody. He said he'd watch the muscles in the center's hand because he'd squeeze the ball just before he was going to snap it, and the muscles in his hand would tighten up on the ball.

Now how many athletes would think about timing their charge with the center squeezing the ball and be making their move just as the ball is coming up to the quarterback? Most guys, they wait until the ball moves and then they move, but Willis anticipated the snap based on the guy squeezing the ball. Everybody used to think he was offside, but he wasn't, he was just moving at the same time that the quarterback was getting the ball. In the annals of football, there has *never* been a middle man over the center like Bill Willis.

Then the Browns had Motley and let me tell you, he did not let Otto Graham get touched. He'd hit one guy and knock him back and then go back and get somebody else. You don't find too many backs like that. He was the only guy I ever saw who could block Lenny Ford. They would go at it in practice and nobody else, on our team or any other team, could block Lenny one on one except Motley. Plus Motley was a great linebacker. Even Jim Brown would admit that he couldn't do all that Motley did.

Motley being the only one who could block Lenny Ford is saying something because Lenny was some player. I played against him when I was a rookie with the Yankees because he started in the All-America Conference, too. He taught [Doug] Atkins everything he knew when Atkins started out with the Browns. He used to work with him after practice showing him how to get around the blockers and everything.

That was the beginning, I thought, of the era of recognizing blacks in pro football. It began right there in Cleveland with the Cleveland Browns. After that everybody said, "I'm going to try and get me a Motley or a Willis or a Gillom." I haven't even talked about Gillom. He started the 15-yard drop because he kicked the ball so far. Before that it was 10, 12 yards, and they'd kick it right quick. But with Horace being 15 yards back, it gave him enough room and enough time to kick that ball far and high. He kicked it so high that the guys on the Browns had more time to get down to the receiver. You had a lot of fair catches when you played against them. Even guys like Tunnell who prided themselves on never calling fair catches had to call them because of Horace.

I understand that when Horace played for Paul in Massillon, he would kick the ball above the lights and the return man would have to try and pick it up as it came down out of the darkness. He had such leverage for that ball. I have never seen anybody kick it like that in my life. I mean *kick* it. And Horace wasn't just a kicker, he could play some football. He was a big guy and a good athlete.

I always tell kids I was taught to be prepared so when the opportunity came, we were prepared to enter into the situation. Once things got going, coaches were going to get guys to help them win. The attitude became, "I don't care what color he is, I want to win." Even Bear Bryant changed. He played out west someplace when Alabama had one of its good teams and there were three black guys on that other team. After the game, Bryant asked them where they were from and it turns out they lived about three blocks from the University of Alabama. Bryant decided that was the last time that would happen to him and he changed his whole philosophy after that.

Knowing all about Motley and Willis and Gillom going up with Cleveland, I was thrilled when I first met them. They welcomed me and encouraged me and showed me around and let me meet people. It was very much like a family. I used to eat over at Motley's house and go over Bill Willis's house for the holidays. That was great because I looked up to them. To me, they epitomized athleticism and how football should be played.

I played that one year with Emlen Tunnell at Iowa and then against him in the NFL. Terrific athlete and a regular guy, just having a good time all the time. I was on the New York Yankees and he was on the New York Giants and we'd always be together. If the Giants went out of town, they'd come back the same night and then you'd look up and there would be Tunnell, back in town, and we'd go running around together.

He was one of those guys that had all kinds of skills. He had terrific agility and a sharp football mind. He could diagnose plays based on which way the quarterback was looking, and he saved Landry and Schnellbacher and all those guys a lot of times. I know many times that I played against him, I beat the guy covering me but there was Tunnell. He just had a knack and a football mind and he knew where that football was going. I remember once a girl asked me, "How can I get close to Emlen?" I said, "You have to turn into a football."

The All-America Conference could match its best teams with any team they had in the NFL. We came in with a lot of the Yankees in 1950 and we gave everybody a fight. If we had beaten the Rams, we would have been on our way to the Championship Game. They beat us, though, something like 40–35 [43–35] and the difference between us was Woodley Lewis. He upset your passing game just like Tunnell. He had good range, a good feel for the ball, and we had two passes that would've been touchdowns when he came out of nowhere and knocked the ball down. He was new in 1950 and I don't know if they would've been able to do that to us before that.

That's where the black athlete came in. Once Paul Brown started it, a lot of teams didn't keep up. The Browns and the Rams were the teams that had the most blacks and those were the only teams we had trouble with in 1950. We could match up well with the Bears, the 49ers, and the Eagles, but the Rams had Woodley and they had a terrific receiving corps with Elroy Hirsch and Tom Fears. Now the Browns, they had everything. They had the speed, they had the defense, they had everything.

But see now, we didn't even have the full Yankee team. When the leagues merged, the Giants had a chance to select five players off our team. If we could have maintained the team we had in '49, we would have had a better chance because they took some good ones. They took Schnellbacher, Landry, Mastrangelo, Weinmeister, and Rowe. They really took away our championship chances because that was almost our whole defense.

[New York Yanks owner] Ted Collins and [general manager] Frank Fitzgerald just said, "Take any five you want." The Giants knew what they were doing. Our coach Red Strader complained about it, but they had two guys negotiating who didn't know anything about football. When they said five players, those two thought any five players was just the same as any other five players. It could have been us and Cleveland in the Championship Game because if we still had that group we could've beaten the Rams.

We were real strong on offense. Ratterman was a good quarterback and we had me, Buddy, and George Taliaferro in the backfield. I was a good receiver and we had Dan Edwards, who was a good end. The other end, Art Weiner, was pretty good but he couldn't play in cold weather. We played the Bears and the Rams in cold weather and they were double-teaming me and Dan which meant Weiner could get open, but he couldn't catch the ball in cold weather. He played in college down South somewhere and he had never played in cold weather before, otherwise we could've won those two games.

But the real reason we lost is because the Giants got to take our whole secondary. That's why we couldn't keep up with Hirsch and them. And Weinmeister? He was great. Let me tell you, *he was great*. He was so great, they wouldn't run to his side the whole game. They would run off-tackle plays and sweeps to the other side, but nobody would run to his side. And with all those guys, the Giants stopped everybody. They were the only ones that beat the Browns. They played that Umbrella Defense and everybody wondered why they were so successful. Well, they had Weinmeister and they had Landry, Schnellbacher, and Rowe back there with Tunnell and you couldn't do anything.

I had three good years with New York before I went to Cleveland. For some reason, I always had a good day against the Lions. One game I had three touchdowns including a kickoff return. Bob Smith of the Lions was on the team with me at Iowa and whenever I would see him over the years, he would always say, "Did we fire you up?" I said, "No, I just always had a good game against the Lions." Even when they had that great team, I always had a good day against them, even on defense.

One time somebody got hurt and I had to play defense against them and I played pretty good, and Doak Walker said, "I didn't know you played defense. No matter what I tried, I never could out-fake you," because he would out-fake them and leave them. I had to remind him I played against Buddy Young on our lunch break in high school, and he was about as hard a guy to catch as anybody. Doak was one of my favorite people and a great runner. He wasn't real fast but he seemed to be able to get to the right spot at the right time.

When I got traded to Cleveland, I thought it was a blessing. Watching Paul Brown operate, that was an education for me. You were off Monday and Tuesday and everybody else practiced on Tuesday. Then in November, he cut practice down ten minutes to keep everybody fresh. Everything was so precise, no time was wasted. With the Yankees, if you messed up a play at the end of practice, you had to run it until you got it straight. That's the way it was with most coaches. They'd get mad and you had to stay out there. With Paul Brown, if you were scheduled to get off the field at 4:05, you got off at 4:05, I don't care what happened. If you didn't do it right that time, you found out who messed up and came back the next day.

Maybe I underestimated my own talent because I wasn't sure I could play for the Browns, they had so many great players. Once I got there I found I could match myself up good, but at first I guess I wasn't sure. They had Willis, Motley, Otto Graham, Mac Speedie, and so many others. Otto threw that ball so it arrived right when you turned your head. You didn't have to wait for the ball to get there.

What helped me with the Browns was my speed. They ran sprints the first day and I came in first and I didn't think I would because Bill Willis was always first. The guy who challenged me the most was Ray Renfro. He was a track man and he was very, very fast, and after that he usually won, although it was never by more than a yard. But the first day I finished first and I think Paul Brown noticed. You know, sometimes you don't know your own ability until you get out there.

What caused my effectiveness to drop was that I needed glasses. I could not follow the ball directly into my hands the way I could before and I found out I needed glasses. Many times I was feeling the ball to my hands rather than seeing it into my hands. It was especially hard with night games. And see, Paul Brown's greatest strength was his passing game and a lot of the passes were to the halfbacks, like with Dub Jones. Contact lenses were not that stable then and when a guy would get hit he would lose it. I remember one time I saw guys looking around on the ground during a game for a contact lens that somebody had lost.

In 1952, I caught a pass against the Washington Redskins and [Joe] Tereshinski jumped on top of me and pressed down to knock the ball out of my hands, and I heard my shoulder crack. That was on the infield in Cleveland and the ground was hard as brick. Guys would hit the ground and break their legs, that was how hard it was. Tereshinski and another guy jumped on top of me because at that time you could get up and run if they didn't keep you down, and that knocked me out for the rest of the season.

I had two game-winning catches that year, one for a touchdown against Pittsburgh and the other when Tereshinski got me at the one-yard line. Then Otto took it in and we won. Paul Brown used to always tell me he remembered the first one against the Steelers. It was a tough game down to the wire and Otto threw me a swing pass and I ran it 50, 60 yards for a touchdown. Paul Brown always said that was the high point of my career.

I always got along very well with Paul Brown. I always respected him and he was very respectful of you as a person, very precise, very outspoken, didn't pull any punches, no bullshit. If you were messing up he would tell you. He had a favorite saying where he asked if you were running as fast as you could. Now if you look at it, that's just a simple question with a simple answer. But if you say yes, then that means you're too slow. If you say no, that means you're loafing. So the best answer is not to answer and we used to tell guys, "Don't answer that question because whatever your answer, it's the wrong one." He's not asking you just to be asking you, he's asking you to get you to think about yourself.

One time Gillom got off a bad punt when we needed a good one. You always say you're doing your best and Paul said to Horace, "Well, your best isn't good enough." He didn't curse you out or anything but he didn't have to because you got the message. The other thing Paul said was, "He's not good enough for our football team," and you understood it. You know, your performance might be good enough for somebody else's team, but it wasn't good enough for *our* football team. That's why he got rid of Doug

Atkins. He couldn't handle Atkins's arrogance or his doing just the opposite of what Paul wanted him to do. Everybody wondered why he traded Atkins to the Bears since he was a terrific player and made the Hall of Fame and all, but it was because he did things different from the way Paul Brown wanted. Now Halas would put up with it just so they could win, but Paul wouldn't.

My second year with the Browns, we were playing Green Bay and a player whose name I won't mention twisted my knee. He admitted to me later that he did it deliberately. He said he did that with all the ballplayers they were trying to get out of the game. I didn't really think about it because at that time, if you got a clear shot, you took it. They were out to win at any cost, and I've seen them do it when they wanted to get certain guys out of the game. They did that with Y. A. Tittle. The Bears put him out of the Championship Game [in 1963] and that's how they won. Later on you say, "You put a guy out and now he's got something he's going to have to deal with the rest of his life." I feel it now, too. My knee is arthritic.

Paul drafted [Chet] Hanulak in 1954, and you couldn't keep but so many running backs and I was the oldest one. I had a talk with Paul and he said I could go on the taxi squad, which paid $100 a week. I had homes in Cleveland and Chicago to maintain and I couldn't make it on a hundred a week, so I went home. The Giants called and they offered me more and I went to the Giants on the practice squad. They never did activate me, though, and what they offered me the next year wasn't enough, so I retired. I was 30 going to be 31 and they were drafting younger guys, too.

After I left the Giants I returned to Chicago and got into education. I was a teacher and a coach and athletic director at Harlan High School. I coached 27 years of high school football and I used to have the guys come out and talk to the students. Graham came one time and Willis came and Tunnell and I had Willie Davis—Willie came out a couple of times. It helped me get started with a lot of kids because I felt like maybe they doubted me or my knowledge, and this was one way I could show them I knew what I was talking about.

I also scouted for seven years and I always remembered one of my professors saying to never make a decision based on improper data or data that is outdated. Sometimes you have to make a decision anyway, but you should always get as much good data as you can and talk to as many people as you can. If I knew a guy was good, I would stand by it. Paul Brown called me at three in the morning and asked me if I was sure [Paul] Warfield was that good. I said, "Who the hell is that calling me at three o'clock in the morning?" And I told him I was sure he was that good. Same thing happened with Dave Robinson, the kid who played linebacker with Green Bay. [Vince] Lombardi asked me why I rated him so high, and I told him, "He's got good skills, he's big, he's quick, and he's got all the moves."

I really had a satisfactory career after I left football. Paul Robeson used to always say, "Live your life so after it's over you can look back and have no regrets." I took his advice and put something back in the soil and the kids I had come up to me now and say thanks. Mark Washington was one of my students. He played for Dallas for years. I see Mark all the time and he always thanks me for the advice I gave him. I always loved working with kids. One time I had Landry send me a film when he was in his heyday at Dallas. I showed it to the kids and they said, "Hey, they're running *our* plays." I got a big kick out of that. "They're running *our* plays."

GEORGE TALIAFERRO

George Taliaferro
Born January 8, 1927, in Gates, Tennessee

Theodore Roosevelt High School in Gary, Indiana
Indiana University

Tailback
Drafted by Chicago Bears and Los Angeles Dons in 1949

When Michael Vick was experiencing some rocky moments in the fall of 2006, a column appeared in The New York Times *that compared Vick the player to George Taliaferro. Authored by William Rhoden, the column referred to George as "the Michael Vick of his day—and then some" and advised Vick "to call George Taliaferro." Rhoden quotes George as saying, "All during my years here, I was never fully accepted and or appreciated as a human being." Despite that, or perhaps because of it, he goes on to say, "I would love to just share with [Vick] what I have had the opportunity to experience in my life."*

George played at a time before specialization, and it was expected that a player be able to play more than one position and do more than one thing on the football field. Rhoden was right when he wrote "and then some": George did a lot more than one thing. Even in an era of multidimensional players, he more than others was called upon to utilize a vast array of skills.

George ran from scrimmage, blocked, punted, caught passes, returned punts and kickoffs, and yes, passed. Playing mostly tailback in the old single wing for five different teams, he threw 255 passes in seven seasons. Willie Thrower is credited with being the first African American quarterback in the T-formation, but George performed

Year	Team	League	Games	Rushing				Receiving			
				Attempts	Yards	Avg.	TDs	Catches	Yards	Avg.	TDs
1949	Dons	AAFC	11	95	472	5.0	5	0	42	—	1
1950	Yanks	NFL	12	88	411	4.7	4	21	299	14.2	5
1951	Yanks	NFL	12	62	330	5.3	3	16	230	14.4	2
1952	Texans	NFL	12	100	419	4.2	1	21	244	11.6	1
1953	Colts	NFL	11	102	479	4.7	2	20	346	17.3	2
1954	Colts	NFL	11	48	147	3.3	0	14	122	8.7	1
1955	Eagles	NFL	3	3	-2	-0.7	0	3	17	5.7	0

Year	Passing						Punting			
	Attempts	Completions	Yards	Comp %	Avg.	TDs	INTs	Punts	Yards	Avg.
1949	124	45	790	36.3	6.4	4	14	27	982	36.4
1950	7	3	83	42.9	11.9	1	0	1	39	39.0
1951	33	13	251	39.4	7.6	1	3	76	2,881	37.9
1952	63	16	298	25.4	4.7	2	6	0	0	—
1953	55	15	211	27.3	3.8	2	5	65	2,437	37.5
1954	2	0	0	0.0	0.0	0	1	0	0	—
1955	0	0	0	—	—	0	0	0	0	—

	Kickoff Returns				Punt Returns			
Year	Returns	Yards	Avg.	TDs	Returns	Yards	Avg.	TDs
1949	13	313	24.1	0	2	53	26.5	1
1950	25	473	18.9	0	9	129	14.3	0
1951	27	622	23.0	0	9	68	7.8	0
1952	6	146	24.3	0	1	4	4.0	0
1953	16	331	20.7	0	10	31	3.1	0
1954	7	134	19.1	0	5	34	6.8	0
1955	1	16	16.0	0	0	0	—	0

Also intercepted 4 passes for 74 yards

Led league in kickoff returns and kickoff return yards in 1951

Played in Pro Bowl following the 1951, 1952, and 1953 seasons *credibly as a passer several years before Thrower's emergency stint with the Chicago Bears.*

Modest to a fault, George takes no credit as the game's first black quarterback. "I never took snaps under center, which is the thing that distinguishes a modern T-quarterback from those who came before," he wrote in the Coffin Corner *in 2005. Although Thrower played just one game in his career before being released, completing three of eight passes, George insists that "Everyone should remember Willie Thrower as the first modern black T-quarterback. He deserves the honor."*

Seeing that others get credit for what they accomplished comes easily to George. He does it when he talks of the Indiana University team he starred for as a freshman. The subject of Robert Arnold's Hoosier Autumn: The Remarkable Story of Indiana University's 1945 Football Championship Team, *the 1945 Hoosiers are the only squad in school history to win the Big Ten Conference championship outright. In addition to George, Indiana featured Pro Football Hall of Famer Pete Pihos and major league baseball great Ted Kluszewski that year.*

Perhaps of greater significance, the Hoosiers featured seven black players during George's time as a student, including Mel Groomes (who played two years for the Detroit Lions), Bill Buckner (father of Indiana University and NBA basketball star Quinn), and Joe Gilliam (father of Pittsburgh Steelers' quarterback Joe Jr.). No school other than the historically black colleges had ever had an athletic team with that many blacks, and George is quick to give Indiana administrators and coaches credit for being ahead of the curve. Typical of the racial schizophrenia of the era, however, George experienced more than his share of slights and outright hostility even as tens of thousands of Hoosier fans yelled their approval of him as a football player.

An outgoing man who speaks with great precision, George has made a point of staying in touch with his contemporaries. He corresponds regularly with players from his professional days like Sherman Howard and John Brown as well as with those of his Hoosier teammates who are still living. George worked for Indiana University in a variety of capacities for many years and is still involved in the school's athletic and alumni affairs. His grandson Raimond

Pendleton is a wide receiver for Kansas University. George and his wife Viola live in Bloomington.

Gary, Indiana, is what I know as home even though I was actually born in Gates, Tennessee. I lived in Gates until I was two months old and then my mom and dad and my two year old brother and I moved up to Gary, Indiana. I have no idea what kind of work my dad did in Tennessee, but there weren't any jobs of note in that part of the country for African Americans. My father had gotten word that the steel mills would be a good place to work and that's why we relocated to Gary.

My mom and dad were both from Tennessee. She was born and reared in Humboldt and I think he was born and reared in Brownsville. My dad had a lot of self-taught wisdom. He only had a fourth grade education but I'll tell you, he was one of the most intelligent people I've ever known. He could do practically anything physically. He could do plumbing, he could do woodwork, he could do masonry, you name it, my dad could do it. The one thing that he couldn't do and had a great fear of was electricity. He didn't understand it at all and he wouldn't so much as change an electric light bulb. All he knew about it was that it was one way to cause death instantaneously.

I have a brother who was two years older than I, I have a brother who is two years younger, another brother four years younger, and a sister who was six years younger, so I am number two of five. My older brother and my sister are deceased and my two younger brothers are alive and doing well in Gary. My youngest brother Claude, who is now retired, became the head football coach at the high school from which all five of us graduated.

The steel mills were the name of the game in Gary. My father got a job at Bethlehem Steel after we moved up from Tennessee and ultimately became a foreman in the tin mill section. My two brothers besides Claude, spent their employment lives in the steel mill and I would say many of the friends I grew up with worked in the mills, as had their fathers and many of their uncles and older brothers.

There is a strong athletic tradition in Gary and all of us plunged right into it. Tony Zale the great boxer is from Gary, as is Tom Harmon. Lester Bingaman played football for Lew Wallace High

School in Gary, went on to play for the University of Illinois, and then played for many years with the Detroit Lions. A lot of outstanding athletes came from there—before me, during my time, and after me.

We don't know where the athletics in our family came from because neither of my parents was athletically inclined. Not at all. My father was 5'7" and 150 pounds, and my mother was not interested at all. The only explanation we can come up with for our athletic ability is that it originated at Gary Roosevelt High School with the three men who were the football coach, the basketball coach, and the track and field coach. These men got many of the boys who had any physical prowess at all involved in athletics, and all of us participated in all three of those sports.

Gary Roosevelt was an African American elementary, junior high, and high school all in one, and those were the only three sports. We were not permitted by the Indiana High School Athletic Association to participate against white athletes or white schools. We had to compete against other African American schools in the Midwest and that was it. I did not play football against white players until I was a senior in high school. When I was a sophomore, the IHSAA permitted Gary Roosevelt to compete in track and field in the city of Gary, and Gary Roosevelt won everything in track and field, and then the following year they allowed us to participate in basketball. By my senior year we competed against white schools in all three sports.

Of the high schools in Gary at that time, Roosevelt was all black, and Emerson, Horace Mann, Tolleson, and Lew Wallace were all white. There was one school, Froebel, that was integrated. Roosevelt was in the Central District, which is where most of the black people in Gary lived. The North District was all white, and the South District was all white. But no matter where you lived, except for Froebel, the black kids went to the black schools and the white kids went to the white schools. For example, one of my very best friends was a white kid by the name of Nick Miller, who lived in the 2700 block of Madison Street. That was one block from where I lived in the 2600 block of Madison, yet he went to Emerson High School, which was five miles from where he lived. And on his way to school every day, he had to go right past Roosevelt.

Because of the restrictions on what schools we could play, we competed against high schools in Chicago, St. Louis, and Louisville, Kentucky, in addition to black high schools in other parts of Indiana. The school that Buddy Young went to in Chicago, Wendell Phillips, we competed against them. And Crispus Attucks High School in Indianapolis, where Oscar Robertson went to school, we competed against them. Another black school we competed against was Lincoln High School in Evansville.

When we were doing this, it was during World War II and we did not have bus transportation so we traveled in automobiles with the coaches and some of the male teachers. And even though in some cases we were traveling hundreds of miles, we often went down and back the same day. I believe St. Louis was the longest trip we made. It's 268 miles to St. Louis from here in Bloomington and Bloomington is 200 miles from Gary so you can see that is quite a distance, especially at that time before the interstate highway system. Then, as I mentioned, things slowly began to change. However, even when we began playing white schools, the majority of our games were against black schools from around the Midwest.

The organized sports at Roosevelt did not begin until junior high school so while we were in elementary school the athletics were centered at the Campbell Community Center. It, too, was in the Central District and it was all African Americans. There was basketball and boxing and all kinds of athletics as well as things like arts and crafts. There was no swimming pool, but we did have swimming at North Gleason Park where the Calumet River ran through the Central District. On the south side of the Calumet River was an eighteen-hole golf course and South Gleason Park, which were designated for whites. North Gleason Park and a little stream that ran off the Calumet River were designated for African Americans.

In addition, like many children of that time, we played street ball. We had a football team made up of guys who lived on the street on which I lived called the Madison Street Tigers. All of the boys on the team were black except for the boy I mentioned earlier, Nick Miller. There was no equipment, but what we did was collect glass, tin, copper, rags, paper boxes, and anything else we could find and take them to the salvage yard. We then put our money together to buy a football, and because I lived in the center of the three block area that made up our team, my house was designated to be the place where we kept the football. That meant I had access to a football and I could practice with it whenever I wanted. So in addition to playing with my friends, I spent time practicing by myself, which I did very frequently. I got to a point where I could kick a football high enough so that I could run and catch it, and I believe that helped me develop my ability to field punts.

On the next street over from mine was a vacant lot and that's where we would play. I could walk out the back door of my parent's house and play football to my heart's content. In addition to the neighborhood kids who were my age, there were several older guys who had attended Roosevelt High School and they encouraged me when they saw that I had some ability. Very, very much so. They would give me pointers that were very useful.

Gary was very segregated at the time and there were parts of town where you were most definitely not welcome. My parents were very strict about observing boundaries, especially heading into the South District, which was south of Gleason Park. If you went there, you did so at your own risk. That did not stop me from riding my bicycle to the Gary airport to watch airplanes take off and land. I was able to do that without any difficulty. However, when Joe Louis knocked out Max Schmeling, Mr. Pitts, an African American man who owned a dry cleaning establishment, drove through a white neighborhood tooting his horn, and he got into all kinds of difficulty because of that.

We followed the Chicago teams through the newspaper. My father didn't understand football and had no interest in it or in basketball, but he was a diehard Chicago Cubs fan. In fact, I think it was my father who invented the phrase, "Wait until next year." I was more interested in the Chicago Bears. In fact, I could name everybody who played for the Bears. And let me tell you, they had some team. In 1940 they beat the Washington Redskins 73–0. I knew all of them. One of the best players on that team, Danny Fortmann, became a doctor and did the surgery on my right knee in 1953.

We also followed the black baseball teams in Chicago. There was no team in Gary, but teams from the Negro Leagues would come and play exhibition games in Gary or when they were barnstorming around the country. There was also a black team in East Chicago, which is between Gary and Chicago. Football was my first love, though, and that is why I was more interested in the Chicago Bears.

I don't know where I got it from, but I told everybody that some-day I was going to play for the Bears. Even though there were no blacks playing in the NFL, I just had something inside of me that told me that. I was like a Boy Scout: be prepared. According to my mother, I was even telling her that when I was eight years old. When I was older she told me that when I was eight years old I told her I was going to take care of her because someday I was going to be a great football player.

When I got to junior high school, I began to play basketball, foot-ball, and track and field for Gary Roosevelt. At first I participated in track and field to keep myself physically conditioned for football be-cause football was always my favorite. However, I developed speed and coordination and I became quite proficient at track and field as well. I could have been a decathlete because I participated, when they allowed me to, in sprinting, shot putting, high jumping, broad jump-ing, and the pole vault. Using a bamboo pole, I set a record for my high school in the pole vault of 12 feet 6 inches that stood for about 20 years, by which time they had the better equipment.

When I got to Indiana University I continued with track for one year, but Bo McMillin the head football coach felt that I needed to concentrate on studying. And Bo McMillin had a big disagree-ment with Robert Royer the swimming coach because I was also a good enough swimmer to compete at the collegiate level. Mr. Royer wanted me to swim and Bo McMillin said, "Under no cir-cumstances." We didn't know anything at the time about how good swimming and aerobics are for conditioning, while today everybody uses aerobics. The myth was that swimming made you soft and that was Bo McMillin's concern. Plus, football was the sport that gener-ated funds for the university. I did not mind, though, because by that time I was really concentrating on football anyway.

Several of my brothers were also very good athletes. My young-est brother Claude received an athletic scholarship to the University of Illinois and I believe one year [1953] they lost only one game. He then played for the service team when he went into the Navy. In fact, he played against Ollie Matson in a service bowl game in Phoe-nix, Arizona when he was playing for Great Lakes and Ollie was playing for the El Toro Marines. Claude was drafted to play in the National Football League and he asked my advice, but he was 5'8" and 175 pounds and I just did not believe he was big enough to play in the NFL as a running back and that was the advice I gave him.

I was not heavily recruited in high school and I would have to say it was because of being black. Indiana always had a Mister Basketball and about fifteen years ago they established a Mister Football. Well, a sportswriter here wrote an article in which he stated that had there been such an award in the 1940s, he knew of two football players from Gary who definitely would have won the award: Les Bingaman and George Taliaferro. I thought it was tremendous that he would write that, but I had to remind him that I never could have been Mister Football. I'm not talking about ability but visibility, because I did not play against the white high schools. I didn't make all-state or all-county or even all-city and they would never have considered me for Mister Football.

Aside from a number of black colleges from the South, the only school that recruited me initially was UCLA. However, UCLA was ruled out because my mother said, "No, you can't go to California because they still have cowboys and Indians there." Even Indiana was not interested in me at first. There were ten of us from my high school who were planning to attend North Carolina Central University in Durham and then we played an exhibition game against Roosevelt High School in East Chicago. They were getting ready to play in the championship game of their league, but it was several weeks away and their coach asked our coach if we would play them to help keep them in shape. Roosevelt High School in East Chicago was an integrated school and a powerhouse in football, perennially considered one of the best teams in Indiana. Many players from East Chicago went on to play at Notre Dame.

I had a very good game and their coach Pete Rucinksi, who was a graduate of Indiana University, recommended me to Bo McMillin. He told Bo McMillin, "There's only one problem: he's black." And Bo McMillin said, "If he can do what you said he can do, I don't care if he's purple, I want him." And that is how I ended up going to Indiana University. One of the other classmates of mine who was originally going to go to North Carolina Central also ended up going to Indiana and the other eight went on down to Durham, North Carolina.

I would say that Indiana had more black players than any college besides the traditionally black schools, which speaks well for Indiana University. And almost 90 percent of the master's and doctorate degrees awarded to African Americans in physical education at that time were awarded by Indiana University. The person who welcomed me to campus and was always available to me was Dr. Herman Wells, the president of the university. Oh, he was light years ahead of his time in the making of a top-flight university. On the other hand, if Ora L. Wildermuth had had his way, I would never have gone to Indiana. He was on the campus at that time and he was unalterably opposed to integration.

The funny thing is, I worked with a man named Mr. Downs taking care of Wildermuth's property the summer before my senior year in high school. Mr. Wildermuth always had a good word for me and was always encouraging me to go to college and do things with my life. I did not know anything about his opposition to integration until I read the Grahams's book [*Getting Open: The Unknown Story of Bill Garrett and the Integration of College Basketball*, by Tom Graham and Rachel Graham Cody]. I was dumbfounded, absolutely dumbfounded. I know Tom Graham and his daughter Rachel and I told them I could not believe the duplicity. I guess that shows you how naive I was at the time.

After Pete Rucinski recommended me to Bo McMillin, Indiana University had J. C. Coffey come to recruit me. They called him Rooster, and Rooster was 5'7", he weighed about 205 pounds, and he was one of the toughest human beings I have ever seen in my life. He was a senior at the time and he was just a tremendous human being. I remained in contact with him until he died about six or seven years ago. He did very, very well. He was a physical educator and he had medical privileges as a podiatrist. He owned a hotel and a taxi cab company and at the time of his death he was very wealthy, although being the kind of man he was, I understand he had no idea how much money he had in the bank.

It was very difficult when I got to Bloomington. I couldn't live in the dormitory, I couldn't eat in the cafeteria, I could not attend the movies except on the weekend, and then we had to sit in the balcony. The restaurants were not open to us. Very little on the campus of a social nature was available to us. All they wanted me to do was play football. They didn't necessarily even want me to be educated except that I had to maintain a certain grade point average in order to be eligible to play football.

We lived in a house one block off campus in the home of Mr. and Mrs. John Mays. They talked with Dr. Wells and he said, "I will approve your home as a dormitory for African American male student athletes." The African American women had to live in two houses off campus and the other African American male students had to live in the town proper. That meant walking a mile to and from the campus. It was quite a small number of black students. I think there were about 100 of us altogether.

Most of the people in Gary did not want me to go to Indiana because of what had happened to one of the most outstanding athletes to ever come out of Gary, an African American by the name of Pat McPherson. Pat was about 6'5", weighed about 230, and he could do everything—football, basketball, track, swimming, boxing—everything. Well, he came to school here in 1938 I think it was, and they treated him very badly and he was out of here after one or two weeks. Everybody in Gary remembered what happened to Pat McPherson and they said, "George, if you go down to Bloomington, you're going to be treated the same way Pat was."

That was another thing I did not find out about until many years after the fact. I was at a reunion 35 years after I graduated from Gary Roosevelt and the man who was the principal when I was attending, H. Theodore Tatum, was there. He was a very special man, the Mahatma Gandhi, the Ralph Bunche, the Martin Luther King Jr. of his time, all rolled into one. At the reunion he asked me if I had ever heard about Pat McPherson and when I said no, he proceeded to tell me the story of this man who had preceded me at Indiana.

Even having said all of that, I can tell you of white people in this city and on the campus who treated me the same way they treated their own children. That was where the role of Herman Wells the president came in. He was an extremely progressive human being. And I must say, people in Gary talked to him expressing their concerns, letting him know that I was to earn a college degree and not be a pampered athlete with no education. After that, Dr. Wells saw to it that everything was put in place for me to earn a degree. I also had a special relationship with Bo McMillin. He was special to me and I was special to him.

Still, it really was a complicated situation. Difficult. Looking back, some of the things amaze me. Picture in your mind's eye a football stadium full of people cheering for me at an Indiana University football game, and yet when that football game was over I walked through that crowd of people to the segregated area where I lived. There would be parties and festivities both on the campus and off the campus that all of the white football players were invited to, but I was never invited to any of those parties or festivities even when we won the Big Ten championship and I was All-American.

If I had allowed it I would have been discouraged and left, but I knew that was the only way I was going to get a college education because my parents did not have the wherewithal to send me to college. I ask young people today all the time, even after I've described to them how difficult it was: If I had left, where would I have gone? I couldn't even enroll at Purdue University. I could not go to Notre Dame, not as an athlete, and that was the only way I was going to be able to go to college. So I stayed.

The only place we had to celebrate was at the house where we lived. One of the things that I remember most was in October of 1947 after we played the University of Pittsburgh in Bloomington, and I had quite a game. Mrs. Mays prepared food and we had a celebration at their home. Well, my dad was there for the game and afterwards he was at the house talking with another African American gentleman, and I was standing a short distance away talking with someone else. This man asked my father if his son played for the football team. At that point I did not even know it was father who was involved in this conversation and I turned to see who the two gentlemen were who were talking, and when I did I saw it was my dad. He was smoking a big cigar—my father always smoked big cigars—and he put that cigar between his index finger and middle finger and pointed to me just as I turned and looked at them and said, "That's my boy." It's the greatest compliment I've ever been paid because I knew that I must be doing something right to have my dad point me out.

Our 1945 team was the only one in school history to win the undisputed championship of the Big Ten. Indiana won it again in 1967 and went to the Rose Bowl, but they actually finished in a three-way tie that year with Purdue and Minnesota. We did not go to the Rose Bowl in 1945 because at that time they did not have the contract between the Big Ten and the Pacific Coast Conference [forerunner of what is today the Pac-10] that said the champions of the two conferences would automatically play in the Rose Bowl.

I would say for the team, 1945 was the peak year while I was there. For myself, I kept developing and getting better as a player until I was my best when I was a senior. I am the only person in the history of Indiana University football to be named to an All-American team three years. I was second team All-American my freshman year, I went into the service in 1946, came back in '47 and made third team All-American, and in 1948, my last year, I made first team.

There were seven African Americans on the football team while I was at Indiana: myself, Mel Groomes, Bill Buckner, Jackie Adams, Simon Range, Leroy Stovall, and a fellow named Joe Gilliam Sr., whose son, Joe Gilliam, became the quarterback of the Pittsburgh Steelers. Mel Groomes, of course, went on to play for the Detroit Lions. We recently had the 60th reunion for the 1945 team and most of those who are living were in attendance. I remain close with some of the white players as well as the blacks, but I must say that not one of the whites has ever said anything to me acknowledging the difficult things that we faced.

There were also important strides being made at Indiana regarding college basketball. Bill Garrett, the gentleman who is the subject of the book I mentioned by the Grahams, was one of the best athletes you would ever want to see. Bill and I were fraternity brothers and the best of friends. In fact, I dated Betty, the woman he eventually married, the year before he came to Bloomington. I am still in contact with his children one of whom is Bill Garrett Jr., who up until recently was the head basketball coach at one of the colleges in Philadelphia. He calls me Uncle George.

Bill was something. He was 6'2", his vertical jump must have been 52 inches, he played center, and in his senior year in high school his school won the Indiana state basketball tournament playing against a school from Terre Haute, whose center was Clyde Lovellette. Bill could also have gotten an athletic scholarship in track and field because he was a tremendous high jumper and quarter miler.

When he got to Indiana, there were four white players on the basketball team who welcomed him. The rest would not even pass the ball to him. Then coach Branch McCracken told them—and I know this because I was at practice on this particular day—"The next time we bring the ball down the floor and Bill Garrett doesn't touch it, the basketball program is over for many of you." The guy who was the ringleader was an older guy who had just come back from the service. His name was Lou Watson and in 1966 he became the head basketball coach at Indiana University.

Bill could have been and should have been the first African American in the National Basketball Association. Instead it was Chuck Cooper, who I got to know very well when I was playing for the New York Yanks. He could have been a two guard or a small forward. The only reason Bill did not play in the NBA is because of the color of his skin. It was such a shame. He did, however, play for awhile for the Harlem Globetrotters. He also became a very accomplished basketball coach. He was the first person in Indiana high school basketball history to play for and coach a state championship team. And then when he was 44 years old, he died while he was painting his house in Indianapolis. He had just called me the day before and said, "George, why don't you organize a reunion for the African American alumni?" And the next day he died. I'll tell you, I mourned his death the same way I mourned the deaths of my mother and father, that's how close I felt to Bill Garrett.

Actually, my very best friend on the basketball team was not Bill Garrett, it was a white player by the name of Jerry Stuteville. Jerry, in a word, was crazy. He would do anything, say anything, wear anything, he just didn't give a shit about anything. But he had a way about him, you just had to love him. Both of us were the first people from our families to ever go to college and we were just two ballplayers on scholarship trying to get an education. He was killed while we were in school on his way to the Indianapolis 500.

A friend of ours who we called Slug and I were supposed to go but when Jerry came to pick us up early on the morning of the race, we could see that he had been drinking. We told him to let one of us drive the car but he refused so neither Slug or I went along. On the way, he came to a one-lane bridge in Mooresville on Highway 37 and hit a truck that was crossing from the opposite direction head on and was killed instantly. His roommate was asleep next to him in the car and didn't get a scratch. That was the end of an incredible friendship and I have never been able to so much as think about the Indianapolis 500 without thinking about Jerry.

I was very aware of the black players who went into pro football in 1946. Yes, sir. That was the year I was in the army. All of a sudden, my dream of playing for the Chicago Bears wasn't so far-fetched. Kenny Washington and Woody Strode for the Rams and Bill Willis and Marion Motley with Cleveland. I got to know all of them because I played against Bill and Marion when I was a rookie and Washington and Strode were living in Los Angeles when I played my first year with the Los Angeles Dons.

The funny thing about it was, the Chicago Bears drafted me in 1949 and it was the greatest shock of my life. For one thing, the Bears had never had a black player, plus no African American had ever been selected in the draft before. I had already signed with the Dons [of the rival All-America Football Conference]. My father was deceased by that time but when I was drafted by the Bears I told my mother my dream had come true. She said, "Remember, you gave your word to the Dons that you would play for them and your father always said a man's word is a measure of the man." As a result, I never played for the Chicago Bears.

What had happened was, the drafts of the two leagues were held around the same time, but the Dons had contacted me and signed me before they actually drafted me. I don't know what I would have done if I had waited but I have no regrets because signing with the Dons simply led me into the rest of my life. My career was much longer than the average and I did everything. Players today run down to cover a kickoff and that is the extent of their playing time. I played seven years both on offense and defense, returned kicks, returned punts, I was a punter, a wide receiver, and a running back so I had a good career. And then in 1956, I was honored by George Halas contacting me about playing for the Bears. I think he was considering making a trade with Philadelphia, who I had played for in 1955, but I told him I was no longer capable of playing the kind of football that he wanted or that I wanted.

In the one year I was there, I loved Los Angeles. Many people welcomed me and helped me to establish myself in pro football. We had a fraternity of football players like Willis, Motley, and Dan Towler who absolutely supported each other when we went to the different cities. Even Washington and Strode, who were no longer playing at that point, were a part of it. And I was very close to Len Ford and John Brown, my teammates on the Dons. It's a bond that has lasted. Marion and many of the others are deceased now but people like John Brown and Sherman Howard, I'm in touch with them on a regular basis.

Several years ago I was invited to an event in Baltimore honoring Lenny Moore's deceased son. Lenny, Art Donovan, Jim Mutscheller, Roger Staubach, and Doug Williams were there, and I remember at one point pointing out Jack Kemp to my wife Vi. Well, a little while later Jack Kemp came by our table and introduced himself. He said, "George, there was no way you could ever know this, but in 1949, when I was 14 years old you used to throw passes to me at Gilmore Stadium after practices of the Los Angeles Dons."

As soon as he said it I remembered there used to be a bunch of kids that would hang around after practice who I used to throw footballs to. He said, "You are on my wall of fame with Muhammad Ali, Dr. Martin Luther King Jr., Thurgood Marshall," and he named several other people. And then when he got up to make his speech, Jack Kemp said, "The greatest football player I have ever seen is in the audience this evening, George Taliaferro." It was quite a thrill, believe me, for this man to say that about me in front of a group of 500 distinguished people.

I would say there was no resentment on the part of white teammates that I was aware of. We were more aware of guys on other teams and how they saw us. For example, in one game in 1950 in Yankee Stadium a little guy for the 49ers named Sam Cathcart received a punt and fell in behind a blocking wall that his teammates had formed. It looked like he was going for a touchdown, and as I was the one who had punted the ball, I was the last man back and I broke through a couple of his blockers to try and tackle him. As we approached each other, he jumped up and tried to kick me in the face and, of course this is in the days before face masks. Well I nailed him and hit him with a couple of shots while he was en route to the ground. Since he was from LSU and none of the ballplayers from the Southern schools had any experience playing against blacks, he had a couple of things to say to me when we were on the ground.

One of the funniest incidents was when I was playing with Los Angeles. I think we were playing the Chicago Hornets and there were four African Americans on the Dons—me, John Brown, Len Ford, and Ben Whaley. We had a guy on the team from Texas named Buddy Tinsley, a huge guy, and we were having a good series and he comes back to the huddle all excited, and these were his words precisely, he says, "You niggers are playing some great football." After the game he had tears in his eyes and he apologized and he said, "That's what we say in Texas."

Well, today Tinsley and John Brown are the closest of friends. They played in Canada together after the Dons and became the best of friends. And to this day, John and I laugh to our heart's content about that. We didn't particularly like it but we understood that he meant it in the most complimentary way. This was the life he had led, and you're not going to forget that, especially in a moment of exultation. I looked at that in a completely different way than the Sam Cathcart situation.

There's a guy I see at golf tournaments, the end from the Bears, Ed Sprinkle. He was a dirty ballplayer. Oh, was he dirty. But I don't think it was necessarily racially motivated because he did everybody that way. He was just a dirty ballplayer. I see him now and he's just lost since his wife died. We play golf and talk about the years gone by but he's in bad shape, just lost emotionally.

The football field was the only place where the black and white players saw each other. We didn't socialize because there wasn't a venue that would accept both African Americans and whites. We had our lives and they had theirs and that's the way it was. I never allowed the social aspects to interfere with me playing the best football I could. The segregation impacted our wives when we were playing in Dallas. Vi and Geraldine Young [Buddy Young's wife] could not sit with the other wives, they had to sit in the end zone, which is the only place where African Americans were allowed. Somehow this was made known to the owners and they said that they could sit with the other wives, but Vi and Geraldine refused as long as no other African Americans would be allowed to sit anywhere but the end zone. It was their way of making a statement.

Young people ask me why I played for so many teams. I say, "It's the same reason why you climb a mountain: because it's there." Seriously, though, the reason is because the teams I played for kept going out of business. The Dons, the Yanks, and the Texans all went out of business. Then I played in Baltimore and got traded to Philadelphia. But that's okay, I played where I was told to play because I wanted to play football.

The Yanks were quite a good team in 1950. Buddy Young, Sherman Howard, and myself were the backs and we were considered to be the fastest backfield ever assembled up until that time. Both Buddy and Sherman were from Chicago and we played against each other in high school. Buddy and I were close right up until his death. I saw him when I was inducted into the College Football Hall of Fame at the Waldorf Astoria. He was living in New York at the time and Vi and I visited with he and Geraldine and then about a week later, he was killed in an automobile accident in Texas. And Sherman and I remain friends to this day.

After the one year in Dallas, I played in Baltimore. Even after I played my final year in Philadelphia I continued living in Baltimore. You hear many stories of the white players who continued to live in Baltimore after they retired, how they were taken into various businesses and did not experience any drop in income. Well the only job I could find in Baltimore was as a used car salesman. And that was not a very prosperous business because, of course, you were on commission and if you didn't bring in business you didn't get paid.

I was able to get some work as a substitute physical education teacher but I could only teach in several schools, not in any of the white schools in the city of Baltimore. The superintendent of health, physical education, and recreation in Baltimore was an Indiana University graduate and when I interviewed with him, I told him I was interested in applying for a job as a physical education teacher and football coach. He said, "There are only two schools here you can teach in, Douglas High School and Dunbar High School," those were his exact words.

That discouraged me quite a bit. I had a degree, I had a letter of recommendation from the dean of the School of Health, Physical Education, and Recreation from Indiana, but all of that preparedness didn't mean a thing. Eventually I went on and got a master's degree from Howard University and took jobs moving up in responsibility and duties each time until I became the dean of students at Morgan State University. Then I came to Indiana and worked in various capacities over the years.

I was chairman of the Special Advisory Commission to the Big Ten Conference from 1974 until 1986. It had been formed by conference commissioner Wayne Duke and consisted of ten people who had been athletes at each of the member schools including Buddy

Young, who was the representative of the University of Illinois. When we met for the first time, I told the others I would not be part of the commission because the proposals that had been made were basically going to benefit white athletes only. I believed in doing everything we could to help more athletes graduate, period, but we also needed a special emphasis on black athletes.

Wayne Duke and some of the others thought the recommendations that had been made were wonderful. I said, "No. There are only three people in this room who have lived through separate but equal: Buddy Young, Bob Dorsey from Ohio State, and myself." Well, they listened to what I had to say, changed the recommendations, and it worked. I was the member of the commission who worked for many years meeting with the college presidents, the athletic directors, and the faculty representatives getting this thing done.

We got a lot done and then eventually the NCAA adopted a couple of the recommendations we made. One of the things we recommended is that there be a fifth year for scholarships. Many universities put many of the scholarship athletes on a reduced schedule. They take 12 credits per semester, which allows them to still qualify as a full-time student, but it makes it impossible for them to finish in four years. So our recommendation in such cases is that the fifth year be a part of the scholarship.

There are people in Bloomington who detest me because I am upright and absolutely a man and won't take any bullshit off anybody. There's a sportswriter here who wrote a series of stories recently about the twelve biggest football games in Indiana University history. One of the games he wrote about was the Purdue game in 1945. Now, in 1945 I was a freshman and I was second team All-American behind Glenn Davis and Doc Blanchard. This sportswriter wrote at length in his story about the contributions of Ben Raimondi the quarterback and Pete Pihos the fullback and then he wrote, "And, oh, by the way, there was a freshman here named George Taliaferro." And I'm the one who was second team All-American.

To show you how far this goes, I am the chairman of the board of directors of the Children's Organ Transplant Association and several years ago Marques Haynes the basketball player came here to play in the golf tournament we have every year to raise funds. A sportswriter approached me and asked if he could ride with Marques Haynes while he was on the way to the Indianapolis airport to catch his flight back to Dallas to interview him for a story. This man's wife is my receptionist at COTA and I said, "Of course." In the story, he said that Marques Haynes came to Bloomington to play in a golf tournament and that is how he got to interview him without ever mentioning that it was a tournament to raise funds for COTA or that it was through me that he got the interview. And it's all because I am a stand-up guy and a lot of people here do not like me because of it.

The situation with Murray Sperber was a part of it because I supported Murray to the hilt. [Sperber was a professor at Indiana and author of several books about the negative impact of big time athletics on university life.] Murray was simply writing about the reality of collegiate athletics and he was absolutely, absolutely on the ball. The criticism of him was something that Bob Knight fostered, and some of the heat that was directed at Murray hit me because I was a prominent person at the university and had been for many years and I supported him. You have never known a more powerful person at a university than Bob Knight. He controlled this university, this town, and the office of the Big Ten commissioner—well, I guess he didn't control it entirely because [Indiana University president] Myles Brand fired him.

Even now that I'm retired, I'm still very much involved with Indiana University. Even amidst the hostility, there are many people who recognize that the intent of the work I have done over the years has been to help this university be what it can be for all human beings. Not too long ago I received an award called the DASA, the Distinguished Alumni Service Award. It is the highest award that an alumnus can get from Indiana University and there are less than 300 people in the history of the school who have received it. And it all started when I was eight years old and I told my mother I was going to take care of her by becoming a great football player.

EMERSON COLE

Emerson Elvin Cole
Born December 10, 1927, in Carrier Mills, Illinois

Swanton High School in Swanton, Ohio
University of Toledo

Fullback/linebacker
Drafted in 12th round by Cleveland Browns in 1950

When he was selected by the Cleveland Browns in the 1950 NFL draft, Emerson Cole became the first African American drafted by the franchise that pioneered integration in professional sports. Growing up in and around Toledo, Emerson starred for the University of Toledo for three years. He set a school single season rushing record and was selected to the all-Ohio team as a senior in 1949.

Told by coach Paul Brown that he was the heir-apparent to future Hall of Famer Marion Motley, Emerson became the back-up full back. When the 31-year old Motley was seriously injured in training camp in 1951, the day of transition seemed to be at hand. Motley carried only 61 times for 273 yards that year as the Browns came up short of a championship for the first time in their six-year history. Emerson, meanwhile, showed great promise, particularly in a Week 4 victory over the Pittsburgh Steelers when he gained 126 yards and averaged 7.4 per carry.

For Emerson, however, the game marked not the springboard to a great career but a high point that would not be replicated. Despite an outstanding 5.5 yard average for the year, he carried the ball just 46 times in 1951. He lasted only one more year in Cleveland and was out of football by 1953 when the Chicago Bears released him in training camp.

| | | | | Rushing | | | | Receiving | | |
Year	Team	League	Games	Attempts	Yards	Avg.	TDs	Receptions	Yards	Avg.
1950	Browns	NFL	12	26	105	4.0	0	0	0	—
1951	Browns	NFL	12	46	252	5.5	1	4	30	7.5
1952	Browns	NFL	6	0	0	—	0	0	0	—
1953	Bears	NFL	1	0	0	—	0	0	0	—

Kickoff Returns

Year	Returns	Yards	Avg.	TDs
1950	1	22	22.0	0
1951	2	28	14.0	0
1952	5	99	19.8	0

Told by several teammates that his career was the biggest waste of talent they had ever seen, Emerson is somewhat mystified as to why Paul Brown did not better utilize him. Although quick to credit Brown for his willingness to sign black players sooner and in greater numbers than other teams, Emerson believes the Cleveland coach did not like the independent manner in which he conducted himself. Emerson also believes Brown was unwilling to employ Motley and other blacks as coaches because he did not consider blacks to be as intelligent as whites.

More than fifty years later, Emerson looks at his NFL playing days as so much water under the bridge. Although there is an element of "what might have been" to his career, he did fruitful work in the years after football. Most notable was his twenty years of service at the Civil Rights Commission of Ohio, where he took on corporations, landlords, and unions on behalf of the underdog.

"As much as anything I did, my biggest accomplishment was all the people I helped," Emerson says. "I walk down the street right now in Toledo or Columbus and people come up to me and say, 'Man, you saved my house, you saved my job, you saved this, you saved that.' It's good to have people say, 'I'd never have made it without you.' To me that's more gratifying than people writing to me with those damn silly ass football cards to sign."

Describing himself as an "above average pugilist" (a cousin won a gold medal as an Olympic boxer), Emerson is not one to back down, whether on the football field or in the courtroom. Despite the unrewarding nature of his tenure with the Browns, he has some good memories and recalls with special fondness the friendships he forged with teammates Motley and Horace Gillom. Emerson is retired and lives in Columbus, Ohio.

I was born December 10th of 1927 in a little town called Carrier Mills in southern Illinois. I left there when I was three months old when my family moved to Toledo. My dad worked in a coal mine in Illinois and when the mines would shut down he would come to Toledo to work in a foundry that my grandfather worked in, so we moved back and forth about seven times when I was a kid. Finally my mother said that was enough of that so we left Carrier Mills for good and moved to Toledo in 1936. We stayed in Toledo three years—1936, '37, and '38—and then moved to Swanton, Ohio, a little farm town about twenty-five miles west of Toledo. We were the first black family there, and I was the first black to ever graduate from Swanton High School.

I went to first and second grade in Carrier Mills, but most of my life has been in Ohio. Carrier Mills was a little one stoplight town. Before my dad passed in 1989, I took him down there almost every year around Memorial Day. I think the population is supposed to be 2,000, but I think they're counting some of the cows because I don't think there are 2,000 people down there.

Working as a coal miner was a very difficult life but that and farming was about the only work in Carrier Mills. My dad was in the mine the day I was born and they wouldn't let him come out. He was a thousand feet down and five miles back and they said, "Wait until your shift is over." I had several uncles and everybody worked in the mines. There were quite a few blacks working in the mines, but there were certain mines that blacks could work in and certain mines they couldn't. Those were the days of John L. Lewis, the president of the United Mine Workers. They thought he should've been president of the United States because he had improved conditions in the mines so much. The wages were only a little better, but he did improve the safety aspect of the mines a great deal.

My dad played baseball, but he was married at nineteen so work came first. He never had an opportunity to do much of anything in athletics, but he was a big fellow, 6'4" and about 240 pounds. My Uncle Herschel was quite a baseball player. That was before integration and Ty Cobb came to Carrier Mills and asked my Uncle Herschel to be on one of his colored teams and he said, "Hell no," and he didn't go. You know, Ty Cobb had three or four colored teams in the old black league. My uncle would pitch a doubleheader for $15 for teams they had around Carrier Mills, but he wouldn't go with Cobb. He told him, "No thank you."

I had another uncle who was the heavyweight champion of Toledo in 1935. He taught me how to fight. His son, my first cousin, Wilbert McClure, won a gold medal in boxing with Cassius Clay in 1960 in Rome. Cassius won the light heavy, a guy named [Edward] Crook won the middleweight, and Wilbert won light welterweight. They had three blacks on the boxing team and three gold medals. He has a Ph.D. and has his own consulting firm in Boston. He was honored in Toledo in 2005 and I was up there for the ceremony.

Toledo was a big city compared to Carrier Mills so it was different. I'd call it a decent town. You had areas where blacks lived, which is universal all over the world—they live in certain areas and other people live in other areas. After we bought the farm, we would still go into Toledo quite often because my grandparents lived there, but we only lived there until '38.

The farm was a little dirt farm of about seventeen and a half acres. Other people that worked at the foundry bought plots in the same area where ours was and they carpooled to go into Toledo to work. My father was more at home on the farm than in the city. He didn't like to be around crowds. Even when it came to seeing me play, he didn't like the crowds. He might have seen one of my college games and he never saw me play professionally. I loved the farm life, but I was also kind of an A personality. I'm more like my mother. I'm outgoing and outspoken, where my father would rather just be left alone.

Me and one of my brothers worked for some of the other farmers in the summertime. Then when we got a little older we started working in Toledo. I worked at B. F. Goodrich and my brother worked at Goodyear for summer jobs. I played football, ran track, and played baseball. We didn't play pickup games because there was nobody to pickup with, just farmers, and their sons and daughters worked after school.

I went out for football when I was a freshman in high school. We had a coach that had all the merchants' sons on the team and they gave me a gray jersey with no number on it. I never missed a practice or a game but I never got in. They got rid of that coach and brought in a new one and right away he said to me, "You're my starting tailback." I said, "Okay, good," and the last three years I started every game. I was most valuable player and was in the second class to get inducted into the Swanton High School Hall of Fame.

My favorite subjects in school were English, history, and sociology. I took up drawing in high school and I drew for the high school yearbook and stuff. There's a funny story about me and this girl who drew for the yearbook with me. After graduation, I told her I was going to the University of Toledo and I asked her where she was going. Her folks owned about ten miles of that area and she said, "I'm going to Paris." I said, "Paris, Kentucky?" And she said, "No, Paris, France," and I've never seen her again since 1946.

I was the only black player on the team and out of all the teams that we played there were only four others. I don't know why but I rode to the games with the coach, I didn't ride with the team. When we would go and play in these towns, he would tell me to go stand under the nearest goal post after the game was over. Then the deputy sheriff or the troopers, whatever they were, the police, they would escort me back to the coach's car. I didn't dress in their dressing rooms, that's how bad it was.

One time we were in this restaurant because the coach was going to feed us after the game. I saw the coach talking to the cook and he got red in the face. He took the whole team out because the guy wouldn't serve anybody on the team as long as I was in the building. My dad had grown up in the South and he told me the southern part of the North was really the South, and that's how it was in those towns around Toledo.

During some of those games I heard everything from those spectators. I've been called so many names that some of them even sound funny. Players on other teams would do it, too, but I was 6'2" and 205 and ran the hundred in 9.9 seconds so I didn't care what they said, I'd just run over them and stomp them in the ground. You get to the point where you're either going to be an athlete or you're going to act a fool about some ignorant people, and I chose to be a scholar and an athlete.

I got along fine with my teammates. I grew up with all the guys on the team so I didn't have any problem with them. They only let the n-word slip one time in the whole four years I was there. It happened during a game. There were only about two or three minutes left until the end of the half and I just walked off the field and sat down next to the coach. When I told him what happened, he shouted at them so bad he lost his voice for ten days.

Although I got along with them fine, I wouldn't deal with them socially at all. Never went to a prom, a dance, nothing. My dad said, "You play football, you go to school, and when the football game is over, take the car and come home." And that's what we did, my brother and I. Like I said, he thought of that place as the South. He said, "Have nothing to do with those people except in class and on the football field. Anything social, leave it. Don't ever be a part of anything they have socially."

My senior year I got offers from about twelve or fourteen colleges, including Ohio State and Toledo. Of course having no money, it all depended on what kind of scholarship they were going to offer. My high school principal was a wonderful guy and he told me to pick out what schools I wanted to go see. Then he drove me personally to those schools and gave me spending money and told me to go talk to the athletic directors. I'd stay on campus and he would go to a hotel.

When the people at Ohio State saw I was black, they changed their offer from a scholarship to half a scholarship and a job in a foundry called Buckeye Steel. I said, "No thanks. We got a hundred and fifty foundries in Toledo. If I was interested in a foundry, I don't have to leave home." It was a guy by the name of Carroll Widdoes. My principal was waiting downstairs and when I came down in about fifteen minutes, he asked me, "What's the matter, wasn't he there?" I said, "He was there but he was talking foolish," so we went from there to Wilberforce.

I ruled out all the Southern schools because I wasn't going South. With Toledo, I didn't have to take the entrance exam because I finished so high in my class and because of the academic rating of my high school. They offered me a full scholarship and I was only fifteen miles away. If things went bad or if I got hungry or financially strapped, I could *run* fifteen miles. Plus, my principal really wanted me to play in Toledo. He never said that, he just said that if I did choose Toledo he wouldn't miss any games. He never told me I should go there—nobody ever told me which school I should pick. One thing I knew, I was determined that I was not going South, that was for damn sure.

I had some buddies in Toledo that played in the schools in the inner city and I was looking forward to playing with them, but none of them could pass the entrance exam to get into Toledo. They all went down to Fort Valley State in Georgia and I was left alone. But I have no regrets because my folks left the farm and moved back to Toledo, so it all worked out. Plus, it was a very, very highly rated school academically. Once they find out you graduated from Toledo, they never ask any questions, so looking back I think it was an excellent choice.

My mother was really pushing for education. The old man only went three weeks into the ninth grade so education wasn't high on his list. But my mother had six children and she wanted six teachers. I was the first one in my family to go to college. Then all my brothers and sisters went to the University of Toledo. She only got two teachers but every one of us were professional people, you know, in supervision or management. My youngest brother's got three degrees from the University of Toledo.

All the boys went on athletic scholarships and the girls went on church and academic scholarships. We had no money, it's as simple as that, so when I got the chance I told the old man, "I can't help feed the family but I can take one mouth that you don't have to feed," and he said okay. My brother Emmett—we were like twins, Emerson and Emmett—they gave him a track scholarship. He ran the hundred in 9.8. They knew my mom wanted him to go to college, and they knew that without me they might as well not even play a football schedule because all but a couple of the kids couldn't have made a good high school team.

When I started in 1946, you could ride all the blacks on campus around in a station wagon. As far as the football team, there were three blacks in 1946, three in '47 when I made the varsity, then in '48 I was the only black on the team, and in '49 there were two of us that were starting and two reserves. That's the kind of numbers we're talking about. I set a school record that lasted twenty years with 1,163 yards one season and I got elected to the University's Hall of Fame in 1983.

It was so soon after the war and all, all the athletes lived in army barracks. I couldn't get a roommate at first because nobody wanted to room with me so I decided that if they're gonna act ignorant, I'll join them. I told them, "I got a big pot in my room and in the middle of the night I'll stoke up a fire and cook and eat my roommate." You know, "If you're going to be stupid then I'll be stupid right along with you." So one guy, a white guy, George Miley, who passed away not long ago, he said, "I don't believe you've got a pot, and I don't believe you're going to cook anybody and eat them. I'll be your roommate." He was on one side of the backfield and I was on the other. A wonderful guy.

We didn't have much talent. I made a lot of yards on my own because I wasn't getting much blocking. I figured if I was going to carry the ball nine out of ten times and take the hammering and the beating I should have something to say about it, so I made suggestions and the coach would listen. I told him I didn't want to run from the same position all the time because they were in the hole waiting for me and he went along. I ran from all three positions in the backfield wherever I saw an opening. I remember I tried that with Paul Brown one time. I said, "I can take an angle like this and cut off that linebacker before he can get to the ball carrier." He said, "You're here to play ball, you're not here to think," and that was the last suggestion I ever made.

I had to improvise when I was in college. When we played against New Hampshire we stayed in Boston and the whole team, except me, went out to get seafood. I belonged to an Alpha Phi Alpha fraternity, a black fraternity, so I asked a cabdriver if they had an Alpha Phi Alpha fraternity in Boston and he took me all the way over there, even though I told him I didn't have much money. It just happened that they were having a big party and they put me up and made me their guest of honor. Meanwhile, the white boys went out and ate some mussels or some shit and every one of them got sick. I had a room by myself and I had the only clean room in the hotel.

The Browns started the same year I started college and they had Bill Willis and Marion Motley, so I knew about them. They played exhibition games at the University of Toledo so I got to see them play. They were in training camp in Bowling Green, Ohio, which is 20 miles from Toledo so I used to go and see them there, too. I met Willis and Motley and I talked to them. We had chats about how it was. Of course, once I joined the Browns I got to know them a lot better.

I was very surprised when the Browns drafted me because they never talked to me. Around my junior year guys from the Giants kept coming to Toledo to talk to me, and that's where I thought I was going to go. Why the Giants waited until Paul Brown got his hooks on me I don't know, but just being drafted was quite an accomplishment for a black. We had five blacks in my rookie year and I was the only one who was drafted.

You couldn't have any bad publicity with the Browns because if you did you got a ticket home. You had to be very careful. Paul Brown would send you packing in a minute. But he was very, very intelligent relative to football. He had a chart three deep for every position that he took out before every game so you knew your status. You might be in two or three positions. I was the number two fullback from the first day in camp behind Motley, I was on the kickoff and punt teams, I was on the goal line defense, and I was a backup linebacker. If you were behind a guy and he came out of the game, you better get in without being told. You better not be sitting on the bench daydreaming. You didn't ask anybody anything, you just went right in, and you'd dash in there because you'd better not get a penalty for being late, either.

Things got off to a funny start with Paul Brown. He had said that he drafted me to eventually take over at fullback for Motley and the first day in the locker room, he's there looking at me like he's looking at an animal in the zoo. He said, "I thought you were bigger." Maybe that was his way of saying, "I want you to play bigger than you are." But I said to myself, "Goddamn it, you know my weight and my height and everything, how could you think I was bigger when you know exactly how big I was?"

I never knew why Paul Brown didn't like me but I believe it was because I looked him in the eye and that offended him. I didn't know you were supposed to bow your head and talk and I wouldn't have done it even if I did know. I had been in white schools all my life and I had a father who said, "Look a person straight in the eye and tell the truth and if you demand respect you'll get respect." He never met Paul Brown, though.

I was very polite, I never said anything out of line, I never condemned anything, but I would just not be a man and then go back to being a boy. You shouldn't have to be a boy, become a man, then go back to being a boy again. That's my philosophy and I got it from my parents. This is only my opinion, but I think he was physically scared that I would kick his ass. There were three people that Paul Brown was really concerned might do something ugly to him and that was me, Jim Brown, and Lenny Ford. He dealt with Jim Brown by raising hell with Bobby Mitchell. He would raise hell with Bobby Mitchell, but it was really intended for Jim Brown. Bobby Mitchell used to say, "I'm catching all this hell and he isn't even really talking to me."

Looking back, it's my impression that Brown thought Negroes were physically superior and intellectually inferior. I just believe that in my heart and if I was under oath I would say the same thing. The impression I got was that you're not smart enough to play quarterback, you're not smart enough to play guard, you're not smart enough to play center—that's what they called the diamond, the center, the quarterback, and the two guards and which are supposedly thinking positions. I don't have anything against him, but I don't think he was modernistic in regards to race.

On the other hand, you can't knock a guy that helped break the color barrier. I have to give him credit. In every opening speech at the beginning of the season he would say, "We have four or five colored"—we were colored then—"four or five colored fellows playing. Anybody that feels that they can't play with them, come to my office and you will get your train ticket home." He said that every year. Of course, nobody took him up on it but I have to give him his due.

I saw him once at a reunion and he had mellowed a lot. Remember Ickey Woods and the Ickey Shuffle? If you did that in Cleveland, you would be on a train home. You better not say anything back to the officials, you better not do a monkey shine in the end zone, you hand the ball back to the official and you get the hell back to the sidelines. All this foolishness they go through now, I look at it and it amazes me, all the shenanigans and the bull. You know, you score a touchdown, act like you've been there before and you're going back again. Don't act like it's a once in a lifetime miracle. That reunion was the only time I saw him and then I went to his funeral.

The other thing about Paul Brown was when Motley wanted to get a coaching job, Paul Brown wouldn't even talk to him. They refused. They said they weren't interested in having him as an assistant coach, but it was in much stronger terms. Even Otto Graham, who owed his life to Motley, wouldn't give him a job when he was a coach. I think Motley was naive. He had a lot of street smarts but he was naive about what white people think about black people. He just didn't get it. He thought they were going to hire him and I knew damn well they weren't going to hire him.

I'd been around Motley long enough. You could look in his eyes and see he was serious. He believed it. He thought because of his faithful duty, he truly thought that Otto or Paul Brown was going to give him a job. Once I saw he was serious, I dropped it. I had nothing else to say, but I knew very well he wasn't going to get any job. I offered him a job, a good job. He said, "Cole, you're the only guy I played with that offered me a job." He worked as a mailman for awhile. He was a beer or a liquor salesman for awhile. He did a lot of odd jobs, a lot of different things. I don't think he got a quality college education and he just had to take whatever jobs he could get. I did get him a job working for the Ohio Youth Commission and that's where he retired from.

There was just one white guy on the Browns who I thought had a problem. I was going to punch him out but Motley said, "Don't do that. You'll set black people back twenty years because they will not look at it as a dressing room brawl, they'll look at it as blacks and whites can't play together." I was a better than fair fighter but when Motley said that, I said, "Okay." I had tremendous respect for Motley, and he was the peacemaker.

I was just not utilized at all in the pros. Motley got hurt in '51 and then I was the number one fullback. That didn't last, though. Dub Jones said, "Never in my entire life have I seen such a waste of talent," meaning that Paul Brown did not use me the way he should have. I ended up with the Bears my last year. Cleveland released me and the Bears picked me up, but they cut me at the final cut the next year. Here I am, 6'2", 220, and run a hundred in 9.9 and [George] Halas kept guys who wouldn't have matched up against a girls' team. Halas said, "Cole, I want to connect you up with San Francisco." And I said, "Yeah, okay," and I got in my car and drove back to Toledo. I joined the sheriff's department and made $2,000 a year more as a deputy than I did as a football player and $2,000 in 1953 was a whole lot. But I had fun. And football got me to college, which I could not afford to do otherwise, and having that degree got me a lot of other things. Plus, I think having NFL experience on my resume helped me out.

When we would go into a city, we would go down to the black neighborhood and they'd throw a big party for the black players on both teams and we wouldn't have to worry that anybody was going to do anything crazy or criminal. You know, nothing was going to get out about us no matter what. Joe Perry, Night Train Lane, Emlen Tunnell, we'd all party together. Tunnell was one of my very best friends. Every town showed us a grand time.

No white player ever attended one of those parties and, frankly, I don't think they would've been welcome. I think they knew that because none of them ever asked. We played football together but once we left the field, we went one way and the whites went the other. We never mingled socially or anything. You know, we'd be in the locker room together, change clothes, we'd go out on the field together, we'd practice or play a game, but when every practice and game was over, one group went to the right and one group went to the left.

Sometimes on the road it was kind of rough. I went in a restaurant in Washington, D.C. and they acted like I wasn't even there. I never was a hell-raiser and I never did complain, I just sat there. After about an hour, here comes somebody I knew from Ohio, Mike DiSalle. He had been mayor of Toledo, governor of Ohio, and he was the head of the Price Stabilization Unit of the federal government, which is why he was in D.C. This was a restaurant that he ate at all the time and all the people working there all knew him.

As soon as he saw me, he came over and said, "Hi, how you doing, Em? Do you mind if I have breakfast with you?" I said, "I'd be delighted," and boy, they came running. It looked like a mob had come to serve us and I had been sitting there an hour and they had pretended I wasn't even there. What I'm saying is, there's a lot of psychological scars. But you know, if you can live through that kind of thing you can live through anything.

Since there were five blacks on the Browns, one of us got to room by himself when we were on the road and the other four got to split two rooms. We were in Baltimore and I wanted a single room and Motley says, "Man, get out of that line." I said, "The hell with you, Motley, you want me to get out of line because you want that single room." He said, "No man, we can't stay here." I looked at him again and he had a look on his face like, damn, this guy is serious. I looked behind me and, sure enough, there was a cab out front and there was Willis and Ford and Gillom in the cab and I knew he was telling the truth. I just got out of that line and we went across town and found some colored hotel they had picked out for us.

Paul Brown took all the letters where they said they were going to kill us with high-powered rifles and all that silly shit. I heard there were lots of them, you know, hate mail and threats that they're going to kill us. We never could get a letter straight from anybody. They all went to Paul Brown if it had a black player's name on it. He didn't want us to worry about getting shot, he wanted us to worry about making a block or a tackle, so he kept all the letters. There were a lot of death threats, which isn't surprising considering the way you got treated in those towns.

None of the white players ever came up and said, "I'm sorry that you had to go to the other hotels, I'm sorry that we didn't mingle socially." They were teammates and that was friendship enough. I didn't seek any additional friendship other than that they block for me when I was running. Two or three of them said my career was as great a waste of manpower as they'd ever seen in their entire lives. That's about as close as any of them ever came. Maybe I got a little of my dad in me because I'm kind of an isolationist. I don't have anything against white people because I can't, having lived with them my entire life. I think I understand people so it doesn't make any difference. And I enjoy myself when I go to the team reunions.

Marion was a heck of a nice guy and a great player. Graham never even looked to his left side because he knew nobody was going to be there. Motley took care of that side. I remained friendly with him all through the years, from 1950 until he died. In fact, I spoke at his funeral at the request of his family. He was kind of the leader of the blacks and the watchdog. He'd make sure we didn't get into any trouble or in any arguments with the white players. He was kind of outspoken, but he was also diplomatic. After I'd been there a while, I told Motley that Paul Brown didn't like me and he said, "He sure doesn't."

During games, guys would hurt you. One time against the Pittsburgh Steelers, I was hitting this guy pretty hard when I blocked him and he was hitting me pretty hard. Then on one play I went down and he stepped in my face with his cleats and cut my mouth up six ways. I couldn't go to the party that night and I couldn't go to the doctor, so I just got a bucket of ice and a wash cloth. The swelling went down the next morning. But, yeah, they would hurt you.

They used to step on Motley's hands and cut his hands all up. One day the ref gave a guy a fifteen-yard penalty and the guy said, "What's that for?" And the ref said, "You know what that's for. That's for stomping on Motley's hands." But Motley would always hit the ground and roll over on his back so if anyone was going to make one of those late lunges, Motley'd kick him. Motley helped me out a lot. He said, "When a guy goes down, get the hell away from the pile because there's always some nut that's going to be rolling in at you. There's nothing to see. He's down and the referee blew the whistle, so get the hell out of there."

I loved Motley and I loved Horace Gillom. We were the three closest among the blacks. Lenny Ford was kind of standoffish, more of a loner, and Willis was more of a family man. That doesn't mean we weren't family people, just that we would go out and have a good time while Willis wouldn't. Every year Motley, Horace Gillom, and myself went around Ohio for a week and had a good time.

Horace was a fun-loving guy, a tremendous football player, and one hell of a nice fellow. He holds a lot of records in punting. You know what he could do? He'd tell us when we were going down on punts: "This one is going to roll and it's going to keep going." On another he'd say, "I'm backing this one up. Don't go full speed because it's coming back this way." I could never figure out how the hell he knew when a ball was going to go forward or backward. He had that much ability.

One time during a game Horace said to me, "You see that guy I got to block today? I won't be able to go to the party blocking that big fellow all night long. Rookie, watch me and you'll learn something." So he lined up opposite the guy and hit him right in the mouth with his fist. After the play was over, he went and told the ref that the guy was playing dirty and the next play, the guy swung at Horace and got put out of the game. It's a good trick if you don't want to block against somebody all night long.

I went and visited with him out in Los Angeles after he quit playing football. He was buried in Massillon after he dropped dead of a heart attack. I went to his funeral and had a heart attack in the cemetery. A guy walked up in the middle of the cemetery and said, "Who's Cole?" I said, "I am." He said, "Your mother is dead." I was supposed to pick her up that afternoon from the hospital. I didn't think I was going to live. Motley and Willis were trying to get me from Massillon to Canton, which is 20 miles, and they decided I wouldn't live 20 miles so they took me to the Massillon General Hospital.

Ford was a devastating player. He was 6'6", 250 pounds, and crazy as hell. Teams would have to put three guys on him. Anytime you have to put three guys on one guy, you're going to weaken your team because there are going to be soft spots somewhere. I had to block him by myself as a rookie and he got mad at me and he raised me up in the air and knocked Otto Graham down with me. That's the kind of player he was.

I didn't get along with him while we were playing after that incident in practice. I made up with him, though. I even saved his life once in Detroit when he got into it with this guy on the street. Lenny said he was a pickpocket, and they got into it and the guy knocked him down and was going to stomp him. I said to myself, "Once he beats up Ford he'll just beat my butt so I might as well jump in here right now," and I knocked that guy crazy. After it was over we went into a bar and this guy said, "You know who that was?" I said, "No, I just know he took one hell of a beating." The guy said, "He's the heavyweight champion of Jackson Prison." I said, "Why didn't somebody tell me that before?"

Paul Brown had a lot of problems with Ford. Ford would go off, on and off the field. He was just crazy, just nuts. I don't have any better way to put it. He slapped a guy in a bar and I think he gave the guy a $1,000 to settle it. Plus he had a lot of problems with alcohol. I think Paul Brown knew Ford had a drinking problem but because of the job he did, he let it go.

I went to work for the sheriff's department in Lucas County in 1953. There were three blacks: two jailers and I was the only patrolman. I took the test for detective sergeant and I came out first, then I asked the sheriff if I could take the test for captain and he said, "You haven't been here long enough. You got to wait a year." So stupidly I waited and after a year was up I asked again. He said, "We don't want no nigger captain and we don't even want you as a black sergeant, so you're never going to take that test."

I had a college degree and the captain had an eighth grade education and the sheriff had a third grade education, so I went across the street and asked the guy that hired me, "Can I go to school?" He said, "Emerson, you can go to school any time you want as long as you can take care of your case load." But the sheriff said, "You can't go to school and work here." I said to myself, "This looks like a dead end to me," and I went to the welfare department. From there I went to the antipoverty program, and then I went back to Toledo as regional director of twenty-six counties for the Civil Rights Commission. After nine years, I was transferred to Columbus as chief of compliance in charge of all regions statewide and that's where I retired from in 1986.

When I was a deputy, I had a lot of problems with other deputies. I went to a house and said to this one guy, "I have a warrant for your arrest," and he says, "Stick that warrant up your ass." I usually don't get mad, I hold my temper pretty good, but I said to myself, "Oh, lord have mercy." He resisted and I beat the shit out of him and took him in. He's bloody as a hog and I asked him, "Why in the heck would you be stupid enough to do what you did?" He said, "Well, two officers told me you weren't really a policeman." I made him tell me who they were and they took about two or three weeks off work, you know, avoiding me.

I had a white partner who got killed because of that shit. We went in to get our assignments and the sheriff's assistant sent me to pick somebody up and sent my partner to the East Side to pick up this other guy, and then after that we were supposed to join up. I asked some of the deputies about the guy I was supposed to arrest and they said, "He's 6'9", 300 pounds, and mean as hell." I realized they sent me alone because they wanted me to get beat up. Well I went and the guy gave me no trouble whatsoever, but on the way back, I hear on the radio something's going on on the East Side. What happened was, my partner approached a suspect and another guy stepped out of the back door and shot him, which wouldn't have happened if there had been two of us. Just for them wanting me to get beat up, they cost this other man his life.

I did most of my life's work in civil rights. My last twenty years, I worked in the Civil Rights Commission, but I was always working on civil rights before that when I was in the antipoverty program, the welfare department, and the sheriff's department. People always want to know about football, but I'll tell you what, I like the work I did getting people jobs and getting jobs back for people who were illegally fired and all the companies I integrated that had never seen a black face and getting houses for people where they wouldn't rent to them and dealing with insurance and loans and redlining and all the thousands of little tricks that they got. I took on factories, all the automobile companies, all the utility companies, the city, the police department, unions that were not protecting their black members. Nothing made me happier than taking on those corporate goons when you got the weight of the state of Ohio behind you. But you better know your trade, your law, and I just had one code I had to know, but it was updated on a yearly basis so I had to stay current.

One time I told the ex-mayor of Toledo, "Look here, I need some records for this report," and he told me to go to hell. I said, "Look sir, I just want the records for my report and I'll return them to you." "Go to hell." I had the sheriff's department pick him up and bring his ass over to my office with the records in a squad car. He said, "You didn't have to do that." I said, "I had to do it because you told me to go to hell." I have always been of the opinion that the smoothest and least complicated and least confrontational way you can do something is the best, but I would use those extremes if I had to.

The KKK had a price on my head in Sandusky, Ohio and other people in Sandusky who I helped get a street paved wanted to name it after me. It was a street in a black neighborhood and they couldn't even get a fire truck in there. I said, "No, this is no good. If a fire started back here it would kill all these people." I was able to get people together and they put a street in. They said they were going to name it after me, but that was right at the time that Dr. King was killed so I said, "Name it after him."

Swanton High School asked me to speak at the school not too long ago and I told them, "No, I'm not going to speak." They said, "Well you're in our Hall of Fame." I said, "Yeah but you don't have any black students, you don't have any black teachers, you don't have any black janitors or groundskeepers, you don't have any black anything, and I am not going to come out there and speak. What the hell am I going to tell you?" See, I lived in Lucas County and the high school is in Fulton County, and it was all right with people in Fulton County as long as there were just a few blacks. But they must have had a little trouble because they changed it so they wouldn't have to take anybody from Lucas County.

I'll tell you what, it's hell being first. I've been first enough to know. Now blacks have every opportunity they want as long as they don't act a fool and mess it up. We had a kid here who blew his future a few years ago, Maurice Clarett. He's in jail now. He could be making $8,000,000, $9,000,000 a year. The worst of all is Terrell Owens. It's a good thing he wasn't around when we were breaking the color line because he would've set things back twenty years. They don't know anything about what happened in 1946 or 1950. Somebody had to blaze a trail and I'm proud that I was a part of that, even if a lot of these people don't know and don't care.

Bill Willis lived just around the corner from me until he died. The last time I saw him was at a reunion for the 1950 team at the

Browns' stadium and he was in a wheelchair. I pushed him from the upper tiers down the ramps to the field and he got up and walked on the field with his cane. Somebody told me that now that Bill's gone, there's only eight from that 1950 team still living.

All in all I'm in pretty good health. My mother's influence is still with me. She said, "Just tell the truth and do the right thing." It's that simple. People can learn all they need to know to be successful in kindergarten and that's three little things: don't hit your partner, stay between the lines, and if you make a mess, clean it up. If you adhere to that your whole life, I don't think we'd have all these problems we have now.

CHARLIE POWELL

Charles Elvin Powell
Born April 4, 1932, in Dallas, Texas

San Diego High School in San Diego, California
No college

Defensive end/linebacker
Undrafted, signed by San Francisco 49ers in 1952

Muhammad Ali, Bill Veeck, and Bobby Layne. Aside from the fact that each was a prominent figure in the world of sports, there's nothing obvious that links these three men. One way in which they are linked, though, is through the person of Charlie Powell. Powell is almost certainly the only person who can say he played baseball for Veeck, fought Ali, and sacked Layne.

Of all the thousands of athletes who have played professionally, only a very small percentage have done so in two different sports. An even smaller number—probably less than 1 percent of athletes going back to whenever—played professionally in three sports. And unless events like celebrity poker and Dancing With the Stars *someday gain recognition as professional sports, it is not likely to happen again anytime soon.*

Charlie (he hates when it's misspelled "Charley") is one of the few who played three sports at the professional level. An unassuming man, he talks about his accomplishments matter-of-factly, with no traces of boastfulness in his voice. He enjoyed the things he did, he was good at each of them, and he was paid fairly, although he hastens to add that what he earned "was nothing compared to what these guys make today."

Year	Team	League	Games
1952	49ers	NFL	7
1953	49ers	NFL	12
1954	Out of football to pursue boxing career	—	—
1955	49ers	NFL	12
1956	49ers	NFL	12
1957	49ers	NFL	12
1958	Out of football	—	—
1959	Out of football	—	—
1960	Raiders	AFL	14
1961	Raiders	AFL	14

1 reception for 27 yards

1 kickoff return for 2 yards

1 safety

Played in Western Conference Playoff Game in 1957

Probably the most noteworthy of Charlie's athletic accomplishments was walking into the training camp of the San Francisco 49ers in 1952 and winning a starting job as a defensive end in the National Football League. Charlie was 20 years old and, although he had been a standout player at San Diego High School, he had never played college football for the simple reason that he had never gone to college. In training camp, he was called on to prove himself in a series of one-on-one drills against Leo Nomellini, one of the best linemen of the time. Charlie held his own, made the team, and was a starter by the end of the season.

In debates about whether pro football is more difficult today than it was in 1952, there are good points to be made on both sides. There's one thing for certain, though: The NFL was a much more primitive place then. "Mayhem" is a word that comes to mind, and there was no place for the shy or the hesitant. This is the world Charlie walked into that summer.

Already able to take very good care of himself when push came to punch, Charlie soon became one of the better defensive ends in the NFL. That he did so with only high school football on his resume is remarkable. Charlie is not the only one to make it in the NFL without playing college ball, but few others have done so at such a young an age or for as long as Charlie did.

In his rookie season, after tangling with Hall of Famer No-mellini, Charlie went head to head with Hall of Fame offensive tackles Lou Groza and Lou Creekmur. Charlie played against a number of other Hall of Fame offensive linemen. He also sacked another Hall of Famer, quarterback Norm Van Brocklin, for a safety that season. In one of his other careers, Charlie fought Ali and Floyd Patterson and sparred with Sonny Liston and Archie Moore. Those men are all Hall of Famers, too, and each was either the heavyweight or light-heavyweight champion of the world during their careers.

Today, years removed from the ring and the gridiron, Charlie lives a rather bucolic life in California. A tough day no longer involves ducking blows to the head but rather keeping the yard clean. He keeps in touch with people he grew up with and is a member of an organization that helps ex-fighters down on their luck.

I played professional baseball, I played pro football for seven years, and I had almost 60 pro fights and was the number one contender for the heavyweight crown, and let me tell you, being a boxer was the hardest. You have to do your roadwork, you have to get your sleep, you have to eat right and keep your weight under control, you have to put in long hours in the gym, and you have to get your rest. When you're in training for a fight, you can't be out keeping late hours. You've got to be in bed by eight, nine o'clock because the next day you're up at four to do your roadwork and start another day of training.

I participated in all different sports when I was a kid growing up in San Diego, including boxing. We lived about two blocks from the Boys Club and I used to go there all the time. I saw the boxing rings there and the next thing I knew, when I was about eleven or twelve years old, I was boxing. They used to bring kids who were incarcerated and others from the youth camps and I knocked them all out, so they stopped it. But I kept on with it with some of the older guys there giving me pointers and I got to be pretty good.

My dad was a hell of a baseball player. When Satchel Paige and the Negro All-Stars would barnstorm, they would call him and pick him up when they got to California. Satchel would call and say, "Get ready. We're coming out that way." He would go barnstorming with them all over California and then he would come back home when they moved on. I got to meet all those guys.

Both my dad and mom were originally from Texas and that's where I was born, too. We moved out here when I was about two or three years old. He was a cement finisher. As a matter of fact, I think about my dad a lot when I drive out of the driveway in the house I'm living in now because when I bought it, the driveway was all messed up. He came over and fixed it up and I haven't had to do anything with it since. He could do all that kind of work.

My dad didn't really have much to do with me getting interested in sports. I had five brothers and three sisters and I was the oldest of the boys and the second oldest in all. I think my dad was more concerned about what the younger kids were doing. He knew that I had enough sense not to do anything wrong and that I could take care of myself. He used to say, "Charles, if you want to do it, do it."

One thing I did from a young age was work to help put food on the table. I used to shine shoes and bring home a little money. Then after they stopped the boxing at the Boys Club, I used to box at the training center on the Marine base in San Diego. They used to have exhibition fights to entertain the service men and afterwards the officers would take me to the officers' quarters and give me a big brown paper bag full of butter and steaks. Oh man, that made me feel good. Here I was, thirteen years old and bringing butter and steaks home and the whole family was eating good off me.

The part of San Diego where I grew up is Logan Heights and it was very mixed. After I was grown I had some friends who used to tease me and say, "Man, San Diego was nothing but a little one-horse town," but if I had to do it all over again, that's the place I would want to grow up. I still say it was one of the greatest cities because we had all races and nationalities and everybody got along. We had blacks, Japanese, Hispanics, Irish, Jewish, and we lived together, played together, and the whole bit. I would eat as much Hispanic food as I could and I could speak Spanish real good. Then I took Spanish in school figuring I'd get me an A, but it wasn't the same Spanish that I could speak and I only got a C, so I didn't take it any more after that.

I never had any kind of racial problems growing up. The only thing I remember was when I was shining shoes. Some of the guys, I would shine their shoes and they would pay me and give me a tip, and after they paid me and gave me a tip they wanted to rub my head. I said, "No, no, that don't go with the shine. And don't ever touch me." And they'd say, "Oh, excuse me. I didn't mean any harm." I'd say, "It's no harm as long as you never touch me." I'd run into that every now and then but outside of that, I never had any problems.

I never will forget when I was about ten years old, these army trucks came into the neighborhood one day. This was right after World War II started and it was really something to see these army trucks practically in front of your house. It made you think that the neighborhood was going to be invaded or something. Well, they were there to pick up all the Japanese and take them away. One of the boys we played with was Bobby Omada and they took him and his family. I ran home and said, "Mom, dad, look what they're doing. They're taking Bobby." My dad said something about how we were at war with Japan, but I couldn't understand it and I cried like a baby.

Bobby was one of the kids I used to play with all the time. We played football, baseball, and basketball. We played tackle football with no shoulder pads or helmets and we used to run races in this park in bare feet because nobody had track shoes. My brothers were good, too. Art went to San Jose State and played in the American Football League as a receiver and my brother Jerry played in the World Football League. My brother Ellsworth was better at basketball. He ended up making a career out of the military.

I went to San Diego High School. When I look back, I realize they were scouting me before I even got to high school. My freshman year one of the coaches said to me, "We've been waiting on you." I got 12 varsity letters: three in football, baseball, basketball, and track. That school opened in the 1800s and I'm the only person who ever went there who got twelve varsity letters. Baseball season and track season were at the same time so what would happen was, they would drive me to wherever the track meet was, and then after I did the shot put they would drive me across town and I would change into my uniform and play baseball.

I enjoyed all of them. Probably I enjoyed football the most of all, but I enjoyed all of them. When I got to high school I was close to 6'3", same as I am now. I weighed about 200 pounds, and then I began to fill out and I was about 230 or 235 pounds by the time I graduated. I had the San Diego High School shot put record for 47 years, up until a few years ago when some kid broke it by a quarter of an inch or something. What was ironic, the kid was the grandson of Earl Gilliam, who I went to school with and who was a very good friend of mine. In fact, Earl and I remained good friends right up until he died about five years ago. He went to the University of California and became one of the first black judges in the state of California, and then he became United States district judge. Anyway, they had a little thing where I met the kid because my record stood for all those years. I said, "I'll be doggone. So that's Earl Gilliam's grandson."

I used to read the sports pages in the newspaper all the time and they had stories about Kenny Washington when he came up with the Rams. The Rams had just moved to Los Angeles and Kenny was from Los Angeles and UCLA, so there were a lot of stories about him in the local papers. Jackie Robinson was from LA, too, and he had played for UCLA, so it was the same thing with him. Even before he joined the Rams, I saw Kenny Washington play in San Diego. They had a team called the San Diego Bombers and I remember going to see him and a little scatback by the name of Steve Bagarus play. We used to climb the fence and sneak into the stadium. Then a few years later I was packing that same stadium with people when I was in high school.

I got a lot of offers when I was a senior in high school. I could've been the first black football player at Notre Dame. Eddie Erdelatz, who later coached me in pro ball, was coaching at Notre Dame and they wanted me to go there. Other schools like UCLA were interested, too, and so were the St. Louis Browns. I really wanted to be a boxer but the baseball thing appealed to me because I could start earning money right away, plus I got a signing bonus.

Tony Robello was the scout from the St. Louis Browns who started coming around when I was finishing up the baseball season my senior year. This would be 1951. I talked with Bill Veeck, too, the owner of the Browns. I got offers from other teams but one day I came home and Tony Robello was at my house and he said, "We'll give you more money than any of these other teams and more than you can make as a fighter. Besides, if you become a fighter, it's just a matter of time before you get hurt." I said to myself, "Man, I can fight better than you think I can." But I was the oldest son and I always believed in helping my family, so I signed.

I played right field for the Stockton Ports in the California League. I thought I was good enough to make it to the major leagues, but I got bored with it. There wasn't enough action. Plus, I had a lot of power and I always wanted to pull the ball as hard as I could. They told me, "Charlie, you've got to go with the pitch and hit those curve balls on the outside corner to right field." I knew they were right because you can't pull the curve ball good unless they hang it, but I used to like to hit the ball as hard as I could and as far I could to left field.

I was the only black player on the team when I played for Stockton. I stayed in a rooming house where some porters who worked on the trains stayed. It was alright. Some of the players from the other teams would say some stuff, but I'd tune that out. You tuned all of that out because if you let that get to you, you can't concentrate on what you're doing. The only thing that was a no-no is if they came up to me and tried to start some bullshit. As long as they didn't do that, everything was alright.

A lot of times, I couldn't eat in the restaurants. The same used to happen when I was fighting and going around the country on the highway or Route 66 or whatever. They'd say, "No, you can't eat here," and I'd have to take the food with me. I'd say, "Man, you're out here in the middle of nowhere and I can't sit down here?" And I'd get pissed off. Now, most of these places had a flagpole out in front, so I used to take my food and go sit under the flagpole and eat. That was my way of saying, "The hell with you."

One day in 1952 I was sitting out on my front porch with an old saxophone trying to play "Sentimental Journey" when this distinguished, silver-haired man pulls up in a gold Cadillac convertible. He says, "Excuse me. Which one of these houses does Charlie Powell live in?" I said, "You're talking to him." He says, "Can I come up and join you on the porch?" I said, "Yes sir." He says, "I'm Buck Shaw, head coach of the San Francisco 49ers." That didn't really mean anything to me. Then he says, "We understand that in a few years when your college class graduates, you'll be eligible to play pro football." I said to myself, "Pro football? He's got to be kidding." I thought it was a joke. The last thing I was thinking about at that time was playing pro football.

I guess the 49ers had heard about me from when I played in high school. What they didn't know is that I had played professional baseball and that meant I didn't have to wait until my class graduated. See, because I had already turned pro, even though it was a different sport, I didn't have to wait. Once Buck Shaw heard that, he told me he was serious and asked me if I wanted to come up to the 49ers training camp. I went in and asked my dad and he told me what he always told me: "Take care of yourself and go up there and see what you can do."

Well, they sent me a plane ticket and a letter about where to report. That was the first time I was ever on an airplane before and I was shaking, I was so scared. Once I got there, I joined the rookies in the drills they were doing. I did pretty good but I could hear some of the guys saying, "Wait until [Leo] Nomellini gets here." So when the veterans got there, they put me on Nomellini and when we went at it you could hear the rattling of the helmets and shoulder pads. He knocked me back and I had to check to see if I still had all my teeth. I had a good mouthpiece I used when I was boxing and once I saw that all my teeth were intact, I went up to go at it again. I fought him to a standstill—sometimes he got the better of me, sometimes I got the better of him. But I held my own and each time I got more confidence.

See, I had speed, quickness, good coordination, and good hand–eye coordination and all of those things allowed me to do pretty well against Nomellini. And even though I was a big guy, I was always light on my feet. My sister taught me how to dance when I was in high school and that helped a lot. Up until I was maybe a senior in high school, I never used to stay out late or go to parties. I was like Jack Armstrong, the All-American Boy: I'd drink my milk and go to bed early. But my sister was a good dancer and she used to go to dances at Navy Field and I used to go to watch the guys and keep them off her. At first I used to just watch, but then she taught me to dance and I got to be pretty good. She could really get down.

Nomellini was one of the best in the whole league and after I saw that I could match up with him, my confidence really started to build. It got to be a piece of cake because I was the quickest one off the ball. They had all these veterans and rookie prospects from big-name colleges and I was kicking ass. I was twenty years old, had never played college football, and won a starting job in the NFL with the San Francisco 49ers. The first time they introduced me with the starting lineup, that was really something. The guy came on the loudspeaker and said, "At right defensive end, number 87, from San

Diego High School, Charlie Powell." People were like, "What? San Diego High School?" They couldn't believe it.

I was the third black player who ever played for the 49ers. Joe Perry and a tackle by the name of Bob Mike were the first two. Then we brought in John Henry Johnson and R. C. Owens. Joe Perry was so quick coming out of his stance and through the hole, that's why they called him The Jet. Frankie Albert named him that when we were in camp. He faked to somebody and turned to give Joe the ball and Joe was already through the hole. Frankie said, "Damn, man, you take off like a jet," and it stuck with him throughout his career. Joe the Jet.

I heard a lot of tales about Bob Mike. I don't know if they were true or not and it wasn't none of my business anyway, but they said he was dating a white lady and that was a no-no, and I heard that's why they got rid of him. I don't know if it's true or not, but I wouldn't be surprised because that's the way it was back then. I never felt like Buck Shaw or [49ers owner Tony] Morabito were like that, but who knows?

Mike wasn't on the team when I got there in '52 but I met him and we would talk. We didn't talk directly about the rumors I had heard, but I know he was disgusted about the whole thing because he felt like he should've still been on the team. I know they weren't doing that stuff with the white players, keeping up on who the women were that they were running around with. But that's the way it was back then. Segregation. Segregation was definitely out there.

I don't remember any racial stuff on the 49ers or from the fans in San Francisco. I would hear epithets and stuff from the fans when we played on the road, though, and sometimes from players on the other team. But, see, they wouldn't do too much of that stuff because the dressing rooms were usually right next to each other and both teams used the same exit. After the game, you'd go through the tunnel at the same time so if somebody did something or said something you didn't like, you could get his ass right there in the damn tunnel. A lot of stuff goes on in football and the cussing and everything was all part of the game. When it was over, you'd shake hands with the guy and tell him, "See you next time," and go about your business.

I never will forget one time when we were going to play an exhibition game in Dallas and the promoter called up Morabito and said, "It sure is going to be a nice exhibition game but leave those two colored boys there. Don't bring them down here." Morabito told us the whole story in a team meeting. He told the guy he could take the game and do what he wanted with it, that the 49ers weren't coming. All the guys clapped and it was good because it kept the team together.

It was the same way when we got to a city and they told us that me and the other black players couldn't stay at the hotel with the white players. Morabito would say something like, "You mean you're going to rent rooms to all these players and not these two? Well, I'll tell you what. You just lost your money for everybody." And he would find a resort hotel or a country club or some kind of place and rent the whole damn thing to keep the team together. It was nice. The 49ers were a good experience for me and San Francisco was a hell of a city. I had a good time in San Francisco. I sure did.

I've heard some guys say they had problems in Baltimore, but I liked Baltimore. I never had any problems there and I thought they had the prettiest women that I'd ever seen. I liked going up and down Pennsylvania Avenue—in fact, I would say Baltimore was my favorite city. A good friend of mine and his brother had a place there I used to go to, and he'd take me out on his boat. Then he'd send me a box of fish and crab and different things. I enjoyed Baltimore.

One guy I got to be good friends with was Bobby Layne. He was such a great guy. When we played Detroit, he would take me out and we'd go nightclubbing. We would just get through playing and either the Lions would whip our butts or we would whip their butts, and he would say, "Charlie, go get dressed. I'll wait for you outside your dressing room." And it seemed like anyplace we went, everybody knew him. We'd go to a place with a band and Bobby knew everybody in the whole damn band. He would introduce me to everybody he knew.

He would take me to the nicest clubs in Detroit and they would roll out the carpet for him. He would even take me to the black clubs in Detroit and everybody in those places knew him, too. They loved him in Detroit. Anywhere we went, people were crazy about Bobby Layne because he was a character and a beautiful person. We had a hell of a relationship. And he was a good football player.

There was no bullshit with him on the football field, though. He was a real drillmaster. If somebody sacked him, he would get the guy's number and chew out whichever one of the Lions was supposed to be blocking him. Whenever we played the Lions, I was up against Big Lou Creekmur. He was The Man, a good one. In one game, I sacked Layne for 67 yards. I used to have a scrapbook here and it said right in the newspaper that I sacked Bobby Layne for 67 yards. I know it was a record but the NFL says they don't keep sack records from back then. And you know, even after that game, Bobby and me went out nightclubbing together.

Roosevelt Brown from the New York Giants was another good tackle. I look back on it and, man, we used to really go at it. We'd start in the tunnel before the game. He'd say, "Man, I'm going to whip your ass." Or I'd say, "God damn it, I'm going to knock the shit out of you," or something like that. It was all in fun. But it was no joke when you got out on the field. They would encourage you to go after the quarterback or the halfback or whoever. The owners would say, "We got a pot for whoever knocks him out of the game. Nothing dirty but we want him out of the game." Then everybody would be after him because you wanted that pot.

I remember we had Hardy Brown. He played outside linebacker right in back of me, and he would say, "Hey, Chas"—he didn't call me Charlie, he called me Chas—"Hey Chas, just turn them inside and I'll get them." He had that shoulder tackle and he would knock guys out. If he missed he looked amateurish but if he connected, those guys went down. Hardy wasn't that big for a linebacker, maybe 200 pounds. I'll never forget, we played the Rams down in the Coliseum in front of 100,000 people with Bob Waterfield at quarterback and that big Bull Elephant backfield of Tank Younger and Dan Towler and Dick Hoerner that was all about 225 pounds, and he knocked the whole backfield out of the game with that shoulder tackle. That son of a bitch could hit.

Another guy who could hit was Marion Motley. Him and Bill Willis started with the Browns around the same time Kenny Washington started with the Rams. We went to Cleveland for an exhibition game my rookie year and they gave Motley the ball on a draw play, and when he came through that hole he sounded like a rhinoceros. I said, "Oh shit," because if he got going for even two steps, you knew he was going to be a handful to tackle. But I hit him low, got him down, made sure I still had all my teeth, and got up feeling petty good. People ask me and I tell everybody: There has never been *anybody* who came through the line like Marion Motley. I'm telling you, that's exactly what he sounded like, a rhinoceros.

Cleveland had a hell of a ball club. I mean, they were a machine. I guess them and Detroit were about the two best teams when I was playing. They were all tough but those two were the toughest. And the Rams with that Bull Elephant backfield, like I mentioned. We had a good team, too, but we always came up a little short. Still, if I had to do it all over again, that's where I would want to be, is playing for the 49ers in the city of San Francisco.

I never socialized with any of the black players from the other teams. We spoke after the game but once we got to the locker room, we went our separate ways. One guy I did meet was Jackie Robinson. I met him in New York and spent a little time with him. He had a warm personality and he made me feel he was glad to meet me. He was a real person, not standoffish or anything like that. I had kept up with him when he went up with the Dodgers and I knew the things he went through. They would sharpen their spikes and go into him at second base and those suckers hurt because they're sharp as a razor. Then they'd be dropping black cats on the field, all kinds of shit like that.

At first, he took it because that's what he had to do to make it a success. But he could fight a little bit and then he let those people know he wasn't taking any bullshit. It was really a Martin Luther King type thing. He opened a lot of doors and that's what it's all about. I tip my hat to him and everybody else should, too. But he paid the price because that's what killed him at such a young age. I look back on it and I met some great people in my life and Jackie Robinson was definitely one of them.

These kids today, they don't know anything about us, how we helped open some doors for them. They've forgotten the old ballplayers. I don't watch football that much on television. It's more like entertainment, all these young players making all that money. I don't know if many of them today could have played back then. We used to be able to knock the hell out of each other. Now there's so much money in it. Same thing with college football. That's all big money.

I used to tease Deacon Jones. I would say to him, "Man, we were using the head slap before you even knew what football was." Because they talk about him like he invented the head slap. They did away with that. They did away with a lot of things. Guys would use rolls of tape on their arms and on their hands and they would put things under the tape to hit somebody with. I mean, they would be knocking the hell out of the guy across from them.

It's like that in all sports. Like the boxing thing has gotten so bad because there's no teachers around. These kids today can fight, but can they box? Do they know how to move? Do they know the art of self-defense? They're all things of the past. You don't see guys doing like Willie Pep and Ray Robinson used to do. Every once in awhile I'll see a guy who can fight and box and move a little, but there aren't too many.

My wife Irma and I have known each other since grammar school. We started going together when I was playing for the 49ers and we got married in 1954. A lady named Mandy Moore had a rooming house on Golden Gate Avenue in San Francisco and I got me a room over there and then I would move back to San Diego my first couple of years after the season was over. After I got married, Irma got a job with the phone company in Los Angeles and she stayed there during the season and came up once in awhile for a few days during the season. I lived in Los Angeles during the offseason and moved back and forth, San Francisco during the season, LA in the offseason.

We used to hang out at a black hotel called the Booker T. See, when Count Basie and Duke Ellington and them would come to town, they couldn't stay at the hotels downtown so they stayed at the Booker T. You name it, any of the black entertainers, if they were in San Francisco, they stayed at the Booker T: Count Basie, Duke Ellington, Red Foxx, Billy Eckstine, Dinah Washington, Billie Holiday, all of them. I met Billie Holiday—oh boy, what a lady. I sent for my wife to come up to San Francisco to hear her sing and I introduced her to Billie Holiday.

Music, that was another one of my things. My record collection was unbelievable. I used to spend a couple of hundred dollars a week buying records—33s, 78s, everything. I had a closet and some cedar chests full of them. There was an article in the *LA Times* once that said the two greatest collections of jazz records belonged to Miles Davis and Charlie Powell. When I was boxing, I would turn on something real smooth before a fight, something with a soothing saxophone sound to calm me and relax me before I went into battle. I even tried to play the saxophone for awhile when I was young, but I didn't stick with it.

All through the time I played for the 49ers, I was still boxing during the offseason. I couldn't fight during the season because I had to put weight on for football. As soon as the season ended, I would trim down to 214, 215, but once football started I'd go back up to around 230 or 235. Whenever I came up to San Francisco or Oakland for a fight, guys from the 49ers would come. I remember Billy Wilson and some other guys came to see me fight a few times.

Finally, I decided that I didn't want to just box in the offseason, I wanted to do it full-time. I decided to try and just box, you know, not to go back and forth but to really get down with it. I knew that was the only way I would be the best I could be and if I had to give up football to do it, so be it. So after I played for the 49ers a few years, I told them this is what I was gong to do and that I wasn't going to come back the next year. I didn't tell them I was *never* coming back, but I knew I had to try boxing full-time, and if it turned out I never played football again, then I'd do something else.

People think football training camp is tough, but let me tell you, it's nothing like the training you go through to be a pro fighter. The main thing is your roadwork. I was blessed because Joe Louis trained me for awhile. He took me to Griffith Park and he was riding in this big Cadillac alongside me. I'd be running and he'd say, "Now, sprint until you get to that tree there," and I'd sprint. When I got to the tree, he'd say, "Now don't stop, just slow down." And every quarter mile or half mile, he'd tell me to sprint and then go back into a jog. I'd say, "You've got to be kidding me," because I never ran like that before.

I had lied to him and told him I was doing my running but I wasn't, I was just doing bullshit running. He could tell. After he got through with me, my muscles were trembling and I couldn't lift my legs. But I was glad he thought enough of me to come and train me. Every fighter in Los Angeles wanted to spar with me once Joe Louis came around. He got a bunch of them lined up and I guess he told them to really get on my ass because this one guy busted my lip and I went after him and didn't stop even after the bell rang. Joe jumped in the ring, and he said, "That's what I wanted to see. You've been too nice. I wanted to see you get mad."

I don't mean to say that football was easy or anything because it wasn't. No, sir. There were always guys coming out of college with a good bonus and with a chance to make more money than I was who couldn't take it. We'd have those two-a-day practices and scrimmages and they'd have roll call the next day and some of those guys would be gone. Somebody would say, "Where's so and so?" "Oh, he's gone. He left camp last night." I guess they figured there had to be an easier way than that to make a living. I'd see it every year.

I had a good manager when I was fighting and I got along good with the promoters. I knew some of them was in the Mafia but I never had any problems. My word was my bond and I never did anything wrong, never got in no trouble. That's all they cared about, plus they saw I was serious about it. I'd go to Las Vegas and they'd treat me good. They told the guys at the windows in the casino to give me money if I wanted it. They'd give me $500 or so in chips, and I'd just walk around with them in my pocket and then cash them in when I was ready to leave. I never gambled but it was nice that they would do that. It was good. I never felt like anybody ripped me off or took advantage of me.

One time when I was in New York, one of the guys told me he wanted to take me out for lunch. I said, "Sure," and he took me to this restaurant and I sat down and ordered a sandwich and an iced tea. The guy I was with gave his order and then the owner of the place said, "Will there be anything else?" And the guy said, "Yeah, the money that you owe." The owner looked at me and he looked at the other guy and that's when I realized why he brought me.

The owner says, "Oh shit. They sent you for the money." The guy says, "Look, just be cool," and the owner went and got the money and put it on the counter. That was it. We brought the money back and after they counted it, they gave me some and said, "This is for you, Big Charlie." I told them thanks and they told me that anytime I wanted to I could make some money, but I told myself I wasn't going to get involved in anything like that. It would've been easy money, but I wasn't going to get hooked into doing that kind of stuff.

When Archie Moore was getting ready to fight Nino Valdes, they asked me to come and work out with him because Valdes and I were about the same size. I knew Archie when I was a young kid because his niece and I were in school together. He and Bob Murphy were two fighters I looked up to and I used to work out with both of them, so when they asked me I went up to train with Archie for a few days. Archie beat Valdes by a decision in Las Vegas and he got a shot at the heavyweight crown. Then when it came time for me to fight Valdes in Miami, I knocked him out on national television but I never did get a chance at the title. It just goes to show you how these things happen sometimes.

When I knocked out Valdes, he was the number one contender for the heavyweight crown so then I got to be the number one contender. Floyd Patterson was the heavyweight champion then, but for whatever reason they didn't give me a shot at him. I did fight Patterson, but that was later on after he lost the crown. Then when Muhammad Ali was coming up I fought him. I think it was two fights before he fought Sonny Liston for the title. They were looking ahead to him fighting Liston and Angelo Dundee told me, "You and Liston hit the hardest and we want to see how Ali does with a real puncher."

I was 31 and I was through with football and they kept telling me I could make good money in boxing. I said, "What kind of money are you talking about?" So they set it up right and I fought Ali pretty good until I got cut over my eye in the third round. Then when Liston signed to fight Ali, Liston's manager called me to come work with him because Sonny was knocking everybody out and they couldn't get anybody to box with him. No sooner would a new guy get in with him than Sonny would knock him through the ropes.

I told them, "Send me a ticket and I'll come up there for two days." When I got there, I went right in on him. I wouldn't run or any of that bullshit. I'd get in close so when he tried to get one off, I'd touch him on the shoulders or biceps and nullify it. He couldn't throw anything. When we finished he said to me, "Shit, I thought you were a football player. Where'd you learn all that from?" I said, "I know how to fight. I've been doing this since I was 12 years old."

I fought for a few more years after that. One of my last fights was against Floyd Patterson. He had been the heavyweight champion and he was getting ready to fight Muhammad Ali. All told, I fought against two guys who were heavyweight champions of the world, Ali and Patterson, and sparred with a third, Sonny Liston. Plus I sparred with Archie Moore, the light heavyweight champion, and I fought and beat Nino Valdes when he was the number one contender for the crown. I think I had 56 fights altogether as a professional.

After my last fight they kept telling me I could still make good money. And I could have, too, but I told them I was quitting. They said, "Why?" I said, "Because what good is money if you're too punch drunk to count it?" I said, "I don't need money that bad. Besides, I got other things I can do." I had played professional base-ball, seven years of professional football, been a professional fighter for almost 60 fights, and I had a good career in all of them. I didn't stay too long and get banged up or get to a state where I couldn't enjoy the rest of my life.

When my brother Art went to San Jose State, I was living right there in the Bay Area so I would take him a little money and see that he was okay. I always tried to keep him encouraged and tell him to not let anything get him down. We were close. Like I said, I was the oldest of six boys and Art was third. Then when I was with the Raiders, I played against him when he was playing for the New York Titans [of the American Football League, forerun-ners of the New York Jets]. That was fun. He would be spread out wide and I'd say to him, "Now, don't come cracking back over here or I'm going to have to bring it to you." And he'd come up to the line and he'd say, "Here I come, man," you know, he'd let me know. It was fun.

I was proud of him when he made it. I didn't realize he was the receiver he was until I played against him. He had the size and he had good hands and he could run after catching the ball. I played against some pretty good receivers and we had some pretty good ones on the 49ers so I know a good receiver when I see one and he was good. After I retired, the Titans traded him and he came out here and played for the Raiders. He had a good career.

It was good being part of the AFL. I had been out of football for a few years and the AFL gave me a chance to play two more years. In my second year, the Chargers moved to San Diego and we went down there to play them when I was with the Raiders. I got to play in Balboa Stadium in my hometown and that was something. Oh man, people I knew came from all over for that game. The place was packed. It was nice, getting to play in front of all these people I knew. As a matter of fact, it was a game against San Diego when I ruptured my Achilles tendon. Oh man, that hurt. I have never been in so much pain. But that was the only major injury I ever had in all them years playing football and fighting and everything. To this day, I still have all my teeth. I knock on wood. I was lucky.

I was in business with a partner after I retired. We used to do refurbishing in the aerospace industry. It was a good business because you have all the aerospace industry here and we were getting a lot of work out of it. Now I just kick back and take it easy. I live up in this canyon and I got great big trees on my lot here. I always got yard work to do, cutting the grass or trimming branches off the trees or something. I still get up early. I go out and get the *LA Times* and the Pasadena paper and I get one of each for my neighbor.

I go back to San Diego pretty often. The people there have been real nice to me. They have a wall of honor at San Diego High School, and they inducted me into that about five years ago. They're always having one kind of an affair or another in San Diego. I don't go to all of them, but I go whenever I have a chance. Whenever I do, I always get to see some of the old-timers I came up with. We also have a thing here where we try to help some of the fighters who are down and out. They found out that one of the guys who used to be hooked up with it was stealing money, so that set us back. We usually have lunch and they raise money that way. I've been lucky because I never got hurt from all my fights and the only serious injury I had playing football was my Achilles tendon.

Once I left San Diego I never spoke Spanish anymore so I forgot most of it. If you don't speak it for 50 years or something, you forget it. But I got some tapes in my hall closet and I'm going to listen to them one of these days and get back to it. I figure if I start listening to them it'll start coming back. That way if I see somebody who speaks only Spanish, I can talk to them and have a little conversation.

EDDIE MACON

Edwin Donald Macon
Born March 7, 1927, in Stockton, California

Stockton High School in Stockton, California
College of the Pacific

Running back/defensive back
Second round draft choice by Chicago Bears in 1952

In 1951, the phrase "Undefeated, Untied, and Uninvited" was coined to describe the University of San Francisco football team. The Dons were loaded that year. Their roster included a number of players who went on to play in the National Football League, three of whom are members of the Pro Football Hall of Fame. Their story has been told in a book and in a one-hour television special. The last bit about them being "uninvited," however, is not quite true. USF was invited to play in a bowl game but declined when bowl officials stipulated that the team's two black players were not to come. "Undefeated, Untied, and Declined a Bowl Invitation in Solidarity with Their Black Teammates" is not such a catchy phrase but is actually a more compelling story.

In 1949, the College of the Pacific, featuring standout sophomore halfback Eddie Macon, went undefeated, untied, finished number 10 in the AP's final poll, and truly were uninvited. (For what it's worth, San Francisco finished number 14 in 1951.) Not one bowl extended an invitation. One justification put forward at the time was that Pacific was not a national power. That argument was nicely undermined, however, by Pacific's good showings in the Sun Bowl after the 1951 and 1952 seasons with teams that were probably not as strong as the 1949 squad. There is little question that the main reason was

Year	Team	League	Games	Rushing				Receiving			
				Attempts	Yards	Avg.	TDs	Receptions	Yards	Avg.	TDs
1952	Bears	NFL	11	30	194	6.5	1	8	25	3.1	0
1953	Bears	NFL	12	40	130	3.3	1	6	24	4.0	2
1954	Played in Canada										
1955	Out of football										
1956	Out of football										
1957	Played in Canada										
1958	Played in Canada										
1959	Played in Canada										
1960	Raiders	AFL	14	0	0	—	0	0	0	—	0

Year	Kickoff Returns				Punt Returns				Interceptions			
	Returns	Yards	Avg.	TDs	Returns	Yards	Avg.	TDs	Interceptions	Yards	Avg.	TDs
1952	9	299	33.2	1	7	74	10.6	0	0	0	—	0
1953	13	373	28.7	0	17	68	4.0	0	0	0	—	0
1960	0	0	—	0	0	0	—	0	9	105	11.7	1

the same as in the USF case: Virtually all bowl games were played in the South in 1949 and none wanted Pacific because of Eddie.

It is likely that questions around Pacific's not getting an invitation led to their participation in the Sun Bowl two years later, not to mention USF's at least getting one that same year. From there officials of bowls in the Deep South had little choice. Before the end of the 1950s Pitt, Syracuse, Penn State, and other teams with black players were regular bowl participants. The history of social change is a long chain; each link is important. If you miss one you invariably miss a piece of the story. Pacific's story doesn't detract from USF's, it simply adds to the overall history.

Eddie knows this because he lived that piece of the history. He does not begrudge USF's 1951 team the attention they've received. On the contrary, he sees it as a good thing. He and his teammates know, after all, how good USF was, as they were beaten badly by the Dons that year. Moreover, Eddie later became good friends with Burl Toler and the great running back Ollie Matson, USF's two black players, but he does believe Pacific's 1949 season shone some much-needed light on the "whites only" bowl games and that subsequent events should be viewed through that prism.

Eddie was one of the great players in Pacific history who counts leading the team in touchdowns and scoring three straight years among his accomplishments. He was in the first class inducted into the school's Football Hall of Fame and in the spring of 2008, his uniform number was retired by the school. He had some success in the pros but again ran into the Iron Curtain of prejudice. For jumping his contract to play in Canada, Eddie says he was blacklisted from the NFL by none other than George Halas. As a result, like so many black players of his era, we will never really know how good he was.

My father died when I was a year and a half after he was bitten by a black widow spider and the only father I ever knew was my stepfather. He raised us just like we were his own children. My mother was always in frail health and she died when I was 14. Then my stepfather raised my brother and I and when he remarried, his wife helped raise us. My brother and I were only 11 months apart so we were like twins and the lady my stepfather married had a daughter who was almost the same age as us.

My stepfather worked for the WPA [Works Progress Administration] two weeks out of every month. They put in all the sidewalks in Stockton, paved the streets, all that kind of work. He was born and raised in Stockton and it was always difficult to find steady work. His family was originally from Virginia. His mother sailed from Virginia down past the tip of South America to California back before they built the Panama Canal.

My stepfather wasn't interested in sports except boxing because boxing was the only sport open to blacks at that time. He admired all the great black fighters like Jack Johnson and Henry Armstrong and together we followed Joe Louis when he came up, then later on Sugar Ray Robinson. He'd take me to the corner grocery store when there was a big fight because the guy who owned the store would put his radio in the upstairs window and we'd gather outside to listen. We didn't own a radio, which tells you a little about our financial situation. The first time I went, Max Schmeling knocked out Joe Louis and the black community was sick for a year. Then when Louis won the rematch, we celebrated because we had a champion again. That's the fight I remember the most.

My stepdad even wanted me to be a fighter. I'd stand in front of the mirror and I'd throw jabs and hooks and he'd instruct me. Then one day, I'll never forget, I was reading *Time* magazine, and it had a picture of a punch drunk fighter's brain and I said, "That's it for me." He felt real bad but I did learn one thing: I learned how to take care of myself.

Stockton was an agricultural hub and a lot of people did work in one way or another related to agriculture. My grandfather was an agricultural contractor and he got farm work for members of our family. I started when I was 12 years old, picking onions, apricots, tomatoes, whatever there was that needed to be picked. We'd get in an old Model T Ford and go ten, fifteen miles to wherever there was work in the fields. Me, my brother, and everybody else in the family would work and we'd all contribute what we earned. Money wasn't easy to come by and you just accepted that this is what you had to do.

The Fair Oaks neighborhood where I grew up was a mix of different races—blacks, Mexicans, Japanese, Filipinos, whites. I went to school with a lot of Japanese kids and their families were mostly farmers. Once World War II started, we began hearing that the government was going to take them away. I didn't see people taken out of their homes or anything like that, it was just like one day, they were gone. Their homes and businesses were taken and other people took them over. Years later, the Japanese who were still living and their families got reimbursed.

A lot of my athletic ability just came naturally. I remember one morning before school when I was eight or nine, I was hitting a baseball around and the baseball coach, Mr. Spooner, came up to me and the next thing I knew I was on the grammar school baseball team. I became Mr. Spooner's pet project. We had baseball, football, and basketball at our school and from then on I played all three. Then when I got to high school I also got into track.

When the war started, Fair Oaks changed a lot in terms of the people who were living there. Many of the whites moved away to what you would call the nicer areas of town and more blacks and Mexicans moved in. We didn't move because we couldn't afford to. Then after my first year with the Bears in 1952, I came back and bought two lots in Fair Oaks just a few blocks from the house where I grew up. I built a house on one lot and sold the other one and made a little money from it.

Every day when I wake up, I know that I'm black. I knew that when I was a young kid and I know it today. I wake up and I say to myself, "Good morning, cruel world, how are you going to screw me today?" Hardly a day has gone by in my life where something hasn't happened to let me know that I'm black. You go to a store in a mall and you're looking at things and you know there's somebody following you. Or you're the first one standing in line to buy groceries and the cashier points to the guy behind you if he's Caucasian and calls him to the front of the line. That's when I have to say, "Wait one minute. I'm next."

The first incident I remember was at the YMCA when I was a kid. We used to go all the time and use all the facilities except for one: They wouldn't let us swim in the swimming pool. That was like that until the 1950s. Years later when I started taking my son to the very same YMCA, he was allowed to use all the facilities including the pool, so that's one example of change that I've seen over time right in my experience. The Mexicans also faced discrimination but not as much as we did. For one thing, they could use the swimming pool at the YMCA. I never had any trouble at school, though.

There weren't many blacks in my grammar school or high school, but everybody got along. I had some fights from somebody saying something stupid, something racial, but they were always people from the outside, never from school.

I always thought baseball was my best sport but I messed up my arm trying to pitch. My coach even told me, "Eddie, you're not a pitcher. You're an outfielder and a first baseman. Don't screw around with pitching." But I wanted to be a pitcher and sure enough, I screwed up my arm by throwing too many curveballs. After that I could run and catch the ball but I could only throw it from center field to about second base. My arm is still screwed up today.

I had no thoughts whatsoever about playing sports even in college, let alone pro ball, until one night when I was playing in a high school basketball tournament. The superintendent of schools came over to me after the game and talked to me about transferring from Edison High to Stockton High. He told me if I transferred, they would make sure I got a scholarship to UCLA. This was when UCLA was about the only school that had black players, right after Jackie Robinson and Kenny Washington were on their football team.

I thought about it for a while and then I told this man no. It was a hard decision to make at such a young age but I regret it to this day because the education I got at Edison High School was not the best. At the time I didn't want to leave my friends and they didn't want me to go but sometimes you just have to cut your friends loose and do what's best for yourself. I didn't realize it at the time but I don't think they wanted me to go because I would be separating myself from them and getting something better for myself.

I had actually started at Stockton and gone there for a semester but then they moved all the shop courses to Edison and I transferred over there. The only academic course I took was English and when I got to the University of the Pacific, I was not prepared. I was planning on becoming a carpenter and didn't even think about college. I even had a job as an apprentice carpenter in high school but I can see that might not have turned out too well. None of the unions were accepting blacks and the only way you could work as a carpenter or bricklayer or what have you was to go to Oakland or San Francisco.

Every time I think about the gentleman who was the superintendent of schools and that situation, it makes me realize there have been white people I've known all through my life who have tried to do the right thing and help me out and help other blacks out. They were trying to do the right thing but it was the people around *them* who tried to prevent them from doing it. I found that to be true in other areas like working on the waterfront, where I got a lot of support from whites who wanted to give me a chance to do better in my life. I've always known all of my enemies but you never know all of your friends. A lot of people were on my side.

When I turned 18 in 1945, I had a little ways to go yet with high school, plus I was married, so they gave me an exemption from military service until I finished school. When I graduated in February of 1946, the war was over and I thought maybe they'd forget about me but they didn't, they called me right away. I graduated on February 7th, 1946, I got my notice to go in on February 8th, and on February 13th I was in the induction center at Camp Beale.

The war changed a lot of things. Sometimes I wonder if I would've been able to do all I was able to do if it wasn't for the war. You had the war and then not that long after, the Civil Rights Movement started and there was even what you could call a civil rights movement during the war. World War II was the first time that blacks got hired for certain jobs and it was also the first time we were able to join some of the unions.

I remember I was walking down the street with a friend of mine some time in 1942 and this man came out of this warehouse and offered us both jobs. We had been looking for work before that but we had given up because no one would hire us. In fact, we had been to that very place and they wouldn't hire us and now they were literally pulling us in off the street. They knew we were just youngsters 14 or 15 years old but they took us anyway because they knew we could load trucks.

I was drafted and went in as a buck private and came out a buck private. I was stationed in Yokohama and I played basketball and football. I couldn't wait to get out but the major and the two lieutenants who coached the football team wanted me to stay in and they tried to talk me into re-enlisting. They told me, "Go back home, re-enlist, wait 30 days, then come back over here and play on the football team and we'll make you a staff sergeant."

I didn't want them to know how much I wanted to get out so I said, "Oh man, that sounds real good. That's exactly what I'm going to do." Yeah, right. I wasn't even thinking about re-enlisting. I got back to Camp Stoneman in California, got discharged, and I caught the first bus I could get back to Stockton. I couldn't wait to get out of the army. I've got to say, though, I got a lot out of that experience because of the GI Bill. I got my schooling out of the GI Bill and I was able to buy two homes because of the GI Bill.

One thing I'll never forget occurred in Nagasaki. The basketball team traveled by train to play teams from other bases and one time we had to go through Nagasaki. When we were on the outskirts, the train stopped and some MPs got on, pulled all the blinds down, stood in the car with their hands on their weapons, and they said, "Do not open the blinds or look out the window. That is an order. Anyone who attempts to look out the window will be shot."

We went through Nagasaki, they stopped the train, the MPs put all the blinds up, then they got off the train and we proceeded on to wherever it was we were going. I don't know if they actually would've shot us, but nobody even thought about looking out the window, I'll tell you that. They did the same thing when we went through Hiroshima because they did not want us to see the devastation. I had seen a lot of devastation in a lot of places in Japan, but what happened in Hiroshima and Nagasaki was so bad that they didn't even want military personnel to see it. And that was two years after the bombs had been dropped. I tell people about it and they're amazed. That was really something.

I went back to working in the warehouse and I was playing basketball in a recreation league in Stockton when this guy who was the track coach at Stockton Junior College asked me if I wanted to go there on a track scholarship. He was coaching one of the teams in the rec league and he knew about me because his aunt was my English teacher in high school. I talked it over with my wife and at first I didn't want to go because I had had enough of school, but then my high school football coach became the football coach at Stockton Junior College.

I enrolled and I became the instant star of the football team and the coach of the University of the Pacific in Stockton recruited me to go there. They only offered me a partial scholarship and that still pisses me off because I was the one who was filling the stadium. It was good that I was able to go because I was able to further my education, but not getting a full scholarship is one of the hard lessons of life that I still get angry about.

Pappy Waldorf was the coach of Cal when I was at Stockton Junior College and he was interested in me. He sent word through somebody I had gone to school with to come to his office in Berkeley, but I wouldn't. I wanted Pappy Waldorf to come to me. He had a car, he had a budget, and I just thought he should come to see me. Then years later I met a guy who was one of the big boosters of Cal football and he told me he had pushed Pappy Waldorf to recruit me. He was still angry that they hadn't done more to try and get me to go there.

I really had to work hard in college to keep my scholarship and remain eligible to play football. George Moscone went to school with me. He was instructed to help me because I was so unprepared for college, to teach me to use the library and things like that. He became the mayor of San Francisco and was killed along with Harvey Milk. We remained friends for 30 years. I would see him politicking or speaking, and he would always make a point of acknowledging me to the audience. He'd say, "A good friend of mine is here today, Eddie Macon." It always made me feel good when he did that. The day he was assassinated was the saddest day of my life.

When I started at UOP, I was the only black player on the football team, then after a few years they brought two more in. Altogether, there were six black students in the school. We were undefeated in 1949 but we didn't get invited to any of the bowl games. I guess they said it was because of our schedule but we played a pretty good schedule: Fresno State, San Jose State, the University of San Francisco. Our first game against a big school was against Clemson and we beat them. We played LSU one year. We thought we were good enough for a bowl game. 10–0 is 10–0, but nobody invited us. I don't think any team with a black player had ever been invited to one of the bowl games down South up to that time. We did end going to the Sun Bowl when I was a senior, but that team wasn't as good as our '49 team.

The game I'll never forget was when we went to Hawaii to play the University of Hawaii. They were supposed to be the hotshot team and I went wild. I scored five touchdowns and we beat them pretty good. Late in the game, some Hawaiian guy yelled something to me from the stands. I didn't know what he was saying, I just figured it was some nut saying something insulting. It turns out he was saying "Keolha," which means "great," and after that they called me The Keolha Kid.

I played against Ollie Matson when he played for San Francisco City College and I played for Stockton, and then UOP played against USF when he was there. We also played against each other when I was with the Bears and he was with the Cardinals. He was a great player and a great guy. I understand he's been ill with Alzheimer's disease. I see Burl Toler all the time and he was a good player for USF, too, but he never played in the NFL because he screwed his leg up in the College All-Star Game. I went up to Soldier Field from the Bears training camp in Rensselear, Indiana and I was sitting in the stands when it happened. He was the first black official in the NFL.

I never thought about being a professional football player, even after Jackie Robinson started playing with the Dodgers and blacks started playing in the NFL. I was happy the same way I think all black people were, but I wasn't thinking about it as an opportunity for me, it was just progress for all of us. None of my coaches encouraged me in that direction and I didn't get any national recognition. I wasn't on any All-American teams because UOP didn't spend money publicizing me, which is what the big schools do. Same thing with the College All-Stars. I was drafted in the second round, which in those days was about the 20th pick, but I didn't get invited to play in the All-Star Game.

In my senior year I started getting questionnaires from NFL teams and that was the first notion I had that I might play in the NFL. I still thought it was a faraway idea but then a scout from the Rams came to see us play because they were interested in a teammate of mine named Tom McCormick. He was a running back, too, and he ended up playing three or four years with the Rams. He was talking to Tom and then somebody said, "Oh, and this here is Macon," and he started talking to me about how the Rams were also interested in me.

A part of me was thrilled that the NFL was interested in me, especially the LA Rams, because they were one of the best teams at that time and them and the Browns had the most black players. They had Deacon Dan Towler, Tank Younger, Woodley Lewis, Bob Boyd, and one or two more, plus they drafted Night Train Lane that same year I was drafted. The other part of me thought this guy from the Rams was bullshitting me. I said to myself, "Here we go again," but I listened to what he had to say.

I told him about the questionnaires from the other teams and he said, "Don't answer them. We're interested in drafting you in the third round, and if you fill those out some other team might pick you." I thought my chances were so unlikely it didn't even occur to me that he was giving me a line, that maybe some other team might draft me higher. It could've been a big mistake on my part. Then one day I was in line in the school cafeteria when a lady told me the Chicago Bears drafted me in the second round. I could hardly believe it. I went straight home without even eating and, sure enough, it was all over the radio. The funny thing was, the Rams didn't draft Tom McCormick until about the eighth round.

When I got to training camp, I found out what that national exposure was all about. I'd hear, "This guy is an All-American from this big college, this guy is an All-American from that big college," and then I'd see them play and I'd say to myself, "If these guys are All-Americans, what does that make my sister?" It was all about getting ink and these guys got it and I didn't even though a lot of them weren't nearly as good as I was. Some of them only lasted a few days before they got cut. One thing that I think surprised the Bears was that they thought I was bigger. I was 5'11" and I only weighed 150 pounds. They used to put 175 pounds in the program but I only weighed 150. But I played big. There's an expression, "He plays big." That was me. I played big.

Training camp was the roughest time I ever had. A lot of shitty things happened that I had to go through. I'd go into the bathroom and they'd have "Macon Go Home" and "Macon We Don't Want You" and other stuff written on the mirror or on the walls. Or we'd be at practice and a Greyhound bus would go by the field and a bunch of them would say, "Hey Macon, there's the bus going out of town" or "Macon, there's the bus going to Green Bay," because the Packers didn't have any black players and there were no blacks living there and they knew none of the black players wanted to go to Green Bay. They did all this because they weren't ready to have a black player as a teammate. I said to myself, "What kind of BS is this?" But I didn't let it bother me. I knew that's exactly what they wanted.

One time when we were practicing our kickoff returns, I got so angry that I walked off the field. The ball was kicked to me, but I didn't catch it and the ball went bouncing away and I didn't go after it. [Bears owner and coach] George Halas ran up to me and said, "Goddammit, you're supposed to run after that ball." Oh, he really berated me. I was so angry, I walked off the field and got on the bus that took us out to the practice field and stayed there.

A Catholic priest came on the bus and started talking to me. The priest was there because Halas was a devout Catholic and he came and talked to me for almost an hour. While we were talking, practice ended and the rest of the players were milling around, but none of them came on the bus. When they finally got on, none of them said anything to me except George Connor. He said, "Eddie, you've got this team made so don't even worry about it," and that made a big difference.

One thing I noticed about Halas, he didn't let himself get close to any of the players. The only one he was close to was George Connor and Connor was the only player I ever heard call him George. Everybody else called him Mister Halas or coach. Other than that one incident, I got along okay with Halas at first. Then later on I found out how tough he was. Everybody who was anybody in the National Football League at that particular time was there because of two men: George Halas and George Preston Marshall [owner of the Washington Redskins].

I stayed at the YMCA off Wabash Avenue in Chicago when I played for the Bears because I couldn't afford to live anywhere else. It only cost me $5 a week. Every week when I got my check, I sent most of my pay home to my wife and kids and kept a little for myself to live on. In 1952, I was the only black player on the Bears and then the next year they brought Billy Anderson and Willie Thrower in and there were three of us. [Emerson Cole also played one game for the Bears late in 1952.]

I look at the Bears today and I realize how much things have changed. They have a black coach, black assistant coaches, and well over half of the players are black. When I was playing, forget about it, there were no black coaches or assistants and each team had a quota of two or three players and some didn't have any. When camp started, there would be seven or eight, and we'd say, "We're here now but when the season starts, there'll only be a couple of us." We understood what was happening but it still created hard feelings because you knew there was something else besides ability going on. You resented the guy who made the decision and you resented some of the players because a lot of the blacks who were cut were better than some of the whites who made the team, but they had that quota system.

I hardly had any social life at all. The other players all lived on the North Side and I lived on the South Side. I used to take the tram up to Wrigley Field and then after the game or the practice was over, I'd take it back to the YMCA. The only thing I used to do was go to a little jazz club on State Street and get a whiskey sour for 45¢. I'd sip on it for a couple of hours and talk a lot of talk and listen to the bands that played there. Then I'd go home to my humble little abode at the YMCA.

I didn't socialize with the black players on the other teams, but we'd talk on the field before or after the game. I'd see Deacon Dan Towler or somebody and we'd talk about the problems we were facing or mention any new black players that had come into the league that year. The Steelers signed their first black player the same year I started, a big fullback named Jack Spinks, and he was making a big splash, so we talked about him.

One guy I did socialize with was Marion Motley. When we went to Cleveland, he took me out to this bowling alley he had and we stayed there for a while and talked. I met him and the big end Cleveland had, Lenny Ford. Motley was a hell of a good football player. His knees were bad by the time I met him so he was no longer the good runner he had been, but he was still the best blocking back the league has ever seen and a hell of a good linebacker.

Willie Thrower was with the Bears my second year. He was a backup and he hardly played. He was the first black quarterback but I think that was the only year he played. He didn't get into very many games because he really wasn't a very good quarterback. Halas thought he could be good, but it didn't turn out that way. When he did play, I think it was at the end of the year just so Halas could see what he could do.

After I played with the Bears for two years, I got offered more money to play with the Calgary Stampeders so I jumped my contract. That changed my life drastically and ended up costing me a lot of money. I became the only person who was not allowed to play in the NFL. Halas got pissed off and blackballed me, sued me for $100,000, sued the Stampeders for two or three million dollars and I was never allowed to play in the NFL again. I didn't have any money to pay for a lawsuit, let alone $100,000, but he did it just to show what he could do.

After my first season in Canada, all the players up there from the NFL like Eddie LeBaron who wanted to went back to their NFL teams except me. They had a limit of only six Americans per team and guys would go back and forth. I shopped myself around but nobody would sign me. I came out here to meet the Morabito brothers [Tony and Vic, owners of the San Francisco 49ers] and they told me they couldn't do anything until they talked to Halas. Of course, they never got back to me. Then there was a black guy who worked for the Browns as an assistant trainer who told me Paul Brown was interested, but I never heard from them again, either.

The last guy I called was Joe Kuharich, the coach of the Redskins. I knew him when I was at UOP because he was the coach at USF and I thought he might give me a shot but nothing came of that, either. I don't think that had so much to do with Halas as it did with the fact that the Redskins weren't interested in hiring any black players. But it probably wouldn't have mattered if they were interested, they wouldn't have signed me anyway, that's the kind of hold Halas had.

I talked to Halas's grandson once but I never got an explanation about why his grandfather did what he did. I also asked him why I never got invitations to any of the reunions or other affairs the Bears have and he wrote and told me he would make sure I got invited. You know what? Halas's mojo is still working, the blackball is still in place, because I have still never gotten an invitation of any kind from the Chicago Bears.

My brother lived in Chicago after I stopped playing and he was very sick over the last seven years of his life, and I would visit him two or three weeks a year. One time I stopped at the Bears' office and asked to see Halas. They told him I was there and then they came out and told me he didn't want to see me. Before I left, I said, "You tell him I didn't come here to ask for money," you know, because a lot of times ex-ballplayers will go back to the team looking for a handout. I said, "Tell him I'm not looking for a handout, I just came to renew old acquaintances." They went in and told him and then he came to the door, stuck his head out and looked at me, then he went back into his office and closed the door behind him.

A lot of people advised me to sue Halas and the NFL, but I never could because you have to have money to fight a case like that. This was when the Civil Rights Movement had started and everybody was talking about civil rights, but I never could find anybody who wasn't asking for a lot of money up front. I asked people to take the case and we would split whatever money we won but nobody would.

I did not know I was committing suicide with the NFL by going to Canada. It was just a matter of Calgary offering more money than the Bears were paying and I took it. I didn't have a plan about coming back or not coming back, I just figured if I did decide to come back that somebody would take me if I was good enough, whether it was the Bears or somebody else.

I'll tell you something else about the reach that Halas had. After I left Calgary and was unable to hook on in the NFL, I came back to Stockton and was living and working out here thinking that my football days were over. Do you know that for two years the Hamilton Tiger-Cats tried to reach me so they could sign me, but the Bears refused to give them any information about where I was? I heard all about this from Jim Trimble, the Hamilton coach, who had been the coach of the Philadelphia Eagles.

How I found out was, Hamilton sent a telegram for me to the University of the Pacific hoping that somebody there would know where I was and whoever got the telegram didn't know I was back in Stockton. Well, my daughter had her picture in the local newspaper for some occasion and a lady at UOP who knew me called and told me about the telegram. I had her read it to me and that's when I contacted the Hamilton Tiger-Cats and Joe Trimble told me they had been trying to locate me for two years. So in 1957, I went back to Canada and played for Hamilton for three years.

Canada was okay. Canadians like to think they're more liberal when it comes to race but, like I said, I've never had a day where I didn't know I was black. When you're black, you're black and that's it. When I lived in Calgary, blacks were treated the same as anywhere else I had been. As a matter of fact, if there were 140,000 people there, I'd say 100,000 of them were Americans. Oil was big and there were a lot of Oklahoma oil people in Calgary. Hamilton wasn't much different as far as race. Okay but nothing special.

We had a lot of success in Hamilton. I enjoyed playing and we played in the Grey Cup all three years I was there. We won one and lost the other two. I was 30 years old when I first got there and I'd been out of football for two years so it was tough, but I played well. I feel I could've been playing in the NFL if they had given me a chance. That's why I say going up there cost me a lot of money. Now you have collective bargaining and free agency and it's harder for them to get away with that kind of thing.

When the American Football League started in 1960, the Raiders and the Chargers and other teams were looking all over the place for playing talent and some coaches and scouts came to Stockton. I got a hold of them and the Raiders told me they were interested so I signed with them. Considering what it became, I'm proud I was an original in the AFL, but at the time I thought it was awful. It was very disorganized and you had guys coming and going all the time. Anybody who thinks the AFL was as good as the NFL in the early years is crazy. I don't even think they were as good as some of the teams they had up in Canada.

I played defense and did pretty well. I had nine interceptions and finished second in the league in 1960 and made the All-Pro Team. I went back the second year but I had pretty much had enough of football, plus things were so disorganized. Near the end of camp they told me they were going with younger guys and they would find a spot for me with another team but I told them, "Don't even bother, just cut me." I was 34 and I didn't want to go anywhere away from my wife and kids. It was fine playing close by in Oakland but I wasn't about to leave my family and go off and play somewhere far away the way I had before.

I went back to the docks and I'm still there now. I've been a member of the ILWU [International Longshore and Warehouse Union] for many years. I started doing longshore work when I was 21 or 22. A dispatcher was a Pacific man and he got me and several other players jobs. I was getting $92 a month from the government as a veteran, and with a family I needed more than that. My wife and I had four children so having a decent paying job like that was a big help. All through the time I played football, I came back in the off-season and worked, plus in 1955 and 1956 when I was out of football.

Everything is done by containers now but at that time, you loaded everything by hand. I'd go down in the hull and load the ship with whatever goods it was taking. I still work and I'm still a member of ILWU Local 34. I got almost 60 years in. I'm a ship clerk now. I supervise the loading and discharging of the ships. The containers came in to Stockton about 20 years ago and they're all container ships now. We don't have any more American ships except maybe some oil tankers. All the ships that come in the port fly foreign flags now—Japanese, Chinese, different countries from Europe.

We are a militant union and I've been through a few strikes and other things. [Longtime ILWU president] Harry Bridges was quite a person and quite a leader. He did a lot of things for us, not just for working class people but for Afro Americans. They used to only have a few Afro Americans on the docks, but during the war, Bridges integrated the union. I thought he was a great person. I talked to him quite a few times and I felt like I was close to him because he was our leader and he was doing good things for us. There were mistakes he made but you expect that with somebody who was in office that long. Remember, too, he was just doing what the members wanted.

Bridges definitely was not living the rich life at the expense of the members. After he would give a speech in the meeting hall, he would sit down and put his feet up on the desk and he always had holes in his shoes. Always. From the time I joined the ILWU until the last time I heard him speak. That meant something to me because a man with holes in his shoes couldn't have had much money in his pocket and that made me like him. He was a man of the people, still a working class man even though he was president of the union.

He was from Australia and I remember the government was after him when [Senator Joseph] McCarthy was starting his deal. That was the time when the Taft-Hartley Law and other things against the unions came in. They were trying to deport Bridges because they didn't like the fact that the ILWU was militant. Most all of the people in the ILWU supported him because we supported what he did for the members. That's why he kept getting re-elected, even when they were trying to deport him. I'm a union man and I supported him because he was one of us and did what was good for us.

We were all called communists. Anybody who was a good union member was called a communist. McCarthy and them ruined a lot of people simply because they believed in unions. I even heard that communist stuff from people with the Bears. One teammate asked me what I did in the offseason and I told him. This was when the whole business with the union and the Red Scare was in the news practically every day, and as soon as I mentioned the ILWU he said, "Oh, that commie outfit." I didn't want any problem with the NFL so from then on whenever anybody with the Bears asked, I said I worked for the Stockton Department of Parks and Recreation.

A lot of guys on the Bears were from the South, and they thought anybody who had anything to do with unions was a communist, even when the players started talking about starting a union. The biggest change in football has come about because of the Players Association. Just look at the salaries they're making compared to when I was playing. But these guys with the Bears didn't understand that all a union means is that you have the right to bargain as a group.

I've seen what can happen if you don't have a good union or the union doesn't stick together. Look what happened to all the steel mills. We actually shipped steel mills overseas out of Stockton. They would take the machinery and the infrastructure from a steel mill in the United States, transport it out here, and we would load it all on ships that were going to wherever they were moving the plant. Big, heavy machines they didn't want to replace. Of course, they didn't worry about replacing the workers.

I still work three days a week. Most of the docks in San Francisco have dried up because they don't have the space. With these big containers you need a lot of space. One of the docks I work at in Oakland has six or seven cranes and they can berth three ships at a time. You can't do that in San Francisco. Down in Los Angeles, you can berth five ships in some of those docks, that's how big they are.

People always ask me when I'm going to retire but I don't have any plans along those lines. I've noticed that a lot of my friends don't last very long when they retire so the word "retire" isn't even in my vocabulary. I keep myself in excellent shape, my health is good, my weight is good, and I don't see any reason why I should retire. To tell you the truth, I keep working because it's one of the most interesting things in my life. I don't play golf and I don't belong to any organizations, but when I go to work I see people I know and we're all working to accomplish the same thing.

I would've liked to have stayed in touch with some of the guys I knew with the Bears, but if they don't invite me, there's nothing I can do. I'd like to see them to talk about old times and to show them that I've done all right for myself. I don't hear too much from the Raiders, either. They don't seem to have much of an alumni organization because I think I would hear something from them being that I'm an original Raider, plus I see Jim Otto all the time and I'm sure he would've told me about it if they had one. I go to some of the events of the 49ers alumni because they're close even though I never played for them. One guy I see is Bob St. Clair. He used to be the mayor of Daly City, which is where I live now.

I went to my 60 year high school reunion a few years ago. I used to go but I stopped because I would forget how old I was until I got to the reunions. I'll tell you, when you see people you know and see how they've aged and they're all the same age as you, then you know you're not seeing yourself the way you really are. But this time I said to myself, "Eddie, it's later than you think because you're damn near 80 years old." So I went and I really enjoyed being there. I saw four of my friends who played football with me and we sat down and broke bread together and it was really very enjoyable.

HAROLD BRADLEY

Harold Willard Bradley Jr.
Born October 13, 1929, in Chicago, Illinois

Englewood High School in Chicago, Illinois
Iowa University

Guard
Undrafted, signed by Cleveland Browns in 1953

Eddie Bell calls Harold Bradley a Renaissance Man. For good reason. Harold is an accomplished artist, an actor who has appeared in more movies than he can remember, a singer, and one-time owner of a Rome club in a thriving music scene. And, oh yes, once upon a time he was a professional football player for the greatest team in the game's history.

In addition, Harold holds a truly unique place in football history. He and Harold Sr. were the first African American father-son combination in the National Football League. As he spoke lovingly of his father both as a father and as a great football player and pioneer, Harold's voice choked with emotion: "Can you imagine, in the time period that he played, the kind of stuff he would run into? Wow." Like his father, Harold attended Iowa University, where he was voted co-captain and Most Valuable Player by his teammates as a senior in 1950.

After a two-year stint in the Marine Corps, during which he was a tackle on his base's football team, two years in which he played "the best football of my life," Harold signed with the Cleveland Browns. A pioneering franchise in racial integration, the Browns had played in eight consecutive Championship Games when Harold joined the

Year	Team	League	Games
1951	Military service		
1952	Military service		
1953	Military service		
1954	Browns	NFL	12
1955	Browns	NFL	12
1956	Browns	NFL	11
1957	Injured, missed entire season		
1958	Eagles	NFL	12

Played in NFL Championship Game in 1954, 1955

team in 1954. After some words of advice from Marion Motley, Harold moved into the lineup as a guard that year.

Harold befriended many of his teammates, white and black, and refers to them as "top-notch people." The Browns continued their great run in Harold's first two years, winning consecutive NFL Championship Games, 56–10 and 38–14. The experience, Harold says, gave him an appreciation of excellence and "all of the dedication and hard work that go into that kind of achievement." After playing on high school and college teams that finished below .500 in every season that he played, winning championships was a new and enjoyable experience. "The winning thing," he says, "finally caught up with me."

Harold went to Europe for the first time in 1956. At that point he was studying for a master's degree in art, painting, exhibiting his work, and teaching at Karamu House, a famous center for the arts in the heart of Cleveland's African American community. While traveling through 12 countries for the express purpose of exploring the art scene in each, Harold was attracted to the idea of living in Europe and working as an artist. He was especially drawn to Italy. Not only was there a thriving art scene in Rome and other cities, there were music clubs that featured African American singers and musicians.

Harold moved to Rome in 1959, married a German artist, and began to exhibit his work. He also acted in dozens of films, began singing, and was part of a group that opened a music club. It was such a busy and fulfilling period of his life that Harold recalls rarely sleeping more than a few hours at night.

With his wife and children, Harold moved back to his native Illinois in 1968 for 19 years before returning to Rome, where he now lives. While in the United States, he worked in television and continued to paint. Since returning to Rome in 1987, he has revived his singing career.

Fifty years removed from football, Harold's attachment to the game has not been broken. He attended a rally in Cleveland in the mid-1990s after it was announced that the Browns were being transferred to Baltimore. More recently he has attended a reunion of the championship teams he played on, visited former teammates in the United States, and hosted the late Dante Lavelli while Lavelli was vacationing in Italy.

My father Harold Bradley Sr. played one year in the National Football League with the Chicago Cardinals before I was born. He made all-state when he was in high school and then played at Iowa. He knew Duke Slater, who played at Iowa before he did, and I believe Duke had something to do with him signing with the Cardinals. Duke Slater was an All-American when he played for Iowa, was a great player for the Cardinals, and then later on he became a judge in Chicago.

My father was born in Coffeeville, Kansas, and came to Chicago as a boy. My mother was born in Chicago. She was a good sport—Patty Ruth Clay. She was a very warm person and she helped us through some hard times—relatively hard times. I think we were pretty much a black middle class family. She was very intelligent. She did a lot of reading. She and her sisters worked in sales in a sort of discount clothing store over on 47th Street and I remember for awhile she was a hat check girl at a ballroom, then she went to a job training program and eventually became a dietician. She became the head dietician and headed meal preparation at my grammar school. She was also very active in politics, volunteering her efforts in election campaigns, generally for the Democratic Party.

My father was quite a personality. He was a charming guy. Dimpled. Dark-skinned. Just a very charming guy. My father and mother were young when they got married. I think my mother was just 19 and my father 20 or 21, so my parents, my sister, and me all kind of grew up together. My father was a proud U.S. mail carrier.

Sometimes I would be on the blocks where he delivered mail and I got to go with him on his route.

It meant something then to be a mail carrier, especially for an African American. It was a wonderful opportunity. In fact, my father left Iowa University after only a few years when the job with the postal service became available in Chicago. Plus he wanted to get married. He was involved in many social activities that revolved around people he knew in the postal service. He had a steel plate in his leg from an accident he had had as a young boy over in the railroad yard, but it didn't prevent him from playing on the basketball team for his post office unit, just like it didn't prevent him from playing in the NFL.

Outside of his post office duties, he sold appliances. I think he made more money selling appliances than he did as a mail carrier. He was just a very active guy who aspired to improve the life of our family as much as he could. For example, we always had a car. And they bought us a little upright piano and we had piano lessons when we were five or six years old. My dad had a great collection of 78 RPM jazz records that I eventually took over, just great music from that time that I was very influenced by.

My father was a real charmer. He could laugh—he could *really* laugh. He had probably the biggest laugh on the whole South Side. Our neighbors from four or five buildings down would say, "You guys had a lot of fun last night, didn't you? We could hear you laugh all the way down the block." My parents were very good jitterbuggers—my mom especially could really boogie. They hung around with a group of music aficionados and they'd come over to the house and listen to my dad's records—Jimmy Lunceford, Duke Ellington, Count Basie, Charlie Parker. I remember vividly when Charlie Parker burst on the scene.

I have great memories of growing up in Chicago and my sister probably does, too. We lived in the Woodlawn area on the South Side. It was a time when things were pretty safe and sound and secure and people were nice to each other and you didn't have to close your doors or lock your doors all the time. There was a sense of warm neighborliness. Our neighbors were wonderful people. You could sit on the porch or on the stairs or jump rope or play ball with people from all around the neighborhood. My mother would even come out and play with us some times. We enjoyed our life.

We used to shoot marbles out on the street. I used to shoot oddly—I used to shoot "funky knuckle," as they called it, because I couldn't shoot the marble off my knuckle like the other guys. I used to shoot them off my thumb, you know, the unorthodox way of shooting marbles and I actually got pretty good. They didn't like it because I used to surprise them and knock their marbles off with my unorthodox sharpshooting. It was great fun.

We used to always take advantage of vacant lots for playing. There were two or three in the neighborhood and one's imagination just shot off coming up with things to do. We used to play softball—we were softball people, not baseball—and we used to pitch horseshoes and plant gardens and all kinds of other things. And we used to have clean-up week in Chicago, where everybody from the grammar school would clean up the neighborhood. We'd get an assignment and plant gardens and spruce up houses and clean up everything. We had a lot of interaction with the neighbors and a lot of camaraderie and, as one remembers it now, it was a great time.

We would play touch football out in the street and roller skate up and down the block. Our dad bought my sister and I Silver King bikes—those were the glory days of Silver King bikes—and we used to ride around the neighborhood. We were really very well provided for. I wouldn't say my parents gave us everything we wanted, but they did a lot to make our childhood very enjoyable. They also did the best they could to see that we got a well-rounded education.

The world we lived in was fantastically rich. There were Swedish, Irish, Chinese, Mexican—Chicago is just so rich ethnically. Every once in a while you heard about riots here and gangs there, but we had a good opportunity to experience interaction with other racial groups in Woodlawn. I remember this Italian guy, Papacita we used to call him—it's strange how you remember these things. But when we were in elementary school and high school even, we used to all flock to Papacita's wagon for hot dogs and popcorn. He had a very elaborately decorated Sicilian-style horse drawn wagon that he designed, and he was a joy. He made the greatest hot dogs and popcorn. You can still get hot dogs and popcorn like that in these little places here and there in Chicago.

My father's father worked for the Rock Island Railroad and he and my grandmother and my father were very influential in instilling pride in us as African Americans. We were very aware of our culture. My father would buy African American magazines and newspapers to keep up to date on what was going on. We were actually a rainbow family because my grandmother on my mother's side, Pauline Harley Clay, was white. She was German and she came to Chicago from Philadelphia on a covered wagon when she was a girl, and she married a black man, my grandfather Henry Clay.

My mother's brothers and sisters were very light-skinned. They could pass for white but they lived and made their lives in the black community. Actually, they looked Mexican. Every year we had these big Fourth of July picnics and, boy, it was the greatest fun. Everybody would be laughing and joking and I'm sure there were a lot of racial jokes. It was just a great opportunity for me as a young boy growing up in Chicago to be exposed to a lot of wonderful people. And it was a great way to overcome any kind of prejudice one would have.

My father was a very tight friend of E. Simms Campbell, a black man who was a great cartoonist. Elmer was his first name. Originally out of St. Louis, I believe. I didn't get to know him well until a bit later in life, but he was an interesting figure who I certainly enjoyed being acquainted with. He gave me an original cartoon from his Cuties series that he syndicated for the Hearst newspapers. I used to look at them as well as cartoons he did for *Esquire* magazine, and I was also attracted to the illustrators in the *Saturday Evening Post* like Norman Rockwell.

My father used to bring the *Saturday Evening Post* home and that was kind of an influence in a commercial vein. Their covers were like a mirror of American life. Partly because of these cartoons and magazine covers, I began to take art lessons when I was still a pretty young boy. Some of the teachers at my grammar school saw what I could do and recommended me for the Chicago Art Institute. They gave awards for the school they had there on Saturdays and I was one of the awardees—I guess I was about nine or ten. At the Art Institute I got acquainted with fine arts, in addition to commercial art. I was just absolutely intrigued early on with painting and drawing ideas out on paper.

I enjoyed trying to play the piano and music was always a vital part of my life, but my music lessons didn't come off that well. When it came to art, though, my teachers would be amazed by the things I would do. I became the pet artist around my grammar school and that was when they recommended me for the Art Institute. Then when I got to high school, it was the same thing. I remember drawing elaborate illustrations on my chemistry and physics exams. I was known for my art and my athletic ability.

I won a few awards in national competitions with my paintings when I was still quite young. One was something that appeared on a calendar and another was a tempera paint rendition of one of my classrooms. I just sat down at home one night and drew the scene of my physics class from memory—the students in the class and all the details of the room. Everyone was pretty impressed by it and it won one of those national awards.

The high school I went to, Englewood High School, was the same high school my father went to. It was west of where we lived across the Rock Island Railroad tracks just off State Street, which was one of the longest streets in Chicago. We didn't walk, we usually took a streetcar, and growing up there was a great, great moment. You have to understand, the neighborhood was changing drastically at the time to pretty much a mixed neighborhood and there were interactions with all kinds of people, all kinds of races.

My father was very proud of me in many ways and certainly I would say he was proud of what I accomplished as a football player. He got me a part-time job at the post office when I was on Christmas vacation and he kind of showed me off to his fellow workers. He got to see me all through my career, in high school, Iowa, and the NFL. He would joke with me that he was a better player than I was and I would say, "I don't think so." Once in awhile he talked to me about some of the things he faced when he played but not much. Can you imagine, in the time period that he played, the kind of stuff he would run into? Wow. I wish I had thought at the time to talk to him in more detail and record some of our conversations.

Duke Slater and my father lived within close range of each other and I think Duke knew about my father as a high school football player. Since Duke went to Iowa, I'm sure he also knew about my father playing at Iowa. There certainly was some kind of connection. I was at Duke's office on five or six occasions when he was a municipal judge. I also knew him from seeing him at homecomings at Iowa. My father did not aggressively urge me to go to Iowa but through hearing about it, he made it known to me that he had enjoyed it. I know he was pleased that I went there.

I started playing organized football at Englewood High School and I was also a shot putter on the track team. We were not the greatest football team in our league. We were way down at the bottom. Our traditional rival was Hyde Park High School, which was across town and was predominantly white. One school we played was Tilden Tech and those Tech guys looked like monsters, they were so big. Even though we weren't that good, I liked football. I liked working with the other guys. You'd get into a routine and you'd see that everybody was an important part of the game, that your role as a tackle was just as important as the guy carrying the ball.

I aspired to be a good lineman and one thing that helped me was something I learned from my grandmother. She was a Christian Scientist and really into metaphysical thinking and I grew up believing that I could heal myself. Believe me, at Englewood I had a lot of opportunities. The team wasn't that good, the equipment wasn't that good, you just took whatever helmet was available in the equipment room. We didn't have face guards and a lot of times after games I would just feel beat up. It really helped me, that belief that I could heal myself anytime I got hurt. That stayed with me throughout the whole time I played football—it's stayed with me my entire life. I always had this inner strength, the ability to rely on my own powers rather than medical help.

It was when I was in high school that Bill Willis and Marion Motley and Kenny Washington and Woody Strode came along. It had a big impact on me. From then on, I always had my eyes on the Browns. They always had four or five black guys, which was a lot for the time. I followed them the same way I followed the Brooklyn Dodgers when Jackie Robinson came aboard. I became a big Brooklyn Dodger fan because of Robinson and Roy Campanella. That was amazing. Boy, those guys were role models. You followed any team that was willing to break the color line. That was automatic.

What the Cleveland Browns proved was that integration is great stuff. It proved that people can work together more splendidly than the other situation, the all-white situation, or almost all white. I got to be a part of it and in my first two years the Browns won two world championships. It doesn't get much better than that. They had great white players and great black players and that's the way to do it.

Iowa University was an enjoyable experience. There were some families sprinkled around that knew my father from when he had been there and Iowa City became kind of a hub for me. I spent a total of about 12, 13 years there. I went there for four years, graduated in '51, and I was hopping back and forth pursuing a master's degree. Iowa was a groundbreaking school. It became the third school after Yale and Princeton to offer a fine arts program, a forerunner for all the programs that spread across the country after World War II. There were great art teachers and historians, professionals from New York and the East Coast, and I was right there. They were great in the humanities and they had a great creative writing program. It was an absolutely intriguing and buoyant climate, just an absolutely influential experience.

I was one of the last 60-minute men at Iowa. For part of my junior year and all of my senior year, I played both ways just about every play. I was pretty fast for a tackle. I got to be one of the top sprint guys on the team. I was co-captain and the Most Valuable Player on the team in '50, my senior year. Dr. Eddie Anderson was the coach my first three years and he had been very successful back when they had Nile Kinnick. They were never championship teams but good, solid teams. When I played, we had mediocre results and that continued my senior year when we had a new coach. We had some good players—Bill Green, a defensive back, was my co-captain. I enjoyed it despite the mediocre results because I had great teammates and there was great cooperation on the team.

I never heard from any of the NFL teams while I was at Iowa. It was the height of the Korean War or campaign or police action where the United States was policing countries and there was such an air around about guys getting drafted into the service. They knew all of us, or most of us anyway, were going to end up in the service and the NFL was not the monster that it became about getting as many guys as they could to sign contracts.

I was stationed in San Diego and you think of San Diego as being warm, and overall it has a beautiful climate, but those were some of the coldest nights I've ever experienced. Chicago has about the coldest winters so I had a lot of experience but, man, I was never as cold as I was those nights in San Diego. We used to sleep in our boots and all of our clothes. The reason I was in the Marines is because the corps wasn't getting many volunteers because of Korea, so about 18 percent of every draft got raked off into the Marines. My heart was in my throat at the induction center because I knew I was headed for the front lines once we finished basic training. They looked at my forms and saw that I had graduated college and they had me leading the troops in their training. Some miracle happened and I got those guys marching like they had never seen before and they would say, "Private Bradley, I want you to teach these guys over here to march that same way."

I think that was what first caught their attention. Then the football coach looked at my record and saw that I had been co-captain and Most Valuable Player at Iowa and that absolutely attracted *his* attention. I didn't know they had a football coach—I didn't even know they had a team. Boy, that was a saving grace. We called our team the San Diego Bulldogs. That was a lifesaving opportunity because there is no question in my mind that I would have ended up on the front lines.

I probably played the best football of my life in the Marines. Because so many guys were getting drafted right out of college, there were a lot of good service players and it was good competition. We had guys who had been All-Americans in college and plenty of the guys went on to play in the NFL. I can't recall too many of their names but Ed Brown was one. He eventually became a quarterback for the Chicago Bears. There were a lot of excellent teams—Army teams, Navy teams, and part of the motivation to play well was that you knew that if you weren't on the team you were on your way to Korea.

The Browns had a scout come around to look at a crackerjack running back on our team named Tom Carodine. He was an African American guy from Boys Town who had played football at Nebraska, just a slippery guy who you couldn't tackle. I knew he was being scouted and I told him to put in a good word for me. I figured, why not show them what you can do. Show that you're talented and tough and I was probably a more aggressive player even than when I played with the Browns. With the Browns, you had Paul Brown's system and it really did not emphasize that a guard be aggressive. But playing with the Bulldogs, there were times that I felt invincible, that on defense they would just not get any yards on my side of the field, and on offense that they could not stop us.

The scout who was there to see Carodine must have said something good about me because I was approached by the Browns and invited to training camp. Tom was, too. It was unfortunate that we couldn't get out earlier because by the time we got to camp, it was almost over. It was late August or early September, 1953. Paul Brown had wanted me to come earlier but you can't get out of your duties as a Marine. I was in great shape and I was ready, willing, and able, and not long after I got to camp Paul Brown talked to me for about a half hour on the practice field.

I think he had already made up his mind about which players he was going to keep and he kind of talked me into doing a redshirt thing. I didn't have any kind of representative and I probably could have played for Cleveland that year if I had played my cards better. I was naive. I was feeling invincible after playing great ball for the Marines for two years, but I was naive. I shouldn't have gone there alone because he was a very persuasive person, and he just talked me out of playing the 1953 season.

I had told him that one of my goals was to continue my studies and he turned that around on me. He said, "Why don't you spend a year going back to school like you talked about and we'll have a spot for you next year." He also said, "I think in a year you'll be good enough to play on the first team, but because you got here so late, about the best I can offer you is a spot on the practice squad," which meant I could've moved up to the regular squad only if somebody got hurt or something. I would have had to go to all of the practices all year and I thought, "I don't want to be just standing around all year. I can make better use of my time and then come back next year."

I didn't want to jeopardize my chances of playing for Cleveland the next year, so I agreed. I was absolutely deflated. I was naive and I didn't know what would happen if I pushed too hard, so I told myself, "Art is the most important thing in your life. You may not ever play for this football team, but you can absolutely make art, so go do that and see where things stand in a year." But I was absolutely deflated.

When I came back in '54, Paul Brown's original plan was for me to take Bill Willis's spot. Number 60, the great Bill Willis. Boy oh boy, what a great player he was. Absolutely invincible. Anyway, I didn't do too well filling Bill Willis's shoes at middle guard. I had been playing tackle and it takes a while to get oriented to a new position, especially middle guard. Mike McCormack had just gotten out of the military and he played middle guard that year. Later on, after Mike got moved to offense, Tom Catlin took over the middle guard job.

After that they said, "Let's see what you can do at offensive guard," and that's when I became one of the messenger guards. Paul Brown sent the plays in to Otto Graham and whoever else was playing quarterback via the messenger guards and that's what I did throughout the time I was with the Browns. Chuck Noll was the other messenger guard at first and then Herschel Forester for awhile, and then in my last year in Cleveland it was me and Freddy Robinson.

One of the big reasons I made the team was because of Marion Motley. I owe a great deal to him. That was the end of the line for Marion with Cleveland because he had bad knees and the Browns ended up releasing him at the end of training camp, although he caught on with another team for another year or two. But in training camp before he was released, he took me aside and had a little talk with me. He said, "Bradley, you're a great guy and you've got a lot of talent, but you've got to knock the shit out of somebody. That's all I'm going to say to you. You can make this team, but you've got to knock the shit out of somebody." Wise words.

Motley was fed up with me because I was acting too much like a gentleman. I had been back in the university life studying to be a painter, working as an art history teacher, and it's just a completely different atmosphere than the one on a football field. So Marion was right and I absolutely appreciate the fact that he gave me that advice. He was a good guy and unfortunately I didn't have the opportunity to be his teammate besides those few weeks in training camp.

Paul Brown was an interesting character. He was very intelligent and somewhat aloof, sort of like a lawyer. He was balding and he always had a hat on or a cap. He had an intimidating side. What he said went and he could make you feel pretty small. As a football coach, he was always refining things. He also got more nervous before and during games throughout my career. In the beginning he wasn't that way, but by 1957 I noticed he was often quite nervous.

He had big, thick notebook-sized play books and you had to know everybody's job. You had to really study and you had to carry those play books with you to practice every day because before practice there would be a study session. He gave us tests and you would be scratching your head taking those tests. About the only guy who did well on those tests was Chuck Noll. He was a brain, a Phi Beta Kappa. When you came out of the Browns, you came out knowing something. When I went to the Eagles, it was like a holiday compared to the Browns.

The team in Cleveland was absolutely top-notch people—Otto Graham, Lou Groza, Mike McCormack, John Sandusky. Mike and John were the tackles and I worked next to them. Just top-notch people. I worked next to Frank Gatski, just another top-notch guy. I was so unhappy when I heard that Frank died. I had just seen him in Cleveland when they had a ceremony for the anniversary of the 1954 and 1955 championship teams. I hadn't seen him since '57.

I saw a few guys at a rally they had in the '90s when they had the problem with the franchise. But I never saw Otto Graham again after I stopped playing. Never saw Lou Groza. So many good guys. Derrell Brewster. Don Colo. Colo was just a funny, funny guy, full of life and vitality and jokes. And a great defensive tackle. Another tackle we had was John Kissell. Another outstanding player, just a great defensive tackle. He's dead. He was from the Chuck Bednarik school.

Bednarik was something. I played with Chuck one year after playing against him with the Browns and Chuck had an ugly side, a mean side shall I say. I guess you could say that's what kept him going and made him an All-Pro. He was a physical guy from the old school. You know what he represented to me? The old steel factory workers playing in football's early days. He probably was the son of a steelworker and headed that way himself if not for football. He was just a mean, physical guy.

I remember one time after a game he tapped Chuck Noll on the shoulder and when Chuck turned around, Bednarik popped him right in the face. I guess they had some kind of interaction in the game that didn't go down well with Bednarik. He was still wearing his helmet when he hit him, so he was ready for any retaliation. But Noll was so shocked, he didn't retaliate. Plus his teeth were falling out of his head and when your teeth are falling out of your head, you're too shocked to do anything. Bednarik really slugged him.

Lenny Ford was my roommate on the Browns and you couldn't have come up with a worse combination. I was quiet like Horace Gillom, but I got put with Lenny Ford. I liked Lenny but he was a little heavy on the alcohol, plus he was absolutely the biggest snorer of anybody on the team. He would snore like a train and I would be up all night. It got so bad, I had to talk to Paul Brown about changing roommates. I will say this: Lenny Ford was a great player. Boy, was he a great player.

Within the Browns, there were no racial problems that I was aware of. I would hear "black SOB" or something like that from opposing teams once in awhile. Black motherfucker. I didn't care about that stuff. That's like water over a duck's back. I think one of the reasons I was voted co-captain at Iowa was because I managed that stuff and the other guys on the team could see it. I was as talented as anybody and as tough as anybody and all that mattered was the respect and recognition of my teammates. To me, that was as good as being All-American or All-Pro. Same thing with the Browns. The white guys respected me and I respected them. I think Bill Willis, Marion Motley, and Horace Gillom had broken a lot of that ground and their talent showed through. Talent makes respecters out of all kinds of bigots.

I didn't like the label "messenger guard." Messenger, my ass. The implication was that it was part-time work and the focus was on the fact that you were delivering the plays rather than that you were a player. It was okay, though. It kept you on your toes. And that was Paul Brown's system and you would certainly have to say that his system worked.

I would have liked more of a chance to play defense than that brief experience at middle guard. I was a tackle up until I got to the Browns and I was probably better on defense, but tackle and middle guard are two different positions and it was a tough adjustment. After that he moved me to offense and I wish he had at least given me a chance at tackle. I'd look at the guys playing defensive tackle and say, "I could have done that job as good as he did." I spoke with Paul Brown about it, but I guess he never took me seriously.

I learned a lot from Fritz Heisler, our line coach. I was about 225, 230 pounds with all of my equipment and I remember my first year playing against Les Bingaman, who was over 300 pounds and All-Pro. I said to myself, "Okay, here I am up against Les Bingaman. Let's see if the things Mr. Heisler has been teaching me are going to work." Well, we ran and we threw and we beat the Lions 56–10 that day, and I occupied Les so that he wasn't a factor. Otto Graham said to me, "Man, you made some of the biggest holes that I have ever seen."

That whole experience with the Browns was a vital one and it came at a good time for me. It gave me a sense of being a professional and there was an astute sense of winning and being proud of what you accomplished. The winning thing finally caught up with me. You were together with fantastic people, and it made for good interactions and good relationships. I've been in Italy most of the time since so I haven't stayed in touch with many guys, but I still have fond memories of that experience. I've seen Dante Lavelli. He's come over here a few times. And when I was in Seattle, I made a point to kill two birds with one stone and I visited with Tom Catlin, so those things have lasted to this day.

I fractured my leg in the last exhibition game in 1957 and I had to sit out the rest of the season. It was just one of those things that happen. I got my pay and I was on the bench during the games rooting for the team, and I also got to invest more of my time in my art career. I continued to get credits toward my master's degree, I had my first art studio, and I was teaching drawing and painting at the Karamu House in the heart of the black community in Cleveland. That was a wonderful experience.

I felt like I had done a good job as a guard up to that point and I went back to training camp in '58 confident and in good shape, aspiring to get my job back. Maybe I was a half step slower, plus the Browns had drafted [Gene] Hickerson. He was a young guy with a lot of talent and he had a step or so on me as far as speed. He turned out to be a great guard, just one of the great Browns' players, and Paul Brown decided to put me on waivers and keep Hickerson.

The Philadelphia Eagles picked me up so fast, I didn't even get a chance to pack anything. [Head coach] Buck Shaw was a very nice guy and that experience with the Eagles was a good one. I played just the one season, then I started getting established in Rome as an actor and as an artist. I was in Italy in 1959 and one of the guys I was running around with suggested we try to get work in movies as extras. I got a job as an actor with lines right away—lights, camera, action. It seemed like every day I was involved in shooting for one movie or another—big costume movies, small movies, monstrous commercially oriented gladiator movies being shot all over Italy.

The Eagles kept sending me these contracts and I'm saying to myself, "Man, I can't go back to the Philadelphia Eagles. I've got all these movies I'm in, I've got an art show going, I'm involved in this music scene, I'm meeting all these beautiful women. Wow! And you're going to go back to Philadelphia? Man, are you for real? I'm having too much fun. I spent five years of my life butting heads with Les Bingaman and Chuck Bednarik. Why would I want to leave all this to go back to that?" I was having so much fun, doing so many things I wanted to do, I hardly even needed to sleep.

I first went to Italy in 1956. I spent the entire off-season traveling to 12 countries in Europe. I was traveling as a working artist and observing different countries. I wanted absolutely to see as many countries as I could and I was attracted to the Old World view of art. In January of 1959, I decided to come back to Italy to really seriously launch my career. I had played five years by then and that was about the average lifetime of an NFL player, plus I was concerned about hurting my hands. I hadn't retired. My intention at the time was to continue to play football, but I got involved in so many things throughout 1959, I realized I had to make a choice.

I've looked back at it every now and then and asked myself if I did the right thing. It was a shorter commitment then in terms of the length of the season, so I guess I could've gone on for awhile spending half a year in Italy and half a year in Philadelphia. Then when the Eagles won the NFL championship in 1960, I was sort of peeved at myself for not having gone back. I said, "Dang it, Bradley, you missed one." But so what, I missed one. I have no regrets. I made the choice and I'm glad I made the choice I did. I got involved in acting and got on-the-job training. I had some good roles and did about 30 movies in nine years and also did some theater. If anything, I look back and realize that acting distracted me from my painting.

I was studying Italian culture and the Italian language in Perugia when I met my wife. She was studying at the same school. She's German. We were married on April 15, 1960, in the city hall in a chapel that Michelangelo designed. She's a particularly astute woman, an intelligent woman, a very sensitive woman, just a wonderful lady. It's been a blessing and I can't begin to say enough about her.

I started singing because I was hearing all this folk music from the States. I would be up all night listening to this American music on Italian radio stations and it was very inspiring. The Civil Rights Movement was starting, and folk music brought me straight into black history. I used to frequent these jazz clubs and folk music coffee houses and it just started popping all over the place. I was sharing it with students I was meeting at the university in Perugia and absolutely having fun with it.

When I started singing, I got involved in this club scene. We invited our friends to come on Friday and Saturday nights and we would hold these folk music sessions at the studio I was sharing with a sculptor from Canada. We called it a folk studio and we made it on a membership basis to avoid the red tape you would have to deal with if you made it a regular club. I had been to a coffeehouse in Paris, but I can't remember ever being in one in Chicago or New York. It just became this place with these absolutely exciting people displaying these wonderful, interesting talents and the thing just bloomed.

We had three children over the next five years and then we decided to move to the States in 1968. From the time I moved to Italy in 1959 to 1968, I had not been back, and when I went to visit I got this job offer. The Civil Rights Movement was going on and I had been away from it, although I had been representing it in Italy. I got into television work in Chicago. I was interviewed by Studs Terkel and I went around Illinois speaking as a representative of the arts and an organizer of the arts. I helped organize the Illinois Arts Council program on the visual arts and then I got a job offer from the University of Illinois.

I worked full-time at the university and also worked in television in Champaign. First I worked at the CBS affiliate there and then for PBS designing and hosting all kind of programs—talk shows, educational shows. Then I went to Springfield to work for the educational television facet of the Illinois Board of Education for seven years. We did all these things with black people, women, trying to give some in-depth dimension to minority affairs, to broaden the dimension of what it was to be a black person—what it was to be a black woman, a black artist, a black professional. It was very gratifying.

We moved back to Rome after 19 years. We went there to visit when we were on a trip to Germany for Christmas in 1986 and some people organized a sort of anniversary concert for me with all these singers and jazz musicians and people we knew. Within no time I was involved in organizing a few concerts and this circle of people introduced me to club owners and all of my friends there were urging me to come back. Things were moving along quite well and I said, "Oh wow, I've got an opportunity to swing back into the place where so much of my career started."

I had feelers in for jobs in television in New York and Boston, but I had never gotten an offer. Work was coming easily in Italy and I liked the lifestyle. It was my second home and it seemed everywhere I went people were happy to see me, so I was glad to get back. I was singing with a band called Harold Bradley and the Jonas Blues Band. In fact, we got back together just recently. We had broken up 1991. I've also been working for Perillo Tours for 18 years. They gave me an audition and I became the host of their gala evenings with their tour groups.

My daughters are both in the States. My son Oliver's the closest. He's in Germany. They had both a good European and an American experience. They can speak Italian and English and German, so they're all multilingual. They went to the Montessori international schools here and they always had Italian pals and neighbors to play with. We had a nice growing up together family-wise.

I didn't retain any contact with Motley after he stopped playing. I haven't stayed in touch with many guys, so it was great to see them at the reunion in 2004. I was glad some of the wives of guys who had passed away were there. Billy Reynolds's wife was there. So was Otto Graham's wife. I never got to talk to the wives much when we played, so it was good to get some insights. One guy I've stayed in touch with is Sherman Howard. He's also from Chicago and I'm going to see him when I get back there. He's a fun guy. Laughs a lot. Good storyteller. Loves to play golf. I guess if I had played golf I would have stayed in touch with a lot more guys, but I never got into golf.

EDDIE BELL

Edward B. Bell
Born March 25, 1931, in Philadelphia, Pennsylvania

West Philadelphia High School in Philadelphia, Pennsylvania
Howard University
University of Pennsylvania

Defensive back
Drafted in 5th round by Philadelphia Eagles in 1953

Eddie Bell is Philadelphia through and through. Born and raised in the shadow of Franklin Field, Eddie attended West Philadelphia High School and the University of Pennsylvania and played four years with the Eagles. He and teammate Bobby Evans were the first African Americans to play football at Penn. In addition to his football accomplishments, Eddie was also an outstanding sprinter and a member of the junior and senior honor societies.

Eddie's wife Barbara was also a trailblazer. She was the first African American to graduate from the Pennsylvania Hospital School of Nursing. It was while Eddie was at Penn and Barbara was in nursing school that they began a romance that lasted 54 years, until her death in 2005.

Although Eddie was a homegrown talent, his years with the Eagles were not easy. The effects of the team's mismanagement were exacerbated in his case by an unwritten code that allowed black players to play only certain positions. Best suited to play linebacker—a position he later excelled at—Eddie instead played cornerback with the Eagles. Still, he made the most of his opportunity, as he was in the starting lineup for four years until a knee injury brought his stint in Philadelphia to an untimely end.

Year	Team	League	Games	Interceptions	Kickoff Yards	Kickoff Returns	Yards	TDs
1953	Military service							
1954	Military service							
1955	Eagles	NFL	12	1	30	0	0	0
1956	Eagles	NFL	12	4	61	0	0	1
1957	Eagles	NFL	12	2	38	1	7	0
1958	Eagles	NFL	12	2	33	0	0	0
1959	Played in Canada							
1960	NY Titans	AFL	14	2	20	0	0	0

After one highly successful season with the Hamilton Tiger-Cats in the Canadian League, Eddie played with the New York Titans (forerunners of the Jets) as an American Football League original in 1960. Because of his experience and defensive acumen, Eddie served as an unofficial assistant to the defensive coach. Again he ran up against a wall of prejudice, as there were no African American coaches in the pros then, and no coaching offers were forthcoming when he decided to retire at the end of the season. That season was also marked by tragedy as Eddie's roommate Howard Glenn, a talented rookie offensive guard, suffered head and neck injuries in a game in Houston and died shortly afterward.

After football Eddie went on to a successful career in marketing and advertising. Along the way he met Joe Louis and befriended Jesse Owens, two of his heroes from boyhood. Through business he also met Jackie Robinson and forged relationships with such outstanding black athletes as Marion Motley, Emlen Tunnell, Rosey Brown, Rosie Grier, and Joe Black. Eddie also remains close friends with many of his teammates from Penn and from the Eagles. He is retired and still lives in Philadelphia.

I grew up in West Philadelphia about six blocks from Franklin Field and the University of Pennsylvania. In fact, my elementary school, Newton Elementary School, was right on the campus of the University of Pennsylvania. That was at 38th and Spruce Street and Franklin Field is at 34th and Spruce.

My mother was from Philadelphia. She graduated from West Philly High School, the same high school I attended. My father was born in Delaware, at least I assume he was born in Delaware. That's where his relatives were. They both belonged to a tennis club, the West Side Racket Club, so they had an interest in sports. I understand that he ran track when he was younger, but in those days you didn't ask too many questions because they didn't tell you.

The house I grew up in, my parents had lived there for a long time. My father got the deed in 1909 so they had been there for a quite a while by the time I was born. I was a late child, the youngest of four. I was born nine years after my sister, who was the second youngest. My father worked at the post office and my mother did days work. They were able to send my two brothers and sister to college in the 1930s during the Depression.

My oldest brother went to Howard University in 1936, my next brother went to Howard in 1938, and my sister went to Freeman Hospital Nursing School in Washington, D.C. in 1940, so I grew up knowing I was going to go to college somewhere, and not just because of football. Both of my brothers played sports. One brother was very good at track. He won a lot of medals doing high hurdles and he played football at Howard, and my other brother also played football at Howard, so our family had a little sports history.

The street I grew up on was predominately African American, although we did have Caucasians living on the street opposite us. The neighborhood was totally integrated, probably because of its proximity to the university. The schools I went to were mixed. Newton School was about one-third African American and West Philadelphia High School was also integrated—I would guess probably one-third Jewish, one-third Catholic, and one-third African American—so the neighborhood was not totally anything. I still associate with some of my high school friends—African American friends, Jewish friends, and Catholic friends. Every once in awhile we get together for dinner.

There was one minor incident in the neighborhood I remember. I had a little job back in high school at one of the apartment houses about a block away, a totally white apartment house. Two days a week my job was to take the ashes out of the coal burning stoves, which is what we had in those days. There was an incident in that place where a young African American was supposed to have broken into an apartment and the police came to my house to see if I was involved, and my parents got very upset and went down to the police station. They were not neighborhood policemen because the neighborhood policemen knew everybody and we never had any problem with them. But these policemen who came to the house were not the policemen that patrolled our neighborhood. One of our former neighbors from across the street who had moved was a well-known judge at the time, so my mother went down there and straightened that issue out real quick. The police never bothered me again.

Another thing I remember is when we went to Washington to visit my brothers and sister at college, there was always a segregated stop in Wilmington, Delaware where we got our sandwiches. When the Greyhound bus stopped at the rest stop my parents wouldn't let me off the bus. They went to get the food and they had to go to a segregated section to get the food, and when they came back we ate our sandwiches right on the bus. I think it was something they just didn't want me to be exposed to.

When I was still fairly young, I knew through the newspapers that there were lynchings and all of those things going on in the South. But not having those kind of experiences growing up, it came as kind of a shock in many ways when I ran up against discrimination. It wasn't until I was in high school that I discovered that people just might not let you play on a sports team because you were black. I found that out I guess as I got into my later teens.

I found out later my parents were aware of a lot of things we couldn't do even in Philadelphia, but I was never in a situation where I experienced it as a boy growing up. For example, there were places in downtown Philadelphia you couldn't go because you weren't welcome. Actually, I guess I started finding out more of that when I began dating Barbara, the girl that became my wife. She was a student nurse at Pennsylvania Hospital, the hospital at 8th and Spruce in Philadelphia where I was born. She was the first African American graduate from the nursing school there.

One time when I picked her up to go out, we went to a little restaurant not too far away in downtown Philadelphia and they wouldn't let us in. This was I guess in 1952. It was then that I realized that this kind of thing happened right in your own hometown and that it was not unusual. I guess I was fortunate at not having run into it much before that, those kinds of experiences.

Barbara knew a lot more about segregation than I did because she grew up in an absolutely segregated society in New Orleans before she moved up here. After I met her I was more aware of those things that did happen or could have happened from her perspective, although I did not have that many personal experiences. It was really through her I knew a lot about segregation, although as I got older and branched out of the neighborhood I grew up in, these things were not foreign to me. Barbara was quite a lady. As I said, she was the first African American to graduate from the nursing school at Pennsylvania Hospital. We were together from 1951 when I first met her until she passed away in November 2005.

As kids, we were never that interested in baseball or basketball because we didn't have the facilities for it. There was no basketball court in our area anywhere within walking distance and there was no baseball field for miles, so we were never that interested. We played wall ball and handball and touch football in the street. That was our play area because in those days there weren't that many cars.

Even though we didn't play much baseball, we were interested in the Negro Leagues. My father used to take me to the games at Fairmont Park at 44th and Parkside, one of the largest parks in the city. It was just a trolley ride away and he used to take me on occasion to see the Negro baseball teams played there. I think they played at Shibe Park too, but they had to fit it in because both the Phillies and the A's played in Shibe Park. But Shibe Park was too far away anyway.

I went to West Philly High School in 1945 and ran track and played football and also was a reporter on the school paper. My ambition was to be a doctor so my father had me take all the academic courses including Latin and those kinds of things, and I made the all-scholastic football team my senior year in 1948–49. I was primarily interested in track in high school. I ran the sprints—the 50, the 100, and the 220—plus I usually led off all the relay teams. When I was in high school, we'd go to watch the Penn relays, which was a big event held every year right on the Penn campus, and track was my favorite even though I was better at football. We knew about Penn football but we didn't really follow it and I think it was just because there were no black players, no role models there.

There was hardly any interest among people in professional football, less I think among blacks. We followed Joe Louis and Jesse Owens. I mean everything they did was big. They were our idols—mine anyway. When Joe Louis fought, that was one time we could stay up late, to listen to the fights. And when he won we ran out into the streets and cheered. I also remember when I first heard about Jackie Robinson going up to the Dodgers. I was in high school and we were practicing—I think it was spring practice or something like that—and somebody came in and said Jackie Robinson had made pro baseball. At that time I had absolutely no interest in pro baseball. That was their sport, not ours.

As soon as Jackie went up, black people in Philadelphia became Dodgers fans. My parents listened to the games on the radio when the Phillies played the Dodgers and on those days it was like a holiday. And it was really big when Roy Campanella went up because he was from Philadelphia. I was fortunate enough to meet Jackie one time later in life. A friend of mine knew him well and we were able to go to his house in New York, I think it was in New Rochelle. It was a great honor to meet him. Jackie Robinson was every African American's hero.

I got to know Joe Black, the pitcher for the Dodgers, later on after he was out of baseball. When he worked for Greyhound he was in marketing and I was in marketing and we got to know each other real, real well. I knew about the Browns, too, with Bill Willis and Marion Motley. I got to meet Marion. He was a good player and a good person. He was big, really, really big, and he could move the line. [Browns coach] Paul Brown was different because he picked his players solely based on their ability to play. That's my impression anyway. If you were black and you could play, Paul Brown had a spot on the team for you.

I went to Howard for a semester when I got out of high school. We had a trimester program in high school, so we had a January graduation and a June graduation. I graduated in 1949 in January and I was interested in going to Howard because my brothers had gone there. I got scholarship offers from almost all of the black colleges that were within reasonable distance, say, in North Carolina, Virginia, and places like that and from some of the schools on the West Coast like Oregon and Oregon State. I got a lot of letters from a lot of places but I just didn't have the interest. I wanted to be a doctor and go to Howard and I went there early in 1949 and ran on the track team, and while I was at Howard the University of Pennsylvania contacted my parents and said they had been trying to reach me. They were interested in my coming there and I approached the people at Howard because Penn was offering me a scholarship, while at Howard I was paying my own way.

I asked the athletic director at Howard if they would pay my tuition because I had the credentials as an athlete. They said they would probably help me some, but they couldn't pay the tuition. My parents said if I wanted to transfer it was fine with them so I transferred to Penn in September of 1949. I ran track and played freshman football and then I made the varsity football team as a sophomore. I made honorable mention All-American in my junior year in 1951 and first team All-American in my senior year.

At the University of Pennsylvania, by the way, I was among the first two black athletes to play football. There had been no others before they called and asked me to come there. The other young man was Bobby Evans. He was a high school All-American from Philadelphia and they had recruited him heavily. Everybody in the city knew about him. I always told Bobby that Penn recruited me because they wanted me to be his roommate—it was a running joke between us. He was a tremendous athlete and a tremendous person, too.

Bobby ended up having a major, major knee injury, so even though he played four years he was very limited. He and I were members of the junior honor society and he was elected head of the Sphinx senior honor society by the student body and I was elected as a member. I ran track at Penn, too. We ran in the Penn relays and we had the honor one year of being the champs in the sprint medley. I got a plaque for starting on that team and I got inducted into the Sports Hall of Fame at the university.

I don't remember ever having any kind of incidents during high school, although there were some overtones, and we only had one incident in college that I remember. We played the University of Maryland in a scrimmage and we went down there the night before. I went with about three or four of my white teammates to get hamburgers at a little place off the campus of the University of Maryland and they refused to serve me. This was in 1950 or 1951 and all of us just left, you know, they just all dropped their food and we all left and that was it.

We played Southern teams—we played Georgia, we played William and Mary, we played Virginia, but they all came to Franklin Field. We had heard, and I don't know if it's true or not, that when Georgia signed up to play us and they heard there were black players on the team that there was some kind of resistance in Georgia, but I don't know if that was a fact or not. Their schedules in the South were totally segregated but when they came up to Franklin Field they were playing in front of anywhere from 60,000 to 80,000 people. That was a financial incentive for them I am sure.

I think at that point Franklin Field had either the third or fourth largest capacity among college football stadiums. They could put temporary stands up and seat 80,000 people, which in the 1950s was a big number.

Penn was a powerhouse in those days. We played teams from all over the country. We played California, we played Notre Dame, we played Army and Navy, and they both had powerful teams in those days. They always came to Franklin Field to play us. We played a tough schedule, and we had winning seasons. The bulk of our schedule was Ivy Leagues teams—Princeton, Columbia, Cornell, Dartmouth—but we were playing these other major teams when none of the other Ivy teams were doing that.

Things changed, though, because the Penn administration and the other Ivy League schools decided to have less emphasis on football. Harold Stassen was the president of the school and he wanted Penn to go big-time in football. You may know his name because he ran for president of the United States a number of times. But then they instituted what was called a "victory with honor" system, which meant we would not be emphasizing football.

One thing they did was they eliminated spring practice so we went into a national or semi-national schedule with no spring practice, and of course that affected our win-loss record, although we did tie Notre Dame in 1952 when they had [Johnny] Lattner and [Ralph] Guglielmi and those guys. We went out to Berkeley in 1951 to play California, the California team that made it to the Rose Bowl, and they beat us by only 14–7 and they never scored an offensive touchdown. I guess we didn't have fantastic records but we stopped Princeton's two-year unbeaten streak when they had [1951 Heisman Trophy winner] Dick Kazmaier and Frank McPhee and those guys—the names might not mean much to people now but they were big names then.

We didn't have many road games because everybody wanted to come to Franklin Field because of the seating capacity. I think one year we played only one game on the road and eight at home. And then most of the road games we played were short trips like to Columbia or Princeton, except for one game each year where we'd make a long trip to another part of the country. There was the game at Cal and another year we played at Wisconsin when Alan Ameche was one of their star players.

That Notre Dame game in 1952 was probably the biggest game we played in my three years. It was the first game of the year and they were nationally ranked. It was also the first year we were playing without spring practice so everybody expected us to get clobbered and we ended up tying them, 7–7. I caught the tying touchdown pass of 70 yards and then I knocked the ball out of Lattner's hands when they were driving to try and win the game and I recovered the fumble. That stopped their drive, so that was a big thing. And it was one of the few times we were on television because Notre Dame was involved—they had national television coverage. That was a big game.

Our coaching staff was very unique. We had a guy named George Munger as our head coach and he'd been coaching there a long time. He was a very exceptional person. Most of us who played for him still call ourselves "Munger Men" because he was a big influence on all the players. His attitude was, "Always do your best and everything else will take care of itself." We never were win-hungry, but even with the de-emphasis on football there was a lot of pressure—outside pressure, to win, win, win at all costs. We did our damnedest to win, and we won a lot of games and we very seldom got blown out. When they came to play Penn, they had to come prepared. We were, quote, Ivy Leaguers, so we went along with the rules but there was a lot of outside pressure to win.

I averaged 58 minutes a game, something like that. I was an offensive and defensive end in college and my position in the NFL should have been linebacker, but they made me a cornerback in the pros because they did not have any black linebackers or centers or guards or quarterbacks in the NFL during those days. They were the so-called thinking positions and they limited them to whites. I think Emlen Tunnell was the only one they allowed to play safety because that was another mental position. If you played in the defensive backfield, you had to be a corner. Cornerback was somewhat similar to what I played in college because we played a six-man line and a lot of the responsibility of the end was the same as a cornerback. Sometimes you took the first man out of the backfield or you rushed the passer or you closed down for the off tackles or stretched out the end runs, but definitely my best position would have been linebacker.

That's why I say Paul Brown was different. He played African Americans at the positions they played best. Horace Gillom was the first black punter and Motley not only played fullback, they put him at linebacker on the goal line. The Browns also had Harold Bradley and he was either the first or one of the first to play guard. Harold's an interesting person. He was here one year with the Eagles. He moved to Italy to be an artist and I haven't heard from him in decades. He was always interested in art and painting even in those days. I guess he's kind of a Renaissance man.

I ended up majoring in international relations at Penn. The weight of the football schedule just made it too difficult for me to maintain the level I needed to get into med school. I was taking qualitative analysis, chemistry, solid geometry, and trigonometry, and all those courses and my grade level was not medical school level so I changed it to international relations.

I enjoyed my years at Penn. The only thing I regret is I didn't live on campus because being that I lived only four or five blocks away, it didn't make sense to live in the dorms. I think that limited to some degree the amount of contacts I made. But most of the guys I played ball with or ran track with who live in the area have become lifelong friends. It's almost 60 years and I guess that's lifelong. We're in contact with each other and we still get together, the ones in the Philadelphia area. We have a Munger reunion for all the people that played for George. It was a good experience. My brothers are both graduates of the University of Pennsylvania Law School so I have those ties, too.

In those days, the NFL teams sent out questionnaires to college seniors about their interest in playing pro ball and that's when I first heard from the Eagles. [Steelers owner] Art Rooney called and asked if I was interested in coming to Pittsburgh, but I told him I'd rather stay home and play in Philadelphia. This is where everything was for me, including my girlfriend, and I wanted to stay here.

In the meantime, the Korean War was going on, and I was in the New Jersey National Guard. They activated some of us after I graduated and I spent two years to the day in the service after college. They sent me to missile school in Fort Monmouth and I played football, but I also learned computers and electronics and all that kind of stuff. They had a lot of players that had college experience and some with professional experience and they put a team together. We played Army teams around the country and I made All-Army that year.

The computers of that era took up a whole room. I mean literally. Now you can put everything they did in that whole room, all the data, on the tip of your fingernail. They were power circuits and they were just massive and slow but that's how it was. Sometimes I wish I could have stayed in computers, but I didn't have that kind of foresight.

After a year at Fort Monmouth, I went to Fort Mead when they were putting the missiles up around Washington, D.C. I worked with Western Electric engineers putting up the radar and mission control systems, ground-to-air missiles, things like that. Fort Mead had a football team, but it was not well organized and they did not have any medical facilities, which is the reason I didn't play that year. If you got hurt you had to go into Washington, D.C. to Walter Reed, so I decided I wasn't going to play and risk ending my chances with the Eagles because of an injury.

I was never more than a hundred miles from Philadelphia while I was in the service. My training was in the Aberdeen training grounds in Maryland, about an hour and a half by car from my house. I went to Fort Monmouth for my missile training and that's about an hour and a half from my house, and I was stationed at Fort Mead in Maryland, which was about an hour and forty-five minutes from my house. We had every weekend off so I was home a great deal.

When I got home after I was discharged in 1955, I spent most of my time working out trying to get into shape. I was never really out of shape a great deal, but I worked out and ran to build up my wind because it wasn't long before I had to go to the Eagle camp. And I was in the starting lineup by the first exhibition game.

The guys in the NFL were big. I remember while I was in Fort Mead the year before, the Eagles asked me if I wanted to come to a game. I had never seen a pro game so one weekend when I was home I went to see the Eagles play at Shibe Park and they invited me to the dressing room. A lot of the guys were big, and not just big but tall, especially the linemen. When I say tall I mean right around 6'3", 6'4". That made an impression on me.

It never occurred to me that if I wanted to play pro football that I wouldn't be able to. I just had kind of a confidence every time, you know, when I went out for a team that I'd make it. I just thought I could make any team. It didn't seem like an impossible task, I'll just put it that way. If you practice and you do what you're supposed to do and you have the ability you should be able to make it.

There were only two other African Americans on the Eagles that year, Ralph Goldston and George Taliaferro, and George didn't even last the whole year. I think they waived him during the season. George is a fantastic person. George came into town a few years ago, and we had a chance to really get together after so many years. Then my second year with the Eagles, 1956, I was the only African American on the team.

Ralph Goldston's from Youngstown, Ohio and he had been with the Eagles about three years. After he left the Eagles he played in Canada, where he lived for many years, then he came back and became an NFL scout. I talked to him a few years ago. He's living in Columbus, Ohio and I understand he's not doing too well. We played together in Hamilton in 1959 and later on he became a coach at Montreal. When I came up he was very, very helpful.

I started every game and I played special teams my whole four years with the Eagles. Around my third or fourth year, they finally came of age when it came to their attitude about black players, and we got Harold Bradley from the Browns and we got Proverb Jacobs. We also drafted Clarence Peaks out of Michigan State and Clarence became my roommate. In 1957 it was just the two of us. In 1958, my last year, there were four African Americans, all starters. I would say that 97 percent of the African Americans in the NFL were starters. You had none on the bench; if you didn't start you weren't on the team.

I didn't have any problems with any of the whites on the Eagles. A lot of them were from the South, but I did not have any problems. It helped that I was in Philadelphia because I was home with my support system. It's not like I was out of town. I don't know what it would've been like if I had been out of town.

I had some friends among the white players like Tom Scott, who went to Virginia. I had played against him in college and he was the linebacker on my side with the Eagles and we were neighbors. We lived in Abington about six, seven blocks from each other. Several other players also lived in Abington, like Chuck Bednarik. And then when Buck Shaw became our head coach, he lived in Abington. On Sundays we'd carpool to games, but during the week we took our individual cars to practice because we had jobs we went to afterwards. I worked full-time right up until before the season started and then almost full-time during the season because the teams weren't paying you any money.

Bednarik was not a help to me even though he went to Penn, too. When I went to the Eagle camps, guys like Tom Scott and Wayne Robinson, the guys who played on the same side as I did, all those guys were a lot more help to me than Chuck ever was. Quite frankly, we don't see Chuck at Penn reunions and you very seldom see him at any Eagles thing. Pete Pihos was a fine person. Pete helped me a great deal. He was an offensive end, almost like the forerunner of the tight end. He would run little curls and those little short patterns. When the ball came to him you couldn't get through him to get to the ball because Pete was very muscular. Not that tall but very strong. Pete Retzlaff was a very good friend of mine. Still is. He's the one that really was one of the early guys that was a tight end. He and [John] Mackey made the tight end position what it is today. He's still around Philadelphia and I still see him around every now and then. He and [Tom] Brookshier and myself and a number of guys from the Eagles have maintained friendships.

When we went to Washington, D.C. to play the Redskins, the Redskins at that time were the only NFL team without an African American player, and that's the only time I ever heard anything coming from the stands. You'd hear the n-word, but it wasn't any kind of massive demonstration of racism where a whole group would holler or something like that. You might hear a smattering here or there—from the stands, not from other players.

The other thing about the Redskins is that their band would come onto the field playing Dixie, and although the uniforms the band wore were the Redskin colors rather than white, they were just like the Klan uniforms with the big hooded cap and everything like that. I don't know if you can get pictures of the old Redskin band, but they had the pointed hats like the Klan and they'd march on the field playing Dixie. [Redskin owner] George Preston Marshall's team of the South.

When we went south to play an exhibition game it was always a segregated situation. You stayed at different hotels. The damnedest thing was, you'd have the meetings at the white hotels and have your lunch and stuff there, but you couldn't sleep there at night. In hindsight I am sure they scheduled those exhibition games into the major cities in the South because they were trying to increase interest in the NFL.

Our Eagles' teams weren't that good. We had three coaches in four years and the organization was not together at all. There was a lot of tension on the team between Jim Trimble [Philadelphia's head coach from 1952–1955] and some of the older players who had played for Greasy Neale [the head coach until 1951]. When Trimble came in he was a very young guy, not much older than some of the older players on the team, and some of those players really resented him and they had more influence with the owners and they ended up getting rid of him.

The management of the team was not that good and Trimble was a talented coach. As soon as he was fired by the Eagles, he went up to Canada to Hamilton and turned them into a championship team. They won the Grey Cup at least once and he was always a contender up there and it came from his coaching. It's absolutely my opinion that if the Eagles had allowed Trimble time to implement his own system they would have been better off.

We had one coach, Hugh Devore, who had no professional experience at all. He came out of Notre Dame. Buck Shaw, when he came, he brought a whole new system from the West Coast. Eventually they were successful with Shaw, but not while I was there. And we had a lot of good football players, too. Tommy McDonald came in '57. Clarence Peaks was number two in the country in college and in the NFL to Jim Brown as far as running backs were concerned, and they made him a blocking back. Instead of using his running talents he had to stay in and protect the quarterback and block for the other runners, and it made him bitter and rightfully so because he was the premier back in the league after Jim Brown.

I got blindsided about the ninth game [in 1958] and my knee went. In those days if you got hurt and you were black you figured your days were over with that team, and that's the way it turned out. I knew right away that if my knee didn't heal—and it didn't heal right away—that would be the end of it. They put me on waivers right after the season was over, and I got a call from Cleveland. One of their offensive coordinators had been a coach of mine in college and he wanted to know if I wanted to come and play offensive end. Then I got the call from the Hamilton Tiger-Cats, Trimble and Ralph and those guys, and they convinced me to come up there and play.

Ralph and I had been friends when he was with the Eagles and he was an All-Pro in Hamilton. The Eagles got rid of him because they thought he was too small, but he wasn't any smaller than a couple of other guys we had at running back. It was not a coach's decision, it had more to do with management because Trimble liked him and he got him back as soon as he went to Canada.

I chose to go to Hamilton and play for the Hamilton Tiger-Cats instead of the Browns because I knew I would play linebacker, which was my best position. And I did, I played linebacker for Hamilton and I made the all-star team even with a bad knee. We went to the Grey Cup, but we lost to Winnipeg. I have some very pleasant memories of Hamilton and the people up there. We made some lifelong friends even though I only played there one season.

I ended up with the New York Titans [forerunners of the New York Jets] because a guy I knew from Penn named Steve Sebo was involved with them. He asked me if I was interested, so I played the first year of the AFL in 1960 for Sammy Baugh. Sammy was the head coach and he was a fantastic person. I played linebacker, but because of my knee I had to play strong side linebacker with no pass coverage. I played with a lot of pain that year because I got hit in that same knee and re-injured it in Hamilton the year before.

The situation with Howard Glenn was just shocking. We knew it was a pretty serious injury when they took him off the field, but you never think somebody is going to die. He was a rookie and there still weren't that many blacks in pro ball in 1960 and we had to stay apart from the team when we went to Texas, so Howard and I ended up as roommates. It was our first road trip of the year and we had just started to get to know each other a little bit. We had back-to-back games scheduled in Texas, first in Dallas and the next week in Houston. In Dallas, the black players stayed at a hotel in Grand Prairie outside of Dallas, and in Houston we stayed on the campus of Texas Southern University. Howard suffered a head and neck injury in the game in Houston and it was after the game that we found out he had succumbed. He was in the hospital but we never got any details about it, not much more than what was in the newspapers. It was depressing.

The Titans also had me doing some evaluation. I had a 16 millimeter projector and they would give me films to take home and make suggestions and things like that. I used to bring reels of film home and break down some of the things for them. It might have been a form of coaching, I don't know, but they didn't really have African American coaches in those days. But I was doing a little coaching for the defensive coach, although they didn't call me a coach or a player-coach, and they didn't pay me for it.

It's special that I was there in the AFL in the beginning of something that really grew and grew and grew and grew to the point where the NFL had to recognize and combine with them. After I retired, the AFL hired a lot of us during draft time to get some of the draft choices and hide them on draft day. I had a young man from Virginia, a defensive back, and I went down to meet his family a couple of times. I brought him to New York and got him a hotel so that no NFL scouts who might want to talk to him could find him. He ended up not being drafted, but that was the kind of thing that was happening before the two leagues decided to merge instead of fight.

The Atlantic Oil Refining Company was headquartered here in Philadelphia and I worked with them in the marketing department. They were just starting minority marketing, trying to market to the African American communities because they kind of ignored it for years. I worked with them when they merged with Richfield and became the Atlantic Richfield Company, and the headquarters was in Los Angeles. I transferred to Los Angeles and worked for corporate headquarters out there for a long time until we had a personal tragedy. My son of 16 died practicing basketball from a heart attack, so we eventually had to get out of Los Angeles because it was too depressing for my wife and I.

I got to know Jesse Owens very well and I got to personally meet and spend time with Joe Louis. One of the things I did was develop programs for kids and I developed a Jesse Owens track program which ran in 16 major cities. I worked with Jesse and got to be a very personal friend of his to the point where I had the honor of being the pallbearer at both his funerals—one in Phoenix and one in Chicago. I spent time with him at his home in Arizona and his home in Chicago and his summer home in Benton Harbor, Michigan. We spent most of our summers together traveling around the country so I got to know him on a very, very personal basis.

Jesse was a fantastic person. A fantastic person. He had had so many bad experiences, but he never let it make him bitter, which is amazing. I got to know him and his wife, Ruth, and his family. In fact, I used to stay with him when I went to Arizona—he called me his other son. He always had time to talk with people. That's why he was such a popular person and he did well with the kids even though they weren't that familiar with his history, except every four years when the Olympics came up he was reborn.

I was with him when he was featured in the movie *The Return to Berlin*. In fact, I went with him in '72 to the Olympics when the German government honored him. The purpose of it was to make amends to Jesse for the treatment he had received in 1936, which they had discussed with him, so he was well aware that that was the purpose. I stayed with Jesse where the German government had all their honored guests. They gave us a little room in the corner.

I was there when the Palestinians came into the Olympic Village. We didn't know what was really happening until we got the European edition of the *New York Herald Tribune* because it was a complete blackout on television and radio. Then the next day we knew the extent of it when we got the news from the United States. I had been in the Olympic Village the day before, but I didn't go the next day because it was surrounded.

They have a museum for Jesse in Alabama, which is where he's from. They have taken the area where he grew up and turned it into a museum and a park. They reproduced his house and the museum has a bunch of his stuff. It's near Huntsville and I've been there several times to see it. It's an interesting place.

I also had a chance to spend some time with Joe Louis. He had a group of friends who worked for Ballantine Brewery and they were on a promotional tour here in Philadelphia and Joe was part of the tour. I knew most of them because I was in marketing with the oil company, and when they brought him to town I got to meet him and talk to him.

After working with the oil company, I worked for the United Negro College Fund. I headed up one of their major fundraising campaigns, a $60,000,000 capital improvement program for the black colleges. When the campaign was over I went to work for an advertising agency in Baltimore. The U.S. Military Academy at West Point had asked for a marketing plan on how to get more African American recruits and that was my assignment, and I put the presentation together. The day I was supposed to make the presentation was the day the hostages came back [from Iran in 1980]. My wife and I were in the car, we were driving from Philly to West Point around five in the morning, and we heard it on the news. When I got there, of course, my presentation was postponed.

When they were getting ready to set up the lottery in Washington, D.C., they asked if I would help set up the marketing plan. Scientific Games was the biggest producer of instant tickets in the country—maybe the world—and they put a team together and I was on the team that made the proposal. Then I worked on the marketing plan for the lottery, and I worked in the marketing department for the DC Lottery. The advertising agency that I worked for, Bell and Associates, did the advertising for the DC Lottery for a couple of years. Then I moved from there to the Pennsylvania Lottery and worked as director of marketing for ten years before I retired.

Most places I worked, I didn't move my family. My wife would come down or I would come down, and I traveled a great deal. I commuted to New York a great deal when I was with the College Fund. I had a bout with leukemia when I was in my 60s, and I was in the hospital for 36 weeks taking a special treatment that was put together by Memorial Sloan-Kettering Hospital in New York. I didn't want to go to New York, so I stayed in the hospital down here where they worked on my treatment. I'm in remission from that about ten or twelve years now. I had kidney failure, so I had a kidney transplant in 2003. I also got the knee I hurt when I was playing replaced. The other one needs to be replaced, but I can't get it replaced with the kidney. If I get an infection, they can't fight it because I'm on all these anti-rejection drugs that would reject any kind of foreign substance in my body. So I walk with a limp, among other things.

I got to know guys like Erich Barnes and Rosie Grier and Rosey Brown and those guys pretty much after our football careers. And Emlen Tunnell was from this area, from the suburbs here, so I got to know him fairly well. It was not that easy to get to know the African American players from other teams when we were playing because we'd go in on Saturday and come back on Sunday, and you never really got a chance to socialize with them. I've been active in Penn alumni stuff for years, even the years when I was out of town. It was a special time for those of us that played for George Munger. I'm involved some with the Eagles alumni and the NFL Alumni Association. We have our meetings at the Eagles facility. But most of my involvement is with the retired players division of the NFL.

Now of course the Eagles have Lincoln Field. They played for a time at the Municipal Stadium, they went to Shibe Park, to Franklin Field, and then they got their first stadium [Veterans Stadium], and then they built this one. Franklin Field is a traditional college stadium, the open end on it with the track on the inside. They had to modernize it, of course, when the Eagles came there, both the stadium and the training facility, because the Eagles were a lot more sophisticated than what Penn had.

I played all my football at home until 1959—high school, college, professionally—so my support system was here. I guess it was different for a person that would come in from out of town. I had my whole family here—elementary school friends, high school friends, college friends, personal friends. I had my family's history here before me, so there were not those kinds of racial things except the incidents I talked about. If I had gone somewhere else I might have run into those kinds of things.

I was in New Orleans a few years ago for a wedding of one of my wife's relatives. All of her close friends and family are gone or have left the town, and all of the things that she knew, except for her house, which is around Tulane University, were destroyed by the hurricane [Katrina]. It was a depressing trip, other than the wedding. I'm still trying to get over her being gone. Barbara Bell, my baby.

HENRY FORD

Henry Ford
Born November 1, 1931, in Homestead, Pennsylvania

Schenley High School in Pittsburgh, Pennsylvania
University of Pittsburgh

Running back
Drafted in 9th round by Cleveland Browns in 1955

Football was Henry Ford's ticket out of poverty. He grew up in one of Pittsburgh's poorest neighborhoods with a commode in a rat-infested basement that was the family's only bathroom. He never knew his father and met him only briefly on one occasion when he was 22.

Henry was an excellent athlete in his youth. Ultimately that ability is what made a university education possible. He was also an outstanding student and his intelligence made several highly successful postfootball careers possible. He was offered numerous college scholarships because of the former and none because of the latter.

Interracial relationships between men and women were a touchy subject in the 1950s, especially if the man was black and the woman wasn't. Henry met a Syrian woman named Rochelle when he was 18 and fell in love. Six decades later, the two are still in love. Henry believes that his relationship with Rochelle brought a premature end to his football career, that he was blacklisted from the NFL because of it. The fact that he was playing the best football of his life in the days leading up to his release lends credence to his claim.

Remember that it was a time when Rosa Parks was arrested for sitting in the front of a bus. It was a time when a black teenager named Emmett Till was brutally murdered because a white man

Year	Team	League	Games	Rushing				Receiving			
				Attempts	Yards	Avg.	TDs	Receptions	Yards	Avg.	TDs
1955	Browns	NFL	2	2	1	0.5	0	—	—	—	—
1956	Steelers	NFL	12	12	26	2.2	2	3	7	2.3	0

Year	Kickoff Returns				Punt Returns			
	Returns	Yards	Avg.	TDs	Returns	Yards	Avg.	TDs
1955	—	—	—	—	4	15	3.8	0
1956	6	135	22.5	0	25	145	5.8	0

Also intercepted one pass for 17 yards

heard him whistle at a white woman. Is losing a job and a career one loves and is very good at the same as a lynching? No, but racism can corrode as surely as it can kill. It undoubtedly had a corrosive affect on Henry, how much only he may know. But he kept going and, as the saying goes, he got stronger.

In the years after his playing career hit a white wall, Henry nurtured dreams of becoming a coach. A tremendous leader as a player, it seemed a natural way to join his intelligence and football background. But here the white wall was even thicker, higher, more difficult to penetrate.

He worked as a high school assistant with the hope that he would succeed the head coach, who was a year from retiring. Passed over, he quit. He was offered an assistant's job by his alma mater, the University of Pittsburgh, and was all set to move back to his hometown from Washington, D.C. Then, Henry says, a job slated to pay $16,000 or more was turned into two jobs paying half as much. He didn't take it.

Henry finally became a head coach in the 1980s. It was no longer a career move but something he did because he saw glimmers of himself as a kid in the faces of the boys at Menlo Atherton High School. Fans were scarce at the school's games, college recruiters nonexistent. Drug dealers, on the other hand, were abundant. That changed when Henry became coach.

Menlo Atherton became a championship football team. Their story—"a melting pot of Hispanics, Samoans, Tongans, blacks, whites, and Asians"— has been told by Dianne De Laet, daughter of Y. A. Tittle, whose son played for Henry at Menlo Atherton. Henry can tell you exactly how many of his players went to college on athletic scholarships—34. When he talks, one gets the distinct feeling he is as proud of his seven years as a high school coach as he is of anything he has done.

Henry and Rochelle live in Palo Alto, California.

I was born in Homestead, Pennsylvania in 1931 in an all-black community near the Homestead Steel Mill. The majority of the people in that area were on welfare. We lived in an apartment building that housed five families—my mother, my three sisters, and I. There were two bedrooms and a toilet downstairs in a dirt cellar. One morning when I was five years old, I woke up to the sound of men tearing the roof off the building. The house had been sold and was being torn down by the new owner.

We moved to Pittsburgh with another family, the Snyders. Mrs. Snyder had 14 kids and we moved to a two-bedroom house on Orbin Street right off Wylie Avenue in the Hill District in the ghetto. That's how we lived, 20 of us in a house with two bedrooms and a commode in the basement. Mrs. Snyder and her children shared one bedroom and we shared the other. There was no bathroom and no hot running water. Everyone was afraid to go down to the basement to use the commode because of the rats, so we used a slop bucket upstairs.

The heat was coal fueled in a stove in the kitchen. The cooking was done on that same stove, which we also used to heat water for our weekly baths in a tin tub. There was a fireplace in the living room and in each of the bedrooms that provided heat. Nowadays if you have a fireplace in your bedroom it means you're well off, but it didn't mean that then. The icebox in the kitchen held a block of ice and that's how we kept our food cold. All of the children in the neighborhood were on relief and we all wore the same kind of clothes—knickers and brogan shoes. The welfare department provided us with coupons that we used to buy food and clothing.

A few years after we moved to Pittsburgh, we moved to a house next door at 2843 Orbin Street, where we were the only occupants. My sisters and mother used the two bedrooms and I slept on the sofa in the living room. It was the same set-up as the other house, with a commode in the cellar and the cellar full of rats. Everything on Orbin Street was torn down a few years later and nothing has ever been rebuilt in that part of town.

My mother supported us by working as a domestic. She used to commute every day on the streetcar from the Hill District to the Squirrel Hill section of Pittsburgh. Squirrel Hill was an upper middle class white neighborhood. I'll never forget, one day she took me to work with her, and I went into that house and I saw things I had never seen before—a beautiful marble floor, a crystal chandelier, a curved staircase. I don't know where it came from, but I told my mother, "I'm going to buy you a house like this some day."

I didn't have a father growing up, never even saw my father until I was an adult and then only once for about 15 minutes. Whenever I used to ask my mother about him, she resisted ever talking about him. Then one day when I was 22 years old, my sister told me I could find my father in the neighborhood poolroom. She told me to ask for Henry Williams.

It was strange because he was a small man who didn't look like me. I didn't have anything to say to him, really, and I didn't know what to say. He didn't ask me any questions about myself and I thought for a moment that he might ask me for money. But he didn't. All he said was, "I've been following you." You know, following me play football. Then I left. I had met a stranger and all I did was shake his hand and leave.

I went to school in the Hill District and it was difficult when I first started. I was chased over Morgan Hill every day on the way home from school. Then one day I just decided I wasn't going to run anymore. There was this one kid in particular, Harold Brown, and I told Harold, "I'm not running anymore. We can fight right here and now and I'll kick your ass." I never had to run after that day.

Other than Harold Brown and his buddies, I liked school, especially math. I excelled at both academics and sports. I played basketball, softball, and track. Then after school, we played other sports like sandlot football, even boxing. My basketball coach in junior high was Pete Demperio. We were undefeated for three years and I really grew to admire and respect him. You could say we had a father-son relationship. We both considered it to be that. Then right after I graduated Pete left to become the football coach at Westinghouse High School, the number one high school football team in Pittsburgh.

One of the classes I took was a printing class and I printed tickets that my friends and I sold at concerts and dances. I was 14 at the time and two of my running buddies, Jabbo and Lefty, were 18. One day some drug dealers in the neighborhood gave the three of us marijuana to sell at a Dizzy Gillespie concert. We got caught by plainclothes police and taken to jail. While they were fingerprinting me, they realized I was a minor and they took me to juvenile hall, and that's where I stayed overnight.

The next day Pete Demperio came and got me out. He took me to school because he said he wanted to talk to me, except when we got there and entered his office, he didn't say anything, he just put on some boxing gloves and gave a pair to me. Then he started punching me. I blocked as many of them as I could, but he kept punching.

And as he punched, he said, "If you want to be an athlete, you can't mess with that stuff." When I left Pete's office, the other students wanted to know what all the noise was. I never told them and that was the last time I ever touched marijuana.

My counselor in junior high talked me into going to Connelley Vocational High School because she said I would have a trade. I quit after a year and a half and transferred to Schenley High School because I was a good student and I wanted an academic education, plus they had a football team. Connelley didn't. But after I got to Schenley I hurt my knee and couldn't play football so I dropped out.

I got a job as an elevator operator at Joseph DeRoy Jewelers and I started playing for a sandlot football team in Butler, Pennsylvania called the Butler Cubs. We had a game scheduled for a Monday night and I always worked on Monday nights. The manager told me if I didn't work that Monday night, I would be fired. So I played.

The coach of the Cubs was a gentleman named Henry Yandell, an enthusiastic, intelligent black man with a massive amount of football knowledge. I was amazed to see football plays diagrammed on the walls of his house and everywhere else in his house. He was heavily into Clark Shaughnessy and the T-formation. While other guys were out on dates with girls and everything, he had me studying football.

I was 15 and playing quarterback against guys who were 22, good football players who played in high school but didn't have the chance to go to college. We beat everybody. Henry Yandell taught us everything about football. I give him all the credit in the world. And later on, from what I learned from him, I was able to coach my teammates in Spring and Summer practice when I went back to school.

Once I decided to go back to high school, I wanted to go in Butler. The school there offered to help my mother get a job, but she didn't want to move to Butler so I returned to Schenley. I played football in the fall and baseball in the spring and was an outstanding student and athlete. We had a lot of good athletes in the Hill District. I was friends with Josh Gibson Jr., and we played baseball for Schenley and for a sandlot team and both of us were good enough to get invited to a tryout by the New York Giants. I turned them down because I wanted to go to college to further my education and play football.

We used to sneak into Forbes Field to watch Josh's father, Josh Sr., play for the Homestead Grays. He could hit the ball a long way. My friend Bill Nunn's father was a reporter for the Pittsburgh Courier and everyone loved reading that paper because it told stories about the Negro teams. You know, stuff that wasn't in the white papers. Bill's father also wrote a lot of stories about me and I appreciated that, and Bill later went on and became a scout for the Pittsburgh Steelers.

We followed the Grays and the other teams in the Negro Leagues and I remember there was a lot of excitement in Pittsburgh when Jackie Robinson went up to the Dodgers. I would say wherever there were black people there was excitement about that. There were better ballplayers than Jackie in the black leagues like Josh Gibson, but there was no one with the education Jackie had and that's why they went with him. Whenever black players like Roy Campanella and Larry Doby got signed with a major league team, we would keep track of how they were doing. We especially liked hearing about Satchel Paige, who is now recognized by everybody as one of the greatest pitchers in baseball history.

In my senior year at Schenley, we went to training camp for the first time in Ligonier, Pennsylvania, which is about 35 miles outside of Pittsburgh. This is the area where the Mellons and the Scaifes live. Well, in 1950 there were no blacks living in that area at all, and 50 something years later as I'm talking there are still no blacks living there. While we were riding to camp, I saw this beautiful girl standing in the Diamond, which was an area in the center of Ligonier where young people gathered to socialize. I asked the bus driver to stop so I could meet her, but he refused and kept on going. But as soon as I got settled I went back to the Diamond and the beautiful girl was still there. That was the best luck I ever had. She was a beautiful Syrian girl named Rochelle Ann Shamey—very sweet and a little shy.

The funny thing is, at first, I thought she was black. Light-skinned but black. But when I got close to her I could see she wasn't black. At the time I figured she had a tan from being in the sun and I said, "Oops, I'm sorry." She said, "What are you sorry for?" I said, "I thought you were colored." Well things worked out because we've been together ever since. That day began a friendship that lasted nine years and continued on once we got married and we still are after 50 years. I go back to Ligonier now and it's different in a lot of ways, but there are still no blacks living in that town.

I played quarterback at Schenley, and in my senior year we played at Pitt Stadium against Westinghouse, where my mentor Pete Demperio was coaching. Both of us were undefeated and there was a big crowd and it was a close game, very exciting, and we won. After the game I sought out Pete to congratulate him on how well his team had played. Now remember, this guy was the closest thing I ever had to a father, but when I approached him, before I even had a chance to say a word, he spit at me. And then after he spit at me, he turned and walked away and that was the last time I ever saw him.

We ended up undefeated and untied, city champs, beat Westinghouse—the traditional high school powerhouse in Pittsburgh—two of us made high school All-American, and 11 of us went to college on scholarships. I was all-city, all-state, made the Pennsylvania High School All-Star Football team, and played in the state all-star game. I was also the senior class treasurer and played on the sandlot baseball team, the Bobcats, after school—this was when I got invited to try out for the New York Giants. Overall, I have fond memories of my high school days.

Frankly, I had no idea I would even play in college, let alone become a pro football player, because not that many blacks were able to go to college. A lot of schools came around recruiting me, but in the early 1950s hardly any blacks went to white colleges. Most went down South to one of the black colleges. I guess that's one of the reasons I chose Pitt because I wanted to prove to them that I could go to a white school and play. Some of the players from Schenley teased me and said I would never play at Pitt, they would never let me. Most of them went to black schools in the South.

I got a four-year scholarship plus room and board and played four years and never missed a game. At first it was two platoons, so I played just defense: safety and cornerback. I got in some on offense and played running back, which I also did in practice, but mostly I played defense. In my junior year they went to the one-platoon system, and that's when I played quarterback. My first two years I was good enough that I could've played quarterback, but they didn't have black quarterbacks back then. I went to quarter-back meetings for those two years, but I never played quarterback until my junior year when I played six or seven games. For those six or seven games, I was the first black to ever play quarterback at a major university.

They never said I couldn't play quarterback, but they didn't play me there until we lost our first three games my junior year. The newspapers were saying, "They have a quarterback and it's Henry Ford," because some of the sportswriters had seen me play quarterback in high school. Then after I took over they started calling me Model T Ford because I was a T-formation quarterback. We had success after that—I think we won four or five of our remaining games. The next year they went back to two platoons and Red Dawson the coach switched me back to defense. I also played some offense but at running back, not quarterback. I still went to quarterback meetings because they wanted me to be available in case somebody got hurt, but I never played quarterback again. That was one thing that really upset me.

When we went on the road, the black players were separated from the rest of the team. There were times when I was ready to quit school, but instead I decided that I just had to step it up. I tried to figure out how I was going to get through it. It wasn't easy but I did. It was the same thing in the pros. It was even like that after I got out of football. I majored in business administration and they just weren't hiring blacks into marketing and sales jobs in the steel mills or the banks and I couldn't get a job. I went to Duquesne Beer and couldn't get a job. I went to an interview at one company and all we talked about was my playing football with the Cleveland Browns and the Pittsburgh Steelers. It was rough.

Probably the most memorable experience of that type at Pitt was when we went to Florida to play Miami. There were four blacks on the team—me, Bobby Epps, Chester Rice, and Bill Adams. Tom Hamilton, who was the coach then, called the four of us to the back of the plane and started talking about segregation and stuff. He said, "We're going into the South and you know how the South is, so we had to make special arrangements for you boys. You'll be staying at the Lord Calvert Hotel." The coaches and the white players stayed at another hotel and that's where the team meetings were, and we weren't even allowed to go to their hotel for the meetings.

The other players were met by convertibles and taken from the airport through downtown to the stadium by a police escort. The team was going to the stadium to practice and they had a parade, and each of those cars had a beautiful girl and each player rode with a girl in a convertible to the stadium. But the other blacks and I were met by a gentleman named Herb Douglas, a Pitt graduate and an ex-Olympic athlete who was working for Burgmeister Beer in the Miami area. He met us at the airport in a limo and took us to the stadium.

Along the way, we were stopped by a police car so the caravan with the other Pitt players could pass. Then when we got to the stadium and were getting ready for practice in the locker room, some of the other players asked us about the girls in our car. We told them we didn't have any girls and that we weren't in the caravan. It was only then that they realized what was really going on. Afterwards Herb Douglas drove us to the Calvert Hotel.

They put us up in a penthouse, but we had to stay there until the game. We didn't go to the other hotel for the meetings, we didn't eat with the team, we just stayed at our hotel until Friday night. Then after we won the game they had the party at the Calvert so that the whole team could celebrate together.

They gave all of the players tickets for us to give to whoever we knew who came down for the game. They were good tickets, too, right on the 50-yard line, but who were we going to give our tickets to? Blacks weren't allowed to sit on the 50-yard line. So we gave our tickets to some of the white players and asked them to sell them for us, so I guess we made a little bit of money out of the deal anyway.

During the game I had a chance to break the Pitt record for punt return yards, but they weren't kicking to me. I went over and stole a punt from Billy Reynolds and I ran it back 15 yards, which is exactly what I needed to set the record. After the game that night the Pitt coaches even told me I had broken the record, but the next day in the papers they said I missed by one yard. In the game they said I ran it 15 yards, but the next day somehow it became 14, so they said I was one yard short. I just said to myself, "Well, there's another record gone." It was something.

What really bugged me was that the Pitt coaches didn't do anything to dispute the one-yard discrepancy. I figured after they had told me the night before that I broke the record that they would at least try to set things straight. I'm certain that they didn't, though, because if they had they would have said something to me about how they were trying to fix it and they never did. I know I broke that record, and I believe to this day that even though I was their player and they were my coaches, they didn't care one way or another.

It was tough. You're in this competitive situation and you're playing this game where people are knocking each other on their asses, you're trying to play ball up to the highest level you can, and you've got to deal with this other stuff. But they didn't always get away with it. When we played Rice, one of the guys on Rice called Billy Adams a nigger. Well, they penalized the guy 15 yards and then they called us all together and told them that they would kick them out of the game if they called any names like that again.

The year after I graduated, Pitt had a good team and Bob Greer was the first black to play in the Sugar Bowl in New Orleans against Georgia Tech. He was from Massillon High School in Ohio where Paul Brown is from, and they had some powerhouse teams. Pitt got a lot of football players from there. The Georgia Tech fans didn't want Bob to go down there and they were writing letters calling him derogatory names. He called me and asked me what he should do and I told him, "By all means, go and play." It was tough for him, I'm sure, but he played so things changed bit by bit.

We had Billy Reynolds and some other guys from West Virginia and we didn't know about them at first, but we never had any problems with race. We all played together and got along fine. Once we got to know each other, we'd go out together. They were afraid to go to the Hill District, but I took them there for parties and things. I said, "Come on, that's my part of town." We used to have the Letterman's Club and after the Letterman's Club would get together, I used to take them to the Hill District for parties.

The only thing I remember was one day, and I'll never forget it, we were having a very good practice and coach Red Dawson said, "Boys, we had a good practice and I'm giving you the rest of the day off." And then he said, "The last one to the gate is a nigger baby." And boy, everybody including me and the other black players busted off and started running because practice was over and we had the rest of the day off. Plus, I didn't want to be a nigger baby, so I was running with everybody else, and after I got about halfway I said, "Oh no, what did he say?"

I asked the other black players if they heard the same thing I did. I said, "We've got to go see the coach about what he said," and that's what we did. We told him we didn't appreciate him using that word and the next day at practice he apologized in front of the whole team. It was the only time I ever heard him say it but it was there. He said it slipped and he didn't mean it, but it was there, otherwise he wouldn't have said it.

I was in ROTC at Pitt and I went to camp in Richmond, Virginia with 3,500 other Second Lieutenants. Only four of us were black and one evening Chester Rice and I went to the officer's club for a beer. We sat there for an hour and a half and nobody would serve us. Then we asked them for a glass of water and they wouldn't serve us that, either. The next thing we knew, some military police officers came in and escorted us out of the club, telling us that we didn't belong there. The very next day the commanding officer announced that the club was open to everyone. Then at the end of the camp another announcement was made, which was that I had been chosen as the number one officer in the camp.

The coaches at Pitt used to say it was like having a coach on the field when I was out there. Like I said, I learned a lot from Henry Yandell. Do you know I was probably the first safety to ever be called offside? We were playing Minnesota and I was watching the quarterback and moving up, moving up, moving up, moving up, trying to time it just right, but I went a little too early and they called me for offside. It was one of the only times we were on TV, and I run into guys from Pittsburgh who saw the game and they still remind me of the play when I was offside.

After football season my senior year, I was selected to play in the College Senior All-Star Game in Los Angeles. The year before, Pitt sent Billy Reynolds to play in that game, but when I was selected, I wasn't allowed to go. They said I would miss too much school. Now I had taken all of the credits I needed to graduate in the first three and a half years and was using my last semester to take extra courses to expand my education. Pitt knew that, too, but they still said I couldn't go.

I took business administration at Pitt and there weren't any blacks in the program. They wanted me to major in physical education and I told them I knew how to coach but I didn't know too much about business administration, so I'm going to take business administration classes. There was one professor who I thought liked me. It was the only class I had on Friday and I told her I would not be there whenever we had a road game but I would be there for all the tests, and she told me not to worry. Well one time she told me there was no need for me to go to class that day because she already turned in my grade. I said, "What did I get, an A?" And she said, "No, you failed," so I had to take that course over the next year. That was another of life's lessons that I could have done without.

On the field, there were no incidents that I can recall other than the ones I mentioned, either at Pitt or in the pros. Guys would hit you late but I thought it was just football, not race. There weren't that many of us in the NFL when I played and when we would see each other we would get together and talk. I was very good friends with Lowell Perry and he got his pelvis broken. He was an All-American at Michigan, and I played with him with the Steelers and I really can't say it was racial. It was just football.

The Browns drafted me in the ninth round in 1955. I was a Steeler fan, but we looked up to the Browns because they gave blacks the opportunity to play. Paul Brown had a lot to do with that and that influenced other coaches to bring more in. Bill Willis had retired, but they still had more blacks than any other team. They had Harold Bradley at guard and a big tackle named Tom Jones. He was another one who came from Massillon. And they had a few others, too—Lenny Ford. They put him on defense, and he would just charge in there breaking jaws and breaking noses and all. It was something. He was tough.

I got to meet Willis and Marion Motley. Motley was a great guy and he could run that ball. He used to tease me all the time. I remember he called me "son" all the time. He used to say, "Son, you're too young, you can't do this, you can't do that." He would tease me all the time. He was a great guy. He ended up with the Steelers the year before I played for them. I think the first black player on the Steelers was Jack Spinks. He and I were very good friends. He came out of Mississippi and went to Alcorn A&M. I think he went back to Alcorn and became a coach.

It was rough in those days for black players. There were only 15 or 20 of us in the entire league and the number would increase by maybe two or three each year. Most teams didn't have more than two or three and some teams still didn't have any. If they had two, then those two would room together. If they had three, then all three would have to stay with a family because black and white players never roomed together. Most of us were just happy to be there. And you never knew how long you'd be around. Like what happened with Motley. He hurt his knee or something and Paul Brown said, "Well you can't help me anymore. I guess that's it."

The first time I saw Paul Brown, he was sharp and he was clean. He had a brown shirt, brown tie, brown jacket, brown shoes, brown socks, and a brown hat and he looked the same every day after that, all dressed in brown from head to toe. He had a hat on all the time. He was smart and he was a great coach. He established that messenger system sending the plays in with the guards. That was an excellent idea. Otto Graham was a magician and a great player, but all he had to do was execute, he didn't have to call the plays. Paul Brown called the plays. I thought Paul Brown was great. You know, outside of Clark Shaughnessy, he was it.

I don't know exactly what happened between Jim Brown and Paul Brown, but I know Jim Brown wasn't too happy. I never played with Jim but I knew him, and one time he told me he was thinking about quitting. This was after he'd only played a few years. I told him he was crazy because he hadn't even reached his peak, but he said he couldn't play for Paul Brown anymore. Then Paul Brown got fired so Jim Brown played a few more years, but something happened between them because I know Jim wasn't happy.

A lot of times Paul wouldn't get involved directly with the players, he had one of the assistant coaches do it. Or he just looked the other way, like with Lenny Ford. Lenny was a very heavy drinker, but as long as Lenny was a great player—and he was, let me tell you—Paul would let it go without comment. All of us would have a drink now and then and Paul would send [assistant coach Paul] Bixler to tell the guys to quiet it down. Then we'd quiet it down a little. We'd keep going, just quieter.

Paul Brown tried me at halfback on offense and safety on defense. Nobody ever said anything about me playing quarterback, at least not to me. I doubt if the coaches talked about it with each other because it just wasn't done at that time. Willie Thrower became the first black quarterback around then, but that was just because everybody else was hurt. I think he played one game and that was it.

Mostly I played right safety. They had Don Paul, Kenny Konz, and Tom James in the secondary, and they had been successful. The Browns were defending champions and they went on and won it again that year. I made the final roster, but they ended up releasing me after two games. I wouldn't say I got a fair shot, but I don't think I was released because of race. I knew as much football as the others, but they were veterans and I think Paul Brown felt he had a winning formula. And don't forget, you only had so many players on the roster in those days.

After I was released, I went up to Canada and played the rest of that '55 season for the Toronto Argonauts. When the season was over, I went back to Pittsburgh and kept my promise to my mother. I bought her a house as a Christmas gift. I took her out to see her new house, and every house on the block had a for sale sign on the front lawn. All the whites were moving out. I couldn't imagine where they would go or why they would go—it was a very nice neighborhood.

In 1956 I was back in Pittsburgh and that's when I hooked on with the Steelers. I have an article from when I signed and it talks about how happy they were that I was coming to the Steelers. I was happy, too, because I thought I would be there a long time. I was better than the defensive backs they had at the time, so I felt like I had a career ahead of me. It was one thing to get let go by the Browns, they were the world champions, but the Steelers were not that good. Unfortunately it didn't work out that way.

The thing that got in the way was, they didn't like the fact that I had a white girlfriend. They would listen in on our phone conversations. They told [Steelers head coach] Walt Kiesling and the others that I was dating a white girl and as a result they got rid of me. It was strange how it happened because the week before they got rid of me [in training camp in 1957], we were playing the Detroit Lions and I was playing offense and defense and I thought I really had a hell of a day. I came back the next week to practice on Tuesday and I wasn't on the offensive team, I wasn't on the defensive team, I wasn't on the punt return team, and I wasn't on the kickoff return team.

On Wednesday, same thing. I wasn't on the offensive team, defensive team, punt return team, kickoff return team, nothing. I couldn't figure out what was going on, but since I had just played practically the whole game against the Lions the week before and done well, I figured they were trying somebody else out. I figured they had seen what I could do and they were satisfied and now they were looking at somebody else.

Thursday came, same thing. Friday, same thing. On Saturday I was home looking forward to the game on Sunday, getting myself prepared, getting my clothes packed for the trip and everything, and I get a phone call from the business manager. Not the head coach or even any other coach but the business manager. I couldn't imagine what he was calling me about other than something about the travel arrangements, and he says, "That's it." I said, "What do you mean, that's it." He said, "They told me to tell you that's it and they'll take care of you when we get back from the game," and he hung up. And that's how I was cut, right after I had played a hell of a game against the Detroit Lions.

As to why I was cut, I know why. It's because of my love for Rochelle. Me loving her and her returning my love, that was apparently too much for Steelers management. I thought my world was coming to an end. Being kicked off the team for something that had nothing to do with football or how I played the game caused me a lot of emotional trauma. Rochelle, too. But we believed our love and commitment would outlast the pain we felt, so we stayed together, and from then on I was blackballed. Nobody called.

No question about it, I was blackballed. Eventually I got a call from somebody in Arizona to come out there and coach and play quarterback for a semipro team called the Tucson Cowboys. A lot of ex-NFL players went out there and played. It was a good league, we had a lot of good players, but after two years that was it for me as far as playing football. I coached high school football here in California for many years, but that year in Arizona was it for me as a player.

I couldn't get a job in Pittsburgh, like I mentioned with Duquesne Beer. I went to Trenton, New Jersey and got a substitute teaching job. I was offered an assistant coaching job there and the head coach said he was going to quit the following year and that he would recommend me for the head coaching job. So the next year he quit and the school hired somebody else so I left.

Rochelle and I got married and we moved to Philadelphia when I got hired by Acme Markets. I was the first minority hired into their corporate management program and I stayed there four years. From there I was hired by the Commonwealth of Pennsylvania and worked in their antipoverty program. At the same time I was executive director of the Bristol Township Community Center in Bristol, Pennsylvania, the head football coach of the Wheaton, Maryland championship team, and a coach and board member at the Wheaton Boys Club, plus I had two sons and was involved in their early athletic activities.

It was around that time that the NAACP was putting pressure on the federal government to handle discrimination cases and the Equal Employment Opportunities Commission came into being. They hired me as a technical administrator in 1965 and we moved to Washington, D.C. My first assignment was to investigate the NFL because some of the black players claimed they were threatening to fire every black player who wouldn't cut their afros because they saw it as a sign of militancy.

The EEOC was a good job and we made major changes in the way the government solved discrimination problems. Still, I missed football and, as it turned out, Pitt offered me a job as an assistant coach. Then they took what had been one coaching job that paid $16,000 or thereabouts and split it into two jobs and were offering $8,000. They were going to hire me and somebody else. I couldn't believe they would do something like that. They knew I wouldn't take the job if it was like that, which may be what they wanted all along, I don't know. But today Pitt and I are still in trouble because of it.

I continued to work at the EEOC developing programs to eliminate discrimination and promote minorities in corporate America until I went to work for the American Gas Association as their technical administrator. I wrote, developed, and implemented programs to eliminate discrimination based on race, religion, and gender in all of the gas companies in the United States. From there I went to work for Xerox at their headquarters in Stamford, Connecticut as corporate director of human resources. While I was at Xerox I received the Managing Tasks Through People Award in 1977.

In 1978, we moved to California when I accepted a job with Saga Foods as director of human resources. In 1982, I bought my own business from Coca-Cola, a vending and food service company that I later sold to a Japanese firm. Then for four years I owned a contract sewing company, which I sold when I was 54. Then I retired to do what I always wanted to do—coach football.

I became the head coach of the Menlo Atherton High School football team when they hadn't won a game in two and a half years. They had the longest losing streak of any high school in the state of California at the time. Very few people came to the games. And then on the day I was to be introduced as the new head football coach, there was a race riot at the school and they asked me to address the student body to calm the students.

In the seven years I was the coach there, we had a lot of success, especially compared to what it had been before. The kids really pulled together and the school bonded behind us. We went to the Central California championship game three times and won it once. Thirty-four of my players went to college on scholarships. That was quite an accomplishment and something that I was proud of. The last time someone had gotten a scholarship was seven years before I became coach.

I used to sit in on some of the athletes' classes to make sure they kept up their grades. I felt like I made a difference. Of all the jobs I had, that was the one I held the longest and the one that brought me the least amount of money, which I ended up investing back into the football program. It also brought me the most satisfaction of any job I ever had. The way I looked at it, athletics was what saved my life, earned me a college education, and got me into the professional arena.

Y. A. Tittle's daughter Dianne De Laet wrote about my efforts and the team's success in her book [*Giants and Heroes: A Daughter's Memories of Y. A. Tittle*]. Her son played for Menlo Atherton and she wrote about the school and the team being a melting pot of Hispanics, Samoans, Tongans, blacks, whites, and Asians. Not long after I got there, we would have 4,000 fans watching us—quite a contrast to the way it had been before, when the crowd might consist of a few parents, a half dozen students, and multiple drug dealers with their cell phones and beepers going off. It really gave the students pride in their school.

These days I'm involved in a lot of community work and fund-raising activities. I'm a board member of the Black Athlete's Hall of Fame in New York and also the board of ARETE, a nonprofit organization that raises funds and grants scholarships to qualified high school graduates. I'm also on the executive committee of the San Francisco chapter of the NFL Alumni and I do a football clinic every year for free. Kids come from all over. I also work on the annual golf tournament and other charitable events the NFL Alumni sponsors.

Looking back, I realize how much I wish my father had told me something of what he felt or saw in me when he was "following" me. It's sad, all those years without having a father. But my love for Rochelle and her love for me has helped me overcome that and a lot of the racial discrimination we've encountered, including from people who didn't approve of interracial relationships and didn't want us to be together. In fact, neither of our families was happy about the marriage and many members of Rochelle's family did not welcome me into their family at first. But they changed and we're grateful they did.

Rochelle is a well-known metal sculptor and we live in a lovely old Spanish home in the historic Professorville section of Palo Alto. Our house has been featured on television programs and has been written up in numerous publications, and both the house and Rochelle's sculpture garden are sightseeing destinations in Palo Alto. Our best enjoyment comes from being with our two wonderful sons, Michael and Mark, and our two grandchildren, Ethan and Paisley Ford. The other thing I'm proudest of is that I started out as a poor child on welfare who was able to help so many students get scholarships to go to college. I guess in that way I've come full circle through my love of sports, and so have many of them.

BOBBY WATKINS

Robert Archibald Watkins Jr.
Born March 30, 1932, in New Bedford, Massachusetts

New Bedford High School in New Bedford, Massachusetts
Ohio State University

Running back
Drafted in 2nd round by Chicago Bears in 1955

Bobby Watkins is as likely to recite The Gloomy Night Is Gathering Fast *and discuss Robert Burns as he is to talk about football. Ask him about his interest in the Civil War and he will break down the strategies employed in the Battle of Antietam as enthusiastically as he'll discuss the coaching philosophies of Woody Hayes and George Halas. Bobby, you see, was an outstanding football player, but he doesn't let what he did in football define who he is. He's been a devotee of Burns and a Civil War buff, after all, for a lot longer than he played football.*

Bobby played his college ball at Ohio State, as much a football power then as it is today. His first year in Columbus was also the first for the legendary Hayes and the school won the national championship when Bobby was a senior. It was an era when Ohio State halfbacks were Heisman Trophy candidates on almost a yearly basis. In the span of a decade, Buckeyes Les Horvath, Vic Janowicz, and Howard Cassady won college football's most prized individual award.

Were it not for the small matter of the color of his skin, Bobby might also have been a serious Heisman contender. In 1953 as now, the Heisman was primarily the province of running backs and quarterbacks, yet Bobby didn't so much as make a dent in the voting.

227

Year	Team	League	Games	Rushing				Receiving			
				Attempts	Yards	Avg.	TDs	Receptions	Yards	Avg.	TDs
1955	Bears	NFL	12	110	553	5.0	8	6	79	13.2	0
1956	Bears	NFL	9	68	276	4.1	2	2	3	1.5	1
1957	Bears	NFL	12	57	212	3.7	1	3	90	30.0	1
1958	Cardinals	NFL	5	3	17	5.7	0	4	62	15.5	1

Also returned 6 kickoffs for 169 yards

Played in NFL Championship Game in 1956

This despite the fact that he finished second in the country in rushing when calculated by yards per game. The only player ahead of him was J. C. Caroline, who Bobby considers the best player in the country that year, but Caroline didn't win the Heisman, either. He, too, is black.

As a senior, Bobby was eclipsed by Cassady in publicity, although not in performance on the field. Despite injuries, he led Ohio State in rushing for most of the season as the team finished with a perfect 10–0 record. The Buckeyes finished number one in the country and capped their season with a Rose Bowl victory over Southern California. Bobby is as proud of the great game he played against USC and his overall contribution to a national championship as he is of anything in his life.

Beneath the surface, though, is the question of whether Ohio State was unwilling to feature a black halfback in a feature role. It is a question that Bobby himself doesn't raise but one that anyone examining the record can't help but ask. Cassady, after all, was the fair-haired, hometown star from Columbus who won the Heisman in part (as many winners do) because the school widely publicized him. When he won the award in 1955, he did so with numbers that weren't all that different from the ones Bobby posted two years before. It was not until a revolution that had begun to rock the country to its foundations that Ernie Davis became the first black to win the Heisman in 1961.

Bobby doesn't spend his time pondering what might have been, whether it be regarding the Heisman, his career in the NFL, or anything else. He is satisfied in knowing how good he was as well as with the recognition he gets from the men who played with him. This last is important because not all of them accorded him that respect five decades ago. Bobby's teammates, whether they be Buckeyes or Bears, have changed much as the country they live in has.

Bobby lives in Massachusetts, not far from where he grew up in New Bedford. It's difficult to tell if he's retired, he keeps so busy. He writes poetry and talks of authoring a book so perhaps it's appropriate that it's to Burns that he turns to express the code he has tried to live by:

*Whatever mitigates the woes or
increases the happiness of others,*

this is my criterion of goodness; and
whatever injures society at large, or
any individual in it, this is my
measure of iniquity.

New Bedford, Massachusetts, was an interesting place to be raised. The neighborhood I lived in was very mixed, a virtual United Nations. I never felt isolated or set apart as black Americans in many places did then. Most people of color lived in the South End of the city, the neighborhood where I lived. The majority were Caucasians, even in the South End. There were some blacks and a lot of Cape Verdeans. The Cape Verdeans didn't consider themselves to be black or Negro, but they were very dark-skinned. I must say, the Cape Verdeans are beautiful people and the girls are stunning. Jim Parker stayed with me one summer to work out and he loved the Cape Verdean girls. And they loved him.

New Bedford is a historic city of about 100,000 known mostly for its 19th-century whaling period, but it once led the world in textiles, too. It's also the largest fishing port in the world. My father's parents moved to this area from Virginia not long after the Civil War and Reconstruction. From hearing stories from my grandfather, I developed a serious interest in the Civil War and American history in general.

My grandfather owned the largest construction company in the south coast of Massachusetts. My father, Robert Watkins Sr., was the youngest of nine and he and his brother William were both outstanding athletes. They were honor students and valedictorians and two of very few blacks who went to college at that time. My father set a touchdown record at Bristol High School that lasted almost until the time I was playing.

I was aware that there were no blacks in pro football but I didn't think about it much. College football was my first love. There was much more news about college football in the newspapers in those days and it became my dream to play in the Big Ten. Northwestern was my favorite and I followed Otto Graham when he went to school there. I was also impressed by Illinois, and after I saw Pat O'Brien in the Knute Rockne story, by Notre Dame.

My uncle William was unmarried and he became like a second father to me. Even though I always liked football much more than baseball, my uncle took me to Braves Field to see the Dodgers play against the Boston Braves in 1947, when Jackie Robinson was a rookie. We sat right along the first base line so we were close to where Jackie was and I had goose bumps during the entire game.

Today they have all the Pop Warner football leagues and everything is so organized. We had nothing like that. Mostly you had ragtag neighborhood teams that kids would put together themselves. By comparison, the sandlot team I put together was actually quite organized. We were fortunate because my father took an interest in us, plus my family had a big backyard. My father constructed a beautiful goal post and tackling dummy in the yard and he taught us the techniques and principles of football. He was working nights building liberty ships and he would give us time when he could.

We lived close to the waterfront so we called our team the Waterfront Bulldogs. The other kids knew I was the best player and that my father had been a great high school player, or at least they knew that he knew what he was talking about, and it didn't bother them at all that we were black. It was the only time in the 16 years I played football where race was never an issue. We used to stuff our shirts with newspaper because none of us had shoulder pads. I was the only kid that had a real football helmet. Some guys played with tank helmets they bought in the army/navy store. Then my father bought me a pair of football shoes, but the other kids wouldn't play. They saw me with these cleats and they said they wouldn't play with me unless I wore sneakers like everybody else.

Saturdays we used to play against teams from other neighborhoods at a park that was right by a railroad depot called Depot Park. It was railroad property and the railroad police would chase us off, then we'd wait until they left and go right back. My father never coached us in these games, but what he taught us really helped. Fundamentals-wise, I consider him one of the best coaches I ever had. And remember, I played for Woody Hayes, George Halas, and Clark Shaughnessy. We were much better than the other teams and kids from around town would come around because they wanted to play on our team.

When I went to high school, my father introduced me to the coach Wynn Dodge. He said, "Wynn, I brought you a football player. Now it's up to you to see what you can do with him." And that's the last time he ever spoke to any of my coaches. He wasn't a meddler. He'd teach me things I could use, but he would never tell any coach of mine how they should coach. Plus, I think he recognized it was better for me that way. When you go to high school, you don't need a parent in the way. I wanted to do it all on my own.

We played basketball in my yard, too, because I had a basketball hoop and that drew a lot of kids, but the basketball we played was no nicky-picky basketball where every time you touched a guy it was a foul. There were no fouls. It was really more a combination of football and basketball. Some kids played ice hockey but I never did. I skated on frozen lakes and frozen ponds but I never played hockey.

I went to New Bedford High School and had a real good four years there. We never had more than three or four blacks on the football team and the schools we played rarely had any. Some had none. One school we played was in Watertown and not only did their team not have any blacks, the town itself probably had no people of color living there. Before the game, I was warming up punting the ball and there were four or five little white kids watching me. I was a good punter and the ball was just sailing beautifully and this one kid said, "Nice kick, nigger." He was praising me but he used that word and it caused me to look up. I laughed because I thought it was kind of funny coming from a little kid. I would get the n-word during the game, too, from opposing players.

I set some records and in my junior and senior years I was the best player in Massachusetts. One of the best schools we played was Cathedral High in Springfield and their coach Billy Wise was a personal friend of Frank Leahy of Notre Dame from when Leahy was the coach of Boston College. Several of Wise's best players had gone to Notre Dame including Angelo Bertelli. Cathedral was the best team in western Massachusetts and I had an outstanding game and we just destroyed them. The day after the game, Wise called my dad and told him I was more than good enough to play for Notre Dame. He told us he would arrange a trip to New York for us to see Notre Dame play North Carolina in Yankee Stadium and meet Frank Leahy after the game.

We drove down to see the game and we went to the locker room as Bill Wise had told us to do in order to meet Leahy, but Leahy never showed up. We waited for some time but eventually we left for the long ride home. Neither one of us spoke a word until we were on the Merritt Parkway in Connecticut, when my dad finally said, "Well, what do you think?" I said, "To be honest with you, if I was on the field today I would've been the best back out there." I wasn't bragging, I just based my point of view on what I had seen.

There were two backs in the game who were getting lots of publicity. One was North Carolina's Charlie Justice, who didn't play very much but from what I did see, I had very little regard for him. But Notre Dame had a real football player who went on to the pros, Emil Sitko. He was the type of football player I was and I was very impressed. He ran low with big powerful legs and broke tackles. They called him Six Yards Sitko.

We waited and waited but time passed and we never heard from Notre Dame. I recall that when I talked to Coach Wise, he was very upset about it. All I can say is that Notre Dame had never had a black player on their team and it wasn't a priority for them at that time. The first black player on Notre Dame was a kid from New Jersey named Lewis, a halfback. I remember Woody Hayes was trying to recruit him when I was a senior at Ohio State and he had him stay with me when he came to Columbus to visit.

What happened to me with Notre Dame wasn't unusual. It certainly wasn't just Notre Dame. When I was in high school, I played against a great athlete named Joe Andrews, who played for our rival Fall River and broke my father's touchdown record. A terrific football player. When he was a senior and I was a sophomore, he was considered the best running back in the state. He was white and he had about 80 scholarship offers and he ended up going to the University of Washington.

Two years later, I was considered the best running back in the state but it was a lot different. Not one major school in the country offered me anything. I was obviously limited as far as anything below the Mason-Dixon Line, but none of the major football colleges up North were interested, either. There's no doubt it was a racial issue. Only Fordham, Massachusetts, Connecticut, and Brandeis were interested and none had a major football program. Yale expressed interest but insisted I go to prep school. I was tempted, but I knew I was ready to play at the highest level.

I wrote to a number of the Big Ten schools but none of them had anything for me. I didn't write to Ohio State because their coach

Wes Fesler ran a combination of the T-formation and single wing and that wasn't my style. I was a T-formation back who ran quick hitters to perfection. I didn't like spinning around in the backfield, I wanted to hit that line as quickly as possible. I ended up going to Ohio State because of Roy Climer, a Midwestern representative of the Titleist Company. New Bedford is where they make Titleist golf balls and golf equipment and Climer kept hearing stories from Titleist executives in Massachusetts about a kid from New Bedford who was an outstanding high school football player.

Climer was also an Ohio State Front Liner, boosters committed to making sure the best high school football talent in Ohio went to Ohio State. In the meantime Woody Hayes had replaced Fesler and Climer told Hayes what he had heard about me and Hayes said, "Well, see if he has any game films." Nowadays most high schools film every game but not in 1950. I was able to get my hands on a film of our Thanksgiving game, the only film ever taken of any of my high school games, and it just so happened it was a game where I scored four touchdowns.

Climer sent Woody the film and Woody sent me a letter stating that he would like me to come to Ohio State for a visit. Talk about fortuitous circumstances. Not only because of this guy Climer but because of Woody getting hired the same year I graduated from high school. If they hadn't hired Woody and brought in the T-formation, they wouldn't have been interested in me and I wouldn't have been interested in Ohio State.

I loved Ohio State but it was no picnic when I first went there in 1951. I was the only black player on the freshman team and there was only one on the varsity. In my sophomore and junior years, I was the only black player on the varsity, but my senior year we had a talented sophomore class that included the great Jim Parker and three others. Ohio prided itself on being number one in football and we had freshman who scored 25 touchdowns in high school and averaged ten yards a carry. All but three were from Ohio and that made me even more of an outsider. My first impression was, Am I in the right place? But I was determined and because of the Korean War, freshmen were eligible to play on the varsity.

I should have been a starting halfback on the varsity, except Woody was hesitant. In practice, the freshman offense ran the plays of whatever team we were playing that week against the varsity defense and every week I'd break off several good runs. We lost a lot of close games because the offense was terrible until the defensive players decided they had had enough. Three of them—Joe Campanella, Steve Ruzich, and Dick Logan, all of whom had fairly long careers in the NFL—went to see Woody and they told him, "The best back we've faced all year is not any of the opponents we've faced so far, it's not any of the guys who are starting on our varsity, it's this freshman we play against in practice every week." I didn't know about this then but I heard about it later.

As a result, Woody told me I was going to play the following week against Iowa. Needless to say, I left his office elated. I called my parents and they decided on the spot that they would drive roundtrip from New Bedford to see the game. Keep in mind these are pre-interstate roads I'm talking about. My parents were great. No son ever had more supportive parents than me and they didn't hesitate about traveling that far to see me fulfill my dream of playing big-time college football.

When we played Iowa, three quarters went by and I didn't get in. Finally, just before the game ended Woody put me in for the last two plays. He never said anything to me, but if he had been asked why he probably would have said I wasn't ready. I was more than ready. Maybe Woody thought Ohio State wasn't ready. That's the only explanation I can come up with. After that game I was so upset I seriously thought about leaving Ohio State. I realized later it was his first year and it was just as new for him as it was for me. I'm not defending him because I really was devastated, but I guess time salves most wounds. Woody was one of the least prejudiced people I have ever known.

Because of a housing shortage, I was invited to sleep at Woody's house every Thursday during the football season. That's when I became close with him and his wife Ann. I admired his interest in academics and the importance he put on players earning their degrees. He would stay on the backs of players year after year about returning to school and graduating. He would call somebody when they least expected it and say, "When are you going to get your degree?" Over the years I called him many times for advice, but I think he was under a lot of pressure as far as how much playing time to give me because I found Columbus in the 1950s to be a very prejudiced place.

One example occurred not long after I arrived at school. There was a training table where the football team ate six days a week. On Sundays we would get cash so we could eat at restaurants in the area and I remember all the guys going out while I stood there by myself like a lost soul. Vic Janowicz walked past me, stopped, turned around, and said, "Hey kid, aren't you going out? You got a place to go?" I said, "No, I don't know the area. I've never been off the campus." So he said, "Come with us."

There were three of us—me, Janowicz, and Fred Bruney. Janowicz had won the Heisman Trophy the year before and Bruney was a defensive back and a good one who played professionally with the San Francisco 49ers. The three of us went to a popular restaurant across the street from campus on High Street that still exists. It was busy but we got a table, and we were sitting and talking for some time when we noticed that people who came in after us were getting served but not us. Janowicz got up to find out what was going on and they told him it was because of me. He and Bruney were embarrassed and ready to rumble, but I said, "It's my first time off the campus in the city of Columbus and I don't want to be the cause of any trouble. Let's just go somewhere else."

That was my first experience with overt discrimination in Columbus and it wasn't the last. Columbus was a major city with a large black population but there was a lot of prejudice. Situations of a racial nature happened on campus, too. Not long after the incident at the restaurant, I went to get a haircut at the student union. When my turn came, I walked over to sit in the chair and the barber went into a fit. He was waving his hands around like a crazy man shouting, "No, no, no, no, no, I don't cut black people's hair." It just so happened that he was Filipino and he was considerably darker than me. It was a very embarrassing situation and the other students were looking at me as if it was *my* fault. So dinner and a haircut were my first exposures to prejudice in Columbus, Ohio.

With the housing shortage, all dormitories were turned over to women and the male students either lived barracks-style in the stadium dorms or off campus. I answered over 20 advertisements in person for a place to live off campus without any success. I went to the office in charge of off-campus housing and the provost told me there was nothing they could do. Things changed a little when

Baker Hall reopened in 1955, but until then the university did very little to assist their minority students.

At the time I was really in a goldfish bowl. Ohio State had had Bill Willis and other black players, but they had never had a black player who was an offensive star. Blacks recruited by Ohio State mostly had a negative perception of the school. The feeling was that Ohio State wasn't all that enthusiastic about having them and didn't really support those who did attend. Black recruits definitely noticed my achievements, though, and I think the contribution I made definitely helped Woody get other blacks like Jim Parker and Jim Roseboro. It was a slow process, believe me, but gradually Ohio State was able to whittle away the skepticism blacks felt about the school.

I mentioned Bill Willis. I met Bill while I was at Ohio State at several events on campus, then a short time later he moved back to Columbus. We hit it off and became good friends. I'm a great admirer of Bill Willis, just so impressed at how effective he was at nose guard at his size. He was about 215, 220, not a big guy for a nose guard, but his forte was his quickness. He moved so fast that guys who were almost a hundred pounds bigger couldn't handle him. He was almost unstoppable, he was so quick.

Within the team at Ohio State, things were usually okay. There were times on the practice field when I felt I didn't exist and I knew the way I would make them know I was there was by showing them what I could do. I did extremely well in practice and that's what made it so disappointing that I didn't get a chance to play my freshman year. With a better offense, we would've won more games than we did, and 50 plus years later I still feel I could have made a serious difference that year.

In my sophomore year, I was the starting right halfback until I suffered a real bad high ankle injury just before the first game. I played but I could only run straight ahead, I couldn't cut one way or the other, and Hopalong Cassady replaced me in the third quarter. He was a freshman and it was the same deal—he was eligible to play on the varsity because of the Korean War.

Just like the year before, the offense struggled. I'm positive we would've played better if I had been 100 percent, but our record after seven games was just 4–3 and the wolves began calling for

Woody's job. We had games left against Illinois and Michigan and the pressure was really on him to win them both. For me personally, that was the lowest period of my life. I had decided to finish the academic quarter, leave Ohio State, and reconstruct my life someplace else. It was the closest I ever came to quitting.

Dick Larkin the athletic director sent for me around that time. I couldn't bring myself to tell him how I felt because I wasn't sure where he was coming from, but that meeting restored my confidence because he was very supportive. It made me realize there was somebody at Ohio State who actually cared about me. Then Woody called me into his office and told me he was going to use me a lot against Illinois and I rushed for over 100 yards and we won. I had another good game against Michigan and we beat them for the first time in eight years. Our victory knocked them out of the Rose Bowl and put an end to the "Fire Woody Hayes" wolves. Woody spoke very highly of me afterwards and that ended any thoughts I had about leaving Ohio State.

The next year, the NCAA basically did away with the two-platoon system so players would have to play both ways. A lot of coaches and players had a difficult time making the adjustment because some players were good on offense or defense but few were good at both. We had an excellent defensive halfback named George Rosso and Woody moved him to my halfback spot in order to get him in the game and moved me to fullback. It was a jerry-built system but it worked better than we expected and the offense played well except for a big letdown when we lost to Michigan. We weren't so good on defense, though, and we finished only 4–3 in the conference, 6–3 overall.

It was a somewhat disappointing season for the team but an excellent one for me. I finished fourth in the nation in rushing even though opposing defenses keyed on our running game every week because our quarterback, John Borton, was hurt for much of the season. I was named national Back of the Week after I ran for over 150 yards and four touchdowns against California, and I finished the season with 11 touchdowns.

It was extremely rare for a black to make any All-American team in the early 1950s, especially in the backfield, and it didn't bother me that I didn't. I figured J. C. Caroline of Illinois had the best chance of any black player to be selected. He was the best back I saw that year and he made some of the All-American teams, but he wasn't a consensus selection. I was second in the Big Ten in rushing and the leading scorer and believed my performance was good enough to earn a first team spot on the All-Conference Team, but the selectors weren't convinced. Instead I was second team on the AP and UP teams. I wasn't bitter about it, though, and I'm not bitter about it now because I knew what was going on.

I suffered a shoulder injury in the offseason and it bothered me all through my senior year. Hubert Bobo stepped in and did a nice job at fullback and Cassady and I were the two halfbacks. We were 8–0 and number one in the country and the national championship, the conference title, and a trip to the Rose Bowl were all at stake against Michigan. Cassady was named to every All-American team even though I led the team in rushing yards and touchdowns going into our last game.

I was playing both ways again and I hurt my knee making a tackle early in the first quarter. It was the biggest game of the year and I had to watch from the sidelines. We would've lost if not for our defense. They set up our first score and stopped Michigan on two great goal line stands. Our offense finally got going in the fourth quarter, but before that they dominated us and we were lucky to win. Our offensive coach Doyt Perry told me, "Bobby, we know who the real All-American is. When you weren't in there, our offense wasn't worth a damn." I knew that when Doyt said "we" he meant Woody.

Beforehand, Woody gave me a great honor by selecting me as an honorary captain for the game. I believe it was his way of saying thank you for my contribution during the season and for a great career. He was also upset by the fact that I had been passed over for the second year in a row in the voting for the All-American teams while Cassady made every one of them. I've always appreciated Woody's gesture.

We were on our way to the Rose Bowl but a few days later the team doctor said the injury to my knee was so serious that my football days were over. I was in tears. How could my football career be over? But the trainer took me aside and said, "You listen to me. You'll play in the Rose Bowl." And I'll be damned if I didn't. Not only did I play, I led the team in total yardage and scored the winning touchdown against Southern Cal.

If not for questions about my knee, I definitely would have been a first round NFL draft pick. I was upset that the Browns didn't draft me or show much interest in me given that I was right there in Ohio. I wasn't much of a pro football fan until I got to Columbus, and then I became a big Browns fan from watching them on TV every Sunday. They were always winning and by the time I was a senior, I really wanted to play for them. Instead I lasted until the Bears took me in the second round.

I was chosen to play in the College All-Star Game as one of the best college seniors against the NFL champs from the year before. The people in charge decided to get a pro coaching staff and players who were NFL caliber because the collegians were getting annihilated every year. I was a typical NFL-type running back—hard runner, quick start, good blocker, decent pass receiver, and I was the third player chosen.

The defending champions that year were none other than Otto Graham and the Browns. I had actually played against Graham before that in the Hula Bowl. At that time, it was college players against pros from different teams, and Graham was the quarterback for the pros. We worked out together and he was such a nice person. I was happy to find out he was everything you would hope for from someone you had looked up to. And when he threw the ball, it just floated into your hands, even when he threw it hard. Nowadays quarterbacks throw so hard, I wonder how the receivers catch the ball.

Curly Lambeau was the head coach of the All-Stars and he was quite nasty to me. I couldn't figure it out because I was the kind of player who always listened, never talked back, did exactly what they wanted me to, and always gave my best effort. The whole staff seemed to ignore me and I still can't figure out why. I didn't play until the fourth quarter.

I went over to Lambeau and said, "Coach, if you don't put me in now, I'm going to the locker room." He said, "Alright, go in." I only played part of a quarter and gained 47 yards on six carries. I have a clipping where Chicago sportswriter Bob Russell wrote that the coaches must have regretted not putting me in until the fourth quarter. I was so angry when I got on the field, a defense of King Kongs couldn't have stopped me. Our quarterback Ralph Guglielmi just winked at me when I got in and I started hitting quick hitters and picking up good yardage every run and making first downs.

Defensive end Lenny Ford started coming down the line to stop the quick hitter, so we called a play to go outside. Guglielmi pitched the ball out to me, Ford went inside, and I went outside around him. I almost broke it and ended up gaining 25 yards. That put the ball in scoring position, and Tad Weed from Ohio State kicked a field goal and we won the game, the first time in a while the All-Stars had won. The game was in Chicago and George Halas and his assistants were there. He knew how good the Browns were and my performance in the game gave me a leg up when I got to the Bears training camp.

I was the only black on the Bears my first year. They had just had their first black player a few years before that. I read once that Herman Clark was one of the first blacks, but he was actually Hawaiian. He did not consider himself a person of a color and he was not treated as if he was. He was one of the group and was accepted in a way that I wasn't. There was actually another black guy named Henry Mosley who got cut just after the season started. It was sad because he had everything going for him—great build, about 200 pounds, fast, but he never played. He didn't like to get hit, but other than that he had all the requisites to be an NFL player.

After that, I was the only black on the team. The Bears and Redskins were last in terms of black players. The Redskins didn't have any, the Bears had one, and everybody else had at least a couple. Then my second year, the Bears added a few more including J. C. Caroline, who was my roommate. J. C. was a great offensive football player in college but he only played defense in the NFL. Just an outstanding player.

We played an exhibition game in Jacksonville against the Cardinals, the first time in my life I was ever in the South. This was years before there were teams in the South and people in Jacksonville made a big deal about it. Chauffered convertibles met us at the airport and a girl sat with two or three players on the back of each of the cars and there was a parade through the city. I fell in line to get into one of the cars and this guy said, "No you don't. We've got a special car for you." Finally Mosley and I were the only two left, and this old car with a black driver pulled up and they told us that was the car for us. We were the last car in the parade and needless to say, there was no girl in our car.

Of course, we couldn't stay with the team. We stayed in a black section of town in a little fleabag hotel with the black players from the Cardinals. They had four or five including Ollie Matson and Night Train Lane. That was a great opportunity for me, to meet these great men. From then on I considered both Matson and Night Train to be dear friends. Both of them were fabulous football players and here we were together in this terrible situation. That was my first experience of the South.

Halas was looking for a certain kind of black player. He didn't have the highest regard for black people, I'll put it that way, and he wanted a guy who was better educated and came from a school in the Midwest rather than one from the South. He had very little exposure to black people and he was paternalistic just like he was presented in the movie *Brian's Song*. He was completely unconcerned about the things the black players were up against. It wasn't like Ohio State, where Woody Hayes told me, "I promise you one thing, you will go and stay wherever the team goes and stays." And I always did.

I complained about not being able to stay with the team. Training camp itself was alright, but we played exhibition games in Dallas, Memphis, and Little Rock and it was the same as Jacksonville. Because there were no NFL teams in that whole stretch, Halas considered that to be Bear country. He knew the team could make more money if those places were part of the Bears radio and TV network, and that's why we played all those games there. As a result, the Bears were probably the most popular team in the South.

It was like he didn't know that the South had a white world and a black world. The blacks stayed in fleabag hotels or they stayed with black families. If somebody had friends or relatives in one of the cities, they were allowed to stay there. We never stayed in the hotel with the rest of the team, which usually was one of the first class hotels. And we had to take black taxis to team meetings at the hotel where the rest of the team was staying. Then after the meeting, we had to call a black taxi and you might sit for an hour waiting because the black taxis didn't like to go to the white parts of town at night.

Once we even had a problem waiting for a taxi. The hotel lobby was air conditioned so we waited inside instead of standing outside in the heat. The next day, one of the assistant coaches told me that the hotel was complaining about these black men sitting in their lobby. The next night after our meeting, I sat down in the lobby, poured myself a glass of ice water, and we waited inside until our taxi came.

I confronted Halas about these things. He said, "That's how it is down here, Bobby. Things are going to change and people like you are going to help make it change." I solved the problem with the taxis by getting him to let us rent a car. I'm sure the cost to the team was less than all the taxis, but Halas really examined those expense accounts. I'd give him a list of expenses for our meals and the rental car—I called it my swindle sheet—and he wasn't too happy. He had a bad eye and he would hold the sheet up close to his face and play with his glasses. I'd say, "This isn't my fault, Mr. Halas, this is just how it is."

We rented a car with air conditioning and he really didn't like that. If you rented a car back then, air conditioning was extra, maybe 10 dollars, and wow, did he explode. I said, "Mr. Halas, we've got four or five 200-pound guys in a car in the middle of the summer. It's impossible." He finally acquiesced, but he wasn't happy about it. As the leader of the blacks, I was always the one dealing with him about these things. He would get mad but there was nothing on my swindle sheets that he could argue with.

My first year, we played the Redskins in Memphis. Think about the NFL today with 70 percent to 80 percent black players, and then imagine a game with one for both squads. Well, I played a good game and scored a touchdown that turned out to be the only scoring in the game. Halas took me out and while I was standing on the sidelines, I noticed there were no lights in the end zone bleachers, they only extended from goal line to goal line. As the night went on, it got really dark at both ends of the stadium and that's where all the black people had to sit. There was such a contrast between the lights in the middle part of the stadium and the darkness of the end zone bleachers, I've never forgotten it.

The game was dull as hell with the score 6–0 or 7–0 and neither team was playing particularly well, and you could hear murmuring in the crowd. People wanted more action. Then this big booming voice came from behind us: "Hey Halas, put the nigger in. He's the only ballplayer you've got." He kept it up like that for awhile. Of course, Halas ignored it, but that was my experience of Memphis: black people sitting in the dark in a segregated stadium and "Put the nigger in."

The Bears had a lot of Southern guys. Some of them were decent people and some of them were nasty bastards. Doug Atkins came to the Bears from Tennessee the same year I did and he was one of the better guys. He liked to hurdle over blockers and blocking was one of my fortes. I was very strong, only 5'9" but 200 pounds and built very solidly, and I would get under Doug and drive up when he tried to hurdle me. He succeeded in doing it once or twice, but I put him on his back a number of times and he got pissed off. After that he'd come at me in a normal standup charge.

My last year with the Bears was the year Jim Parker was a rookie with the Colts. The week before we played them the first time, I said a few things about how he was a great player. Doug Atkins said, "Yeah, we'll see," and said some disparaging things about Parker. So I said to myself, "Yeah, we'll see." Well, Atkins went head to head with Parker, and Atkins was really a tough nut, but Parker handled him pretty well and Atkins got frustrated. He just couldn't get off the line of scrimmage at all. Afterwards he came to me and said, "You were right. That guy is a football player."

There were other guys on the team from the South that I did not get along with. Some of them I just avoided. Most of them were not very well educated. One guy whose name I won't mention was from the North and went and played college ball down South and fell in love with it. That would happen with Caucasians in that time period: They would go down South and become more of a Southerner than real Southerners. But I never really had any trouble with any of these guys. If necessary, I just avoided them.

I had a very good year as a rookie. One of my goals was always to average five yards a carry and I did that and scored eight or nine touchdowns. I did a little bit of everything—ran the ball, caught passes, ran back punts and kickoffs. Based on how well I did, I thought I was going to have a long career. Honestly, I saw very few backs in the NFL that were better than me, but in my second year I injured my knee again. Again they told me I'd never play again, but

I ended up playing the rest of that year and two more. I was never as effective as I was before the injury, but I played and did pretty well. I just wish I could have played in the NFL without having that first injury.

Art Donovan tackled me on the play I got hurt. He was a right tackle and a great defensive player. I was having a very good game and it was just a freak accident, a freak play. He jumped on me just as I came down on my leg and it hyperextended on me, just tore everything up. I didn't even know he was there, otherwise I could have braced myself. They took me off on a stretcher and I thought my career was over. I came back and played after missing just three games, but I knew I wasn't as effective.

Halas cut me on the last day of the preseason in 1958, which gave me very little chance to catch on with another team. I did, though. I played one more year with the Cardinals. Going from an organization like the Bears to the Cardinals, that was quite a change. The Cardinals were poorly organized and they ran through coaches every year or two, but no coach could have been successful with what they were getting in the way of support from the owners. It had to be the worst organization in professional football.

My knee was painful every day, but I stuck it out. At that point it was the best income I could make. I wanted to get into coaching and I thought I would've made an excellent coach, but I was never given an opportunity. It broke my heart because after my last year, all of my contact with the world of football just ended. It hurt because I loved the game. Ever since, I tell people I would have been one of the greatest coaches ever and I defy them to say otherwise. Since I was never given the opportunity, they can't say I wouldn't have been a great coach because there's no way we'll ever know.

I lived in Chicago for a time and I lived in Stamford, Connecticut. I worked in different professions including for Seagram's. Then about nine years ago I came back to Massachusetts. When I was working for Seagram's, I would see Jim Parker all the time. Part of my area was Maryland, and he had a couple of liquor stores in Baltimore so I would stop in and see him. He was a great guy and I'm sad he's gone.

I keep pretty busy. I'm a big Civil War buff, and I've been to the sites of many of the major battles. I also write poetry once in awhile. I've been to Scotland to give lectures at meetings of the Robert Burns

Society. Burns is one of my favorites but I like a lot of others, too. I guess it started when I was in grade school and my teacher had me recite "In Flanders Fields" by Dr. John McCrae in front of the whole school. You probably know that one. It starts like this:

> In Flanders fields the poppies blow
> Between the crosses row on row,
> That mark our place; and in the sky
> The larks, still bravely singing, fly
> Scarce heard amid the guns below.

I can recite the whole thing through to this day.

INDEX